To Dodge & Heli
xx

Train to australia

LIDIA KARDOS

Bobbin Lace Bookmark
from Jen

TRAIN TO AUSTRALIA © Lidia Kardos

All rights reserved. No part of this publication may be reproduced, stored in a retrieval system, or transmitted in any form or by any means electronic, mechanical, photocopying, recording, or otherwise, without the prior written permission of the author.

National Library of Australia Cataloguing-in-Publication entry (pbk)

Creator:	Kardos, Lidia, author.
Title:	Train to Australia / Lidia Kardos.
ISBN:	9781925388435 (paperback)
Subjects:	Kardos, Lidia.
	Refugee children—Italy—Biography.
	World War, 1939-1945—Refugees—Australia.
	Women—Australia—Biography.
Dewey Number:	945.091092

Published by **Lidia Kardos** and InHouse Publishing

www.inhousepublishing.com.au

Printed using Envirocare paper

Dedication

This book is dedicated to my grandchildren who, through no fault of their own, have no knowledge of the events that shaped their fathers' lives so many years ago.

To Alex, Jamie, Casey, and Kalissa. I love you!

To my daughter Regina, my little queen who started life with difficulties that she overcame entirely on her own just before her first birthday, in spite of well-meaning but inappropriate advice from the 'experts'.

Less than sixteen years separated my older son's first day at school from my own, yet they were so markedly different.

Unbelievably different!

How often I think of those intervening years, and all the dramatic moments about which my children know nothing.

Contents

Surviving That First Day 1
We Have Come a Long Way 4
Bonegilla – 1951 6
Not Your 'Ten Pound Assisted Passage' 10
The 'Luck of the Draw' 13
A Refugee in Australia – 1951 14
The Truly Organic Garden 18
Bartering To Survive 20
Educating Each Other 22
Friendships 25
A Marriage of Faith, Long Ago 28
The Degradation of Family Life 32
The Post-War Years 33
Two Epic Films 35
"You Are Under Interrogation" 37
Whooping Cough 40
What Are We Now? 42
By No Means Alone 44
Another Life 47
There Is Hope for a Better Life 50
Going Around the Long Way 52
Going Nowhere 54
Chaos and Corruption 56
New Kids on the Block 58
A New and Expensive Interest 61
Doing It the Hard Way 64
Rebellion 68

Home from the Dance	76
Towards Independence	80
The Catwalk	84
Going Dancing	87
Marriages	91
A Gift from the Heart	94
My 'Special Day'	96
The Honeymoon	99
New Name – New Abode	102
The New Chloe	104
The Seduction	106
Back Home	111
Getting My Driver's Licence – 1962	116
Labour Is Just Hard Work	119
Planning Our Modest Home	122
History Repeats Itself	126
Spontaneous Combustion	129
My Precious Princess	134
My Green Thumb	140
All In a Day's Work	142
An Enterprising Duo	144
The Legacy	149
Goody-Goody/Baddy-Baddy	159
Residential Development	163
Making Ends Meet	166
A Career Change	170
My First Teaching Appointment	174
Our Changing Neighbourhood	177
Some Recreation	182
Political and Economic Changes	186

Me, an Investor?	189
Holiday House or Investment Property?	193
Trouble Follows	200
Flexible Itinerary – 1984	208
A Shocking Reunion	212
Revisiting The Past	218
From Croatia to Italy	224
Garda – German or Italian?	228
Tosca at the 'Arena Di Verona'	231
Venezia, La Serenissima	237
Lunch by the Pre-Dolomites	240
Mother's Beloved Younger Sister	243
A Medieval Wonderland	246
Nostalgia	253
A Soviet Experience	255
Heading North via South	261
Ah, Gay Paris!	264
Fair Weather in London?	267
A Slight Aside	272
The Homecoming	273
A Generation Apart But Similar	276
Life Goes On	281
Harder Times Ahead	285
The America's Cup	290
The Beginning of the End	297
A Student Among Students	300
Epilogue: Advice I Would Give Myself At 18	304
Many Years Later: To Steve, My Soul Mate	308

Surviving That First Day

For me, school in Australia began as a nightmare. With no language skills, no friends, and no idea of what lay ahead, it was a day my consciousness refused to register. What I know for a fact is that the walk from home was long, the road rough and unfamiliar with hazards all along the way, and I was alone. There were railway lines to be crossed, with no paths, or safety fencing, or barriers. Not even warning lights. The rail tracks were laid on slabs of timber that I later learnt were called sleepers. The tracks and the sleepers were laying on a bed of stones some two to three inches in diameter. That translates to stones around five to eight centimetres. It was very difficult, not to mention dangerous to cross and the morning was incredibly hot. The trains that used that line generally came in the morning and in the evening with a lull in the middle of the day. I could never figure out why trains had an afternoon siesta until I learnt that the heat of the midday sun could cause the steel tracks to buckle, making the trains prone to derailment. That also explained why a little caboose with one, but mostly two men in it, was continually riding up and down the track.

The men were red-faced and wore broad-brimmed hats. They looked big, rough, and scary but after seeing them day after day the sight of them became more familiar. Eventually I got used to their friendly wave and smile. Each day either one or the other would wave and call out, "Top of the day to you, girlie!" Of course I had no idea what they were saying, but eventually I got the courage to wave back. Back in those days, the place where I had to cross, the train line was just a single track with a siding near the station. It needed to be safe and well-maintained as this rail was the only form of transport to the northern and western towns in Victoria. But will I survive this daily negotiation with oncoming trains and slippery rocks underfoot?

Those first few days were traumatic as I came to realise that at eleven years of age, I was being placed in a vast room that contained some forty or more noisy children, who were of an average age of around seven. Class sizes were huge in the 50's in Melbourne's western suburbs. There were not enough schools or teachers to cater for the huge influx of migrants. Of course the same can be said for Sydney, and most big towns, so obviously, cognitive development amongst the students and within the mixed classes ranged wildly between the younger children with a relatively high IQ, and those older children, with perhaps a broader life experience, and survival skills. Teachers coped as best they could. At least sometime they could master some respect if corporal punishment was immediate. But separation of the ringleaders required at least two teachers acting together as soon as these louts started to needle each other. The kids were wild, and discipline was tough. In the dusty schoolyard, fights broke out in all corners amongst girls as well as boys, and with little or no supervision, they often ended in quite serious blood fights. Back then, no boy ever wanted to be called a sissy, or a softie, or mummy's boy, and the girls were always ready to taunt anyone who showed any weakness or dressed differently or had in their lunchbox food that was in any way different. Name-calling was a favourite pastime, and many of the insulting rhymes being chanted around the playground would start a fight. The parents who were summoned to the school because their little Johnny or Jane misbehaved were informed by means of a note from the principal, sent home via Johnny or Jane. How crazy was that? Did they think the kids were stupid as well as naughty? Obviously, either the parents never got the note, or they were too busy working to attend, or could not speak English, so most parents had no idea of what their children's school life was like, or what mischief they got up to.

What I dreaded most was the end of the day when the troublemakers joined their siblings. On the way home, they would pick fights with the more vulnerable. Anyone who intervened was quickly drawn into the melee. Sixth graders can be quite tough and vicious when in a group, and on occasion the constabulary had to be involved in separating them.

Much as we hated the area in which we lived, we had our own miserable property by the time I started school in 1951, in St Albans. At least it was away from the refugees' holding camps. My parents of course were devastated to learn that their daughter, who had already begun grade 4 in Italy, nearly two years earlier, was now in a class of beginners. We understood that it was to be a temporary measure, until my English language skills improved and in fact the ordeal lasted little more than a month. I dare say that the teachers realised that the teasing and taunting I was being subjected to on a daily basis was far worse than my inability to understand the lessons fully. By the end of the first term I was back in grade 4, though still amongst the oldest in the class and definitely the tallest.

We Have Come a Long Way

We had practically nothing more than a seaworthy chest and two, now battered suitcases when we berthed in Fremantle and from there, the powers of the time decided that we were to continue on to Melbourne, then from there, we were taken to a family holding camp in Bonegilla. To arrive at the Migrant Refugee Camp we had to be transported 'en masse' from the port where we disembarked. We must have looked a pathetic, lost, tired, and insecure group. All the immigrants had just their carrying luggage with them. Their sea chests would be delivered to them later.

Old army troop carriers were despatched to pick us up and deliver us some two hundred miles to what would be our 'home' for a while. Initially we travelled through unpainted and rusting iron-sheeted warehouses, then the trucks followed a residential route and we were amazed to see wooden houses suspended on matchsticks (stilts), all with corrugated iron roofing and little buildings all around. Later we learned that these were the outdoor 'dunnies' that were emptied once a week by someone with a truck who carried a bucket on his head—empty on his way in, but full on the way out! Then there was the separate laundry with one, two or sometimes three raised concrete tubs and often with no doors.

As we continued further out we came to some areas where housing styles seemed more along the solid European brick construction and we were told that these were the houses that the Wogs, Dagos, and the Greeks built. Soon we were bumping along the open roads among fields of yellow grass with machinery in their midst. These were the wheat fields that stretched out as far as the eye could see, and interspersed here and there would be flocks of sheep and herds of cattle. Everything was very strange. The heat became unbearable as the day progressed and we had to have frequent stops. A trip that today would take maybe two or three hours, took us all day to complete. What a shock it was to arrive at our destination to find that we would be housed in half round corrugated-iron aircraft hangars!

Bonegilla – 1951

All the families stayed together at the camp for a few days; each family in a single room. Then the breadwinner, my father, who was on a two year bond with the Victorian Railways, was sent away into the bush somewhere, to work on laying sleepers and tracks, and getting derailed trains back onto the tracks. We didn't know where he was and I daresay that most of the time he didn't either. The men were picked up by truck and delivered back the same way when the job was finished, or when another crew was rostered for duty. Migrants did the hard yakka that the locals didn't want to do. We didn't see him again for days, sometimes for weeks. Then he would come back for a few days' rest—a broken man. Demoralised. At the time I didn't understand that he was more than just tired!

Women and children lived in the camp and everyone had their assigned chores according to their individual capabilities, including the older children. Some of the women took care of groups of younger children. Some became self-styled hairdressers. Many more were required to prepare the food, and though many of the dishes were strange to us, some were quite tasty and eventually we acquired some appreciation for ethnic dishes. The ladies in the kitchen were always complaining that they couldn't get the right ingredients and spices to cook proper dishes, but to us the aromas were enough to make us salivate like Pavlov's dogs with anticipation. Some other women did the community washing that had to be rostered for different days of the week. Others, with various skills, were directed to different areas where needed.

So my mother became the seamstress. She also did some ironing and steam pressing which was such an unpleasant job in the heat. The communal iron had to be pre-booked well in advance, and it was heavy and cumbersome. It had a hinged top covering a cast iron tray that held red live coals to heat the metal, and it was my duty to pick up and deliver the clothes. Usually I took my baby sister with me to let mum have her hands free. It was late afternoon and hot on this particular day and I had completed several errands already when I was asked to pick up the iron from the common laundry. Seeing me approach, one of the elderly ladies asked me to take a full basket back to Mum. In my haste to get back, I picked up the basket and the iron without checking if it was still hot. Of course it was hot, someone had just finished using it! Taking my sister by the hand, I placed the iron in the crook of my arm without thinking. My scream must surely have woken up anyone having an afternoon siesta, no matter how soundly they slept. The shock and the stench of burning flesh made me sick and of course there were no doctors around. First aid consisted of smearing butter on the burn because that was the first thing available, but the salt in the butter made the burn even more painful. The burn didn't take long to bubble and go septic. Soon the skin and flesh seemed to fester and disintegrate leaving a horrid, gaping hole that took forever to heal. When a scab formed I had to keep it soft and moist or normal arm movements would make it crack and bleed again. It is a wonder gangrene did not set in because it was ages before it finally healed. For many months a crust would form, dry out and crack, bleed and fall off. Then the process would start all over again. As I grew and my arm grew, the scar got bigger too, painfully stretching the new skin. To this day, whenever I see a burns victim, the memory of my experience makes my skin crawl. But at least today the treatment and care is more gentle, healing and appropriate, so recovery time is shorter. In our primitive compound, nothing was wasted and everyone pulled his or her weight to make the hard, thankless existence more bearable. Everyone realised very quickly that there was no one around to wait upon us, or clean up after us. We had to be resourceful and self-sufficient.

Here I must grimace as I think of modern day refugees, with their legal representatives who instil in the minds of newcomers all their rights, but neglect to make them aware that they also have responsibilities. Some misguided bleeding hearts make excuses for them when they set fire to their accommodation, or organise riots, or go on hunger strikes. If anyone had dared to do that in our day, we would end up sleeping under the stars until *we* fixed the damage. There was no such luxury as Government handouts of taxpayers' money. Now there are gyms to keep refugees fit—back then there was work, lots of it and it kept us even fitter, mentally as well as physically! Now there are doctors and health care workers to monitor the well-being of asylum seekers who have access to television and libraries, but back then we only had the skills and enthusiasm of the children and their parents for entertainment, if we had the time to be entertained!

In the harsh summer conditions of country Victoria, we sweltered in our makeshift accommodation. Actually, there was nothing very accommodating in the half round hangar space that was partitioned off internally into separate rooms. The families with more children, or children of a different sex, were allocated a second room. My mother, my younger sister (not quite two years old), and I shared a room with myriads of blowflies, mosquitos, and the odd snake that wandered inside. Insect screens were a luxury unheard of in those days. There was no shelter from the sun, heat or rain. The corrugated curved iron construction didn't have eaves, so the sun beat down from every angle all day long and the only respite we could rely on was at meal times. We ate our meals at long tables under yet another corrugated iron roof, but at least this one was flat and had mostly open sides for the air to circulate.

We left Bonegilla before the winter set in, so I can't imagine what the conditions would have been like in the cold and wet. But when the men were back on weekends, many trades were represented by these 'inmates,' and I have no doubt that they would have got together to make the dining area more comfortable, draught and water proof because it was used for children's games as well. Of course tempers flared as many of the families had been living there for a good while. There were only a few men in the camp at any one time, and some of those were malingerers. Often when a large number of people are forced to live together in an enclosed area, troublemakers tend to congregate and they were usually found when the various ethnic groups gathered. There were so many different languages spoken that misunderstandings were common.

There are some people who will only be satisfied when they spread discontent, and cause chaos. But the more rational elements of that disparate society thought about their blessings—few as they were! These were the more temperate, resilient, and pragmatic people who kept the rest of us sane.

Not Your 'Ten Pound Assisted Passage'

We had been given the opportunity for a better way of life, in a new country, far away from war-torn Europe, and a chance to rebuild. Most of us were grateful. The only church in Bonegilla was a sombre cabin that some of the women would try to embellish with wild flowers or coloured paper, their own personal embroidered linen or vases. Generally it was well frequented when there was a service because we all needed something to believe in and hope for, while at other times it provided a quiet time for reflection. Reflection that turned to shocked disbelief, and then prayers of thanks to the Lord, when we heard that the converted U.S. troop carrier that had brought us to Fremantle, then on to Adelaide and finally to Port Melbourne, had actually sunk on the high seas whilst on its return journey. Again, we remembered the rough seas of the Great Australian Bight and all the seasickness on board. How lucky we were to have made it unscathed through that long stretch of wild waters and beautiful coastline that conceals many shipwrecks, to disembark on to terra firma in Melbourne before this final calamity.

I vaguely remembered going through the Suez Canal and the colour of the water a long, long way down. We were ever-so slowly travelling along the Red Sea and the water was such a dark red colour in the dusk that I immediately thought of blood. We were being followed by lots of funny little boats filled with Arab men and children, who wanted to barter their goods for cigarettes or American chocolates or preferably for very scarce U.S. dollars. It was a lively trade with goods being continually raised and lowered on ropes that hoisted full baskets. Mum persuaded Dad to sacrifice a ten-pack carton of cigarettes for a pair of ebony elephants, beautifully polished and complete with a pair of white ivory tusks. They were so heavy and glossy, just like I would have imagined elephants to be.

The ship stopped at Port Said for some mechanical repairs, but at my age I was more in awe of the sweating dark-skinned sailors who were brandishing their batons with unrestrained glee and waiting to pounce on anyone on board who displayed too much curiosity or asked too many questions about the nature of the work and repairs under way. It was the first time that I had come vis-à-vis with dark-skinned males, and these were not the slaves that you get to see in films like 'Gone with the Wind'. These African-American sailors were in charge of this ex-war frigate that required constant work to keep it afloat. Surprisingly, these were the two episodes out of only a total of three that I have any recollection about during that long four and a half month voyage. It was a horror trip, and I often wondered if we were drugged, or tranquillised in order to keep the masses under control in this overcrowded ship.

It was the last ship to leave Northern Europe before the end of the year so they jammed in as many refugees as could possibly fit, in fact I can hardly remember any walks on deck. The only other recollection was the fearful experience of seeing my father together with a group of other refugees, carrying huge paint buckets and brushes, and being ordered to paint the decks in the gunmetal grey of warships. No ifs, no buts or useful suggestions. These baton-wielding Afro-American sailors were obviously put in charge of our passage and they were not going to tolerate any back talk. Someone commented that this was another form of slavery, but in reverse, and the chain gangs were made up of the refugees who were given the so-called 'free' passage in exchange for a two-year work bond in the new country. The motto was, "You want to eat? You have to work for it."

Eventually I discovered that many immigrants came to Australia on a 'ten pound assisted passage' and they had a much easier life.

"Italians Celebrate the Time their Ship Came In." The Age, June, 2002. The fifty years' celebration in Port Melbourne by immigrants and their descendants who mainly came from Trieste and neighbouring Venezia-Guilia substantiate their claim of a dream passage to Australia in the early 50s. So very different from our own!

The 'Luck of the Draw'

I have since seen many photographs of happy groups of immigrants from around the globe. Happy and thankful people who have had a dream voyage in comfortable liners, and even cruise ships. And they seemed to be in the majority! When I was younger, I did not believe these reports, thinking they were only stories designed to make us jealous—after all, how can refugees be allowed to go to the theatre? Did a ship have a theatre? And the food stories—they were most certainly designed to make our mouths water with envy. Who had ever heard of dressing up to go to a dining room on a war ship? But of course the majority of immigrants didn't come on a war ship that had been patched up after it was torpedoed.

On ships like the Oriana, waiters served the meals where there were 'Dining Rooms', and the passengers cleaned themselves and changed to dine. And drinks too.... What utter rubbish!

Stories like these, told by happy people who seemed to have all the luck in the world, did not make us want to join them, as we seemed to have nothing positive to contribute and we were not a gregarious family to start off with. By now we all had a chip on our shoulders, and this only got bigger, when we started to hear stories about some refugees who were being flown in by passenger planes.

What did these people have that we didn't? Were we being punished because we had survived the long war?

A Refugee in Australia – 1951

My father was a city man, well-educated, and used to being respected. Now in Australia, 'the land of milk and honey', he bitterly resented working as a labourer, out in the country, sleeping in a community tent, and eating food that he considered indigenous grub. In fact his work mates would say, "Time for some grub" at mealtimes. I believe the 'grub' often consisted of lamb or mutton, which his stomach could not tolerate or digest, so he went without food. Mother and I would encourage him to give up working for the railways, and do what we had heard others were doing. Many were applying to go to school, and having their former professions recognised. But that often depended on the country's need to have more workers engaged in a certain field, or where those with prior experience could contribute to the development of specific projects as and where they were needed.

Father had strong, definite opinions and ideals but we could see that he was becoming more introverted and demoralised. I have heard him say, in his usual negative manner, "These heathens don't even know the meaning of what it is to be a nautical engineer, so what would they do with one."

Our private thoughts were that he was too keenly aware of his poor language skills and his inability to master the English language. Being a perfectionist all his life, he could not reconcile English grammar and spelling with the structure of Latin-based Italian, and he became more and more despondent, not only because he was not able to exercise his profession and make a contribution where he perceived an obvious need in this young and relatively backward country that was Australia in the 50's, but also because for the first time in his life, he was alone. Really alone!

He spent most of his time with people he couldn't understand and didn't like anyway. He felt he was being made fun of because he always started out well-groomed and tried to be correct. But he had a lot of respect for the Aboriginals he came into contact with. He felt that they had to make do with very little and cop a lot of abuse from some of the rail crew, for no other reason than their race and colour. He keenly understood that a nomadic race couldn't be slotted into a pocket of white man's making and that integration would take several generations to transpire. That it was a process that takes time to evolve. I believe there were quite a few indigenous workers with the rail crews. It was 'the boss fella' and his 'shit kickers' that he objected to, because the Ozzies didn't like to do the hard work. Father was doing the kind of menial work that he hated and had never done before, living in worse conditions than ever before, and this lifestyle did nothing for his diminished confidence. On the positive side, the job allowed him to do a lot of overtime and he wasn't likely to be shot at, though he may die of the bite of a brown, black or whatever other colour snakes come in, or even fall off a cliff.

Some of the areas where the work took him he described as inhospitable, hot, dry, chokingly dusty, with the red dust gluing up the nostrils, and drying the throat to make speaking impossible; his eyes were constantly burning and watering. In the early days in the outback, when he could still muster some humour, he would compare himself and his co-workers to the American Indians in war paint. Tears ran down uncontrollably, leaving white tracks as they coursed down cheeks that were burned by the sun. Several layers of peeling skin covered with red dust and spiked dirty, greasy hair that had nothing to do with fashion. It was difficult to cope with the extremes in temperatures and the unpredictability of the weather, the quick and unexpected downpours that took them all by surprise and in a few minutes turned the red dust into rivers of slimy mud that could take an unprepared man into a swollen river, over rapids and to his death, before anyone could get to him with help.

His mood when he came home was invariably dark and morose. He would be dead tired. Too tired to eat, and too keyed up to sleep, so to try to relax he would drink. This drinking became a ritual that affected the rest of the family.

Mother was more forgiving of the people, the country, the conditions, and generally coped better in any given situation. As she said, they had turned their back on the old country, and there was no return trip. I think that I inherited that resilient personality from her, as well as the ability to move on and make the most of what is readily available by way of useable resources. We were embarrassingly poor and too proud to admit it, so we kept away from people. On seven pounds per fortnight, plus food and nomadic accommodation in whichever camp-site the rail crew worked from, plus as much overtime as he could cope with, father took three months to save a deposit for a block of land and put up a one room fibro-asbestos shed on it, which cost thirty pounds. That was our first home and from there, I walked to school over the railway tracks for almost three years. The land cost one hundred pounds, and it was the first time ever that we had purchased anything on credit. For father it was like a noose around his neck. He did more and more overtime, sometimes staying away from us for up to a month at a time so that this shameful debt would be quickly paid off. We were paying Shylock's interest to a moneylender that had been recommended by some other immigrant and we knew we were being screwed.

I don't actually recall how or exactly when we moved to our new abode in St. Albans because I was still feeling very miserable with the pain of my burnt arm. It had to stay bandaged to protect it. Perhaps I was left with someone to care for me while mum and dad shifted our few belongings, and that someone presented me with the cutest kitten I had ever seen, to try to make me forget my pain and misery. Later, when my arm had healed enough to leave it uncovered for any length of time, this kitten always wanted to lick the wound. Our home/shed was in the middle of a cow paddock that had been subdivided into quarter acre allotments. There was no water or electricity initially, and only cattle tracks in place of roads. In summer everything was yellow and burnt-out dry, and in winter the rain made rivulets of mud all around the shed, with patches of clay that resembled quicksand where one sunk down to the knees in the sticky grey ooze. At the time I remember Mum being almost beside herself with fear, which was quite uncharacteristic of her. Stock grazed all around us and at night we three females would lie awake, listening to the sounds that the animals made. Horses raced and neighed and frolicked, and we prayed they would not run into or kick the flimsy asbestos walls of our 'home'. In the morning, we would open the door to be confronted by cows, gazing at us with perplexed, languorous eyes, obviously wondering what on earth we were doing there. So were we!

The Truly Organic Garden

Hygiene was a problem too. The only running water available to us that first year had to be carried by bucket from the original farmhouse about half a mile up the 'road'. About twenty minutes' walk up the hill, and longer coming down the hill, with two full pails! At least there was no shortage of milk or eggs, which we could buy daily from the farmer for a good price.

Because it was so difficult and tiring to bring food home, that first year Father thought he would dig a few shallow trenches and plant potatoes and tomatoes, after all we had plenty of manure both human and animal available on a daily basis and you couldn't grow food more organically than that!

But keeping up the water supply to the plants was too much of a problem and in the end we let the domestic gardening go.

The second year more people came to live in the area and we all got together and lobbied for water mains to be laid in the street, then had the water pipes connected to our property.

Alas, the Health Department couldn't have too many 'organic' gardens in one area and so the 'dunny man' made an appearance, coming weekly to pick up our 'thunder box' too. We could have continued with our planting then, as there was still an abundance of animal manure, but it was all too hard and time consuming. I guess we felt that the effort was not worth the rewards. Electricity never came to us during our time in St. Albans, but in a short time a strange community evolved. A community that we never really became a part of; we somehow never quite fitted in.

My cute kitten quickly grew into a wandering and promiscuous cat, that looked for attention wherever she could find it and when Mum realised that she was about to present us with her own brood of kittens, it was decided to find it another home. We were sad to see her go but we also knew that we couldn't look after a litter of kittens.

On one occasion when I went to pick up some eggs from the lady of the original farmhouse up the hill, she asked me to join their table for lunch the next day when they had a grandchild visiting. I am not sure if it was to show the granddaughter the eccentric child living in the shack downhill, or to give me a break and a chance to taste something different. The food was strange to me, and somehow I don't think I made a very good impression, because I was never asked back again.

I was not the only strange child at the farmhouse that day. There was also a small Aboriginal girl in an ill-fitting dress, who looked just as uncomfortable as I felt and hardly spoke at all. Instinctively we knew that we were both oddities, on show and about the same age, though I was taller. It was many years later that I learnt that this young and timid indigenous creature was a member of the 'Stolen Generation'.

Dentistry for the masses in those days was, to say the least, in its infancy, with a visit to the dentist meaning a tooth extraction. In the first year at school I lost a perfectly good, healthy, strong tooth just because I had a toothache. Obviously the only cure for pain was to remove the offending tooth. Luckily children in primary schools had a daily milk supplement, funded by the government and delivered to the schools in an effort to ensure that all the children had sufficient daily calcium intake. Many of the children refused to drink the milk and sometimes, when it was left out in the sun, I must admit that it didn't taste the best, but my body seemed to tell me that I needed it and so I often ended up with a double dose, which may be the reason that, apart from another unwarranted extraction a few years later, I still have my own teeth.

Bartering To Survive

Mother was an accomplished seamstress and it didn't take her long to have some clientele, but payment was in the form of a badly-needed small table, two galvanized buckets, a small galvanized tub that we used for bathing and doing the laundry, and a kerosene primus with a big single burner that we used to heat up the water in our large saucepan for washing both ourselves and our clothes. We also did some cooking in this multi-purpose utensil.

Needless to say, the meals were very basic and as nutritious as cooking in one saucepan can be. Whatever was cooked had to be eaten immediately, or at least on the same day, as there was no refrigeration in our home. All food had to be purchased on the day it was to be used because, especially in the summer, nothing lasted and the blowflies would have a field day buzzing around any exposed food.

Eventually we purchased two pine chairs. We two kids sat on the battered sea chest that contained all of our other possessions that we had brought over from Italy.

Early in the 50's, Footscray was already a substantial town, halfway between where we lived and the city of Melbourne. It was there that mother found her first real paying job. She worked long hours on her feet at Smorgon's Smallgoods, then she would walk the long track home from the railway station, carrying the food she had bought along the way for our daily meal. But by the time she got home, she was too tired, and it was too late to start cooking. It soon became another one of my chores.

With the end of summer, there was worse to come, as I was now responsible for a young sister. A two year old cannot be left home alone, so we had to find someone to care for her while I was at school. An older lady was recommended, and she charged ten shillings for the five-day school week. Half a pound was a lot of money for us back in those early times, so I was severely reprimanded when one day I lost that precious note.

Each day, before leaving for school, my little sister Ondina (which translates to 'a small wave'), had to be dressed and delivered to her carer who lived a short distance beyond the school, then at the end of the day I had to pick her up again and we would walk home.

It was a real drag in winter, squelching through the mud and cold rain in our galoshes, that we had to meticulously clean before taking them indoors, because for us there was nowhere to leave them, we had no porch. I have often said that at eleven I became my sister's mother, so any issues or hang-ups that she may have developed over the years were probably my fault and as she grew up and developed, we became more distant. But by then, we had long left the hellhole that was St. Albans.

School was the only place where one got away with being an untidy slob and 'monkey see, monkey do', I too kicked my galoshes off, and left them there, in a heap, on the school porch until I needed them for the return home, like every other child did.

Once we had life's basics, like a single bed that I shared with my baby sister, a double bed for Mum and Dad, and a massive wardrobe that also served as a room divider, creating a pleasant separation of the living and sleeping areas, Mum started looking for another job that would be more suited to her talents.

By then, word had gotten around that she was a precise and skilful dressmaker, so she was able to find work more to her liking with a Jewish lady, whose High Couture establishment catered for the upper echelons of immigrant society who lived in the well-to-do areas of St. Kilda, Elwood, Caulfield, etc. on Melbourne's east side, a far, far cry from where we lived.

Educating Each Other

After a short apprenticeship with Madam Bazaar (I can't remember the lady's name but that was the name of her business), it was decided Mum would take work home, to save her all those long hours of travel time that she would otherwise have to tackle on a daily basis. At the end of the week, the completed dresses were then taken back in the two battered suitcases that had come across the oceans with us. I don't think that Madam Bazaar had any idea of how, or where we lived back then.

Soon the double bed had a mountain of Moygashel linen dresses piled onto it and at night they were carefully wrapped in white sheets and placed in a corner of the spotless floor, so Mother and Father, when he was home, could go to sleep. Of course Mum had to buy a sewing machine to be able to work from home, so a beautifully polished Singer treadle sewing machine, with ornate cast iron sides and an expensive price tag, took pride of place under the only window in our 'bungalow'—it had now became more gentrified, but in name only. Life, if anything, became more difficult as the space became more crowded.

In the ensuing months since starting school, every day, without fail, I had to repeat to my mother every single word that I learnt, every sentence composition, and every grammatical structure. I became my mother's teacher and she paraphrased, asked questions, learning exceptionally well and quickly, while her legs kept treading on her new machine and her fingers kept on sewing. Throughout her life she was an avid reader and when she had to deliver her completed work to Madam Bazaar, she would buy an American magazine called 'Grand Hotel' and would read it word by word on the long train trip, then she would get me to translate and explain later in the evening, when together we would work on syntax and pronunciation, learning phonetic clusters and making up our own stories while we worked. Naturally, she would not allow my hands to remain idle either and I became very good at sewing on buttons—millions of them, hooks and eyelets, and hand stitching hems.

In the winter it was bitterly cold in our primitive, barely habitable shack that had only thin, asbestos fibro walls to shelter us from the elements. No lining was ever nailed to the inside walls to provide an insulating barrier. The only heating we had was a kerosene heater that we kept very close to us when we were sewing at night. Thinking back, I am amazed that we didn't set the place alight with the clothes that we were working on always being so close to the naked flames. We had to bring the empty tins of the kerosene that we used for cooking on the primus stove and for lighting the hurricane lantern that provided us with the only light, as well as for the heater that we used in winter, back to the supplier who would refill them for us.

We survived the cold for two winters but Ondina had to have warm clothes for the long walk to her carer each day, so Mother bought her a long white rabbit coat that doubled up as a blanket at night. We certainly lived like the pioneers of times long gone!

As one would expect, I soon became dissatisfied with my own clothes and I begged mum to let me sew too. Surprisingly, she thought that was a good idea and together we went to the local shop that usually had very little variety, but we managed to buy a length of summer-weight grosgrain material that had a band of coloured flowers in red, a band of the flowers in yellow and a band in blue flowers, on a white background. It was really pretty, even by today's standards.

But I could only sew when mother wasn't home. Any other time she was using the sewing machine non-stop herself. She would make some suggestions about the technicalities of sewing but mostly left me to my own devices to figure things out for myself, and of course I made mistakes. That first outfit ended up as a full skirt with a midriff top simply because I didn't cut the bodice long enough to be able to attach it to the skirt. It looked cute anyway!

Friendships

By that time, I had made some friends at school and they always seemed to be better dressed, had more time to socialise, and lived closer to the school and the shops. They had better houses and their own bedrooms, though often they shared them with other siblings. Somehow they seemed to always have more time and money than we did, and didn't mind having their friends around to listen to records or to the radio. Contrary to expectations, and even with Mum earning good money, discontent set in. We should have been happier, but instead we were all getting seriously depressed. Our social life as a family was practically non-existent. Father started to drink heavily and Mother didn't want to go out with him when he was under the influence, which made him angry and then he drank even more.

Arguments broke out and often ended in physical fights. Everyone was getting tired and frustrated. It even got to the stage where we wished he wouldn't be coming home, because with him came a gallon of plonk. The cheap wine that he would pick up at Young and Jackson's, the hotel where he would go with his work mates for a meal, before catching the last train home.

Just after my 12th birthday I started to menstruate. Of course I thought I was dying, never having been told the facts of life. How was I to know what was going on within my own body? To make up for this instance of maternal negligence, my mother bought me my first piece of jewellery and I wanted to live again! I wanted to wear and show off the lovely, heart-shaped locket that opened up to take two photographs. Only problem was that we had no photographs, not even old ones. No camera either. But the locket had a beautiful, bright red ruby. Never mind that it was tiny, it was all mine. Anyway, no one knew that the heart didn't contain any photographs—it never did and still doesn't. I think that was when my three girlfriends accepted me as one of them. The one I liked the most was a gentle Egyptian girl, with glossy, jet black, wavy hair, a little younger than us, but bright and clever, with a good knowledge of English and professional parents, who had great ambition for their only daughter. I heard that later she became a lawyer, and the family returned to Egypt. I was never invited into their home. In fact very few people were, as they seemed to have their own circle of Muslim friends. When the family left Australia, none of us ever heard from her again.

However, it was the other two who protected me from the schoolyard bullies. They were one and two years older than I was, and they often walked with me and my little sister part of the way home. They were our guardian angels and we felt safer walking with them.

Deep down I felt that I was still an only child myself because my sister was a responsibility, and not a companion, so it was a natural progression that I would become closer to one of the angels who was also an only child. Tonia was a girl born in the Ukraine from a Polish father and German mother. The other girl, Vera, had a bigger circle of friends, she had been at the same school for longer, had two siblings and she had been a polio victim who, though she had treatment in the very early stages of the disease, was still left with a slight limp and a big chip on her shoulder.

Vera was the eldest one. Though we kept in touch on and off over the years, we never became really, really close and we didn't include her in our plans on the day when Tonia and I decided to wag school. It was towards the end of sixth grade and just before I left the area for good. It must have been on a day when I knew that Mother would be home with Ondina, because the outing had to be planned the day before. Tonia was the only one with a bicycle so we arranged to meet and she would dink me. Can't say that I remember how that worked on the old bikes, but I think that I sat on the seat and she pedalled standing up. Then we would change places, taking turns.

We had a long way to go to my choice of picnic spot. Probably a couple of miles to the west from school (some three kilometres) there was a stream where (we were told) people could swim. We followed the given directions, eventually coming to a rocky cliff area where a limpid brook flowed into a waterhole below. As neither of us were swimmers, we were sensible enough not to venture into the deep waterhole and were quite content to walk along the stream flowing between the rocks, and cooling our hot bodies by splashing each other, then laying on the rocks to sunbake and eat our cut lunch.

For me it was freedom I had never before experienced. It was also a day of quiet reflection of the impending parting of our ways. We were finishing primary school and I was going away to live on the other side of town. It would be too far away for us to be able to meet often. Soon after, our other friend Vera met a young man who had also emigrated from Hungary, the same country as Vera and her family. He arrived one year after the 1956 Hungarian revolution. They married soon after, and lived a good life together until her demise a few years back. There is a lot to be said for marrying a compatriot.

I also married at barely 19, but my life turned out vastly different.

A Marriage of Faith, Long Ago

Mother and Father were married in 1939 on a bleak, windy, and rainy day in December. She said she wore a heavy, brown, borrowed coat over a skirt and black jumper, black being the colour of mourning. I never knew the exact wedding date, but I think it was sometime during the Christmas celebrations, or between Christmas and Epiphany, my reasoning being, that the birth of Christ signified renewed hope. But then why did she wear black? As I was born early in July, anniversaries were never mentioned. Obviously, I was not a premature baby.

The name of the church *La Chiesa di Sant'Eufemia* where they were married hasn't changed over the years and it had mystic connotations going back to the time of the Crusaders. It was named after a young Christian girl who would not give up her faith even under threat of death.

The legend has been told since time immemorial with a few variations, but essentially this is how it goes: A young, virgin girl named Eufemia was captured and tortured by an invading army of Turks while she was praying on the steps of the church. It was during the time of the Ottoman Empire. She was violated and then her arms were cut off, but still she was a believer who would not renounce her Christian faith, so she was thrown into the sea. Hundreds of years later, her still preserved body was washed up on the rocky beach, from where she had been cast off, but she was inside a sarcophagus.

The story goes that her arms had been restored to her, and her hands were clasped in prayer. She was made a Saint, and her tomb is inside the church, but the marble sculpted sarcophagus remains on the rocky beach, in front of the church to this day, for all to see. This iconic church is one of the few surviving establishments that were relatively undamaged in the furious fighting of the World War Two era, when the indiscriminate devastation of historic buildings, particularly churches, were regularly carried out by the communist partisans who shunned religion.

This church is now one of the most recognisable landmarks on tourism brochures for the region. A region that is still known to survivors as 'La Bella Istria', but now better known globally as Croatia. After the war, the newly formed country of Yugoslavia underwent a horrific period of instability and eventually was carved back into six separate and autonomous republics, and one independent state, in the early nineties.

Mother was born in a town villa, '*in una calle dietro la chiesa*' (in a lane behind the church). Her magnificent contralto voice echoed, and bounced back and forth between the massive stone walls of the ancient buildings throughout her young years, until grandmother died of cancer at a young age after a long illness. The subsequent eviction of the remaining members of the family, for some unpaid medical bills, was a bitter blow, but at least they still had another house that belonged to the extended family. They called it the stables, and it could be made liveable with a bit of imagination and a lot of work. It was half way from town to the family farm and it housed only the mule, now that they had sold all other livestock to pay for the medical bills. They had kept it as a pet for all those years. Now this '*asino*' would come in handy as the working beast she was meant to be. Mother always said that she was a very intelligent beast, and that they kept her on the straight and narrow work path by threatening to make sausages from this ass if she didn't toe the line.

Mother felt that she had given most of her life to nurturing her younger siblings and nursing her ailing mother, and it was now time to look for a new direction to her own life. She went to Algiers that was under Italy's dominion, and there she worked for some time with a French diplomat's family, in the role of governess/instructor to their young children. There were three little girls, bright and pretty, in the latest Parisian dresses, which mother felt were a bit over the top in the sweltering heat of North Africa. Then there was an older boy, who had a male instructor preparing him for college on the Continent. Teaching the girls the Italian language was a paying, live-in job and all the while she was learning French from them. This period, between '36 and '39 was probably the best time of her life! A time that took her away from the pain of losing her mother as well as her home, gave her money, the independence she never had, and taught her a new language as well.

Her siblings were now old enough to fend for themselves and even to help the patriarch on the family farm, which bordered the Adriatic Sea in Rovigno, in the province of Istria. They made the stables into a comfortable home, and all surviving members lived there. Sadly, the communists ruling Yugoslavia exiled them to Trieste in the mid to late 1940's.

From mother's side of the family, I must also have inherited a love of the land, a respect for the fertile soil, and an affinity with the sea. The smell of the biting salty air, the ever-changing surface of the sea—sometimes a smooth calm, pale blue, that was almost transparent all the way down to the rocky bottom that is characteristic of that northern part of the Adriatic. Sometimes an indigo blue-black, windy, ruffled sea would reflect a sky laden with ominous thunderclouds. Howling cold winds would send them rolling relentlessly land-bound and chase the birds from the air to seek shelter in the trees, or under the old tiled eaves of ancient houses. At other times, angry and dark, unforgiving and tempestuous skies would turn, in the blink of an eye, to brilliant rainbows and russet sunsets, with the promise of a perfect day on the morrow. The rugged coastline is continuously hammered by the pounding waves, spraying fountains of salty water onto the footpaths.

From Father's ancestors came the 'Superbia', the pride and arrogance of a long line of Venetian Aristocracy. I am not sure how Father came to be born in Istria, though at the time Grandfather

Tomaso was a Naval Customs officer working on the Adriatic Coast and later, after father graduated, he also went on to work at the Naval Institute in Istria, on the north-eastern coast of Italy. And that is where ultimately I was born. But times had changed.

The Degradation of Family Life

As the war raged in Europe, a whole way of life ended. In Italy, there was no more stability. No more cohesive family life. The ideology of the young was in stark contrast with the age held beliefs of the elders. Arrogance clashed with stubbornness. Women took on a new role, became more assertive and proactive, having to take over jobs that had previously been the domain of their male counterparts, and their lives were at stake as well.

Early in the new decade it soon became evident that there were several major factions, with each one fighting for supremacy. Italy was a monarchy. One faction was Communist, Mussolini was the Fascist dictator who committed Italy to fight alongside Germany; one was Republican and wanted to depose the King; another faction was Democratic. This is a very loose explanation, as I never wanted to become politically involved but I understand that the democrats wanted to change the status quo and there were major upheavals throughout Italy. No party was well-organised or unified. King Vittorio Emanuel lll had Mussolini arrested in 1943 during the major uprising in northern Italy, then he stepped aside in favour of his son, Umberto. The entire political scene was woefully disorganised and the young King Umberto ll worked with the Allied Forces when Sicily was occupied. But the Germans occupied the northern part of the country, and the Nazi Special Forces set Mussolini free. Amongst all this chaos, the last king of Italy from the house of Savoy finally abdicated in June 1946 and Italy was proclaimed a Republic. This did not bring peace.

The Post-War Years

Contrary to common perception, World War Two did not end on a specific day, or month, or even year all over Europe but continued on for much longer than August 1945. For more than another two years, the atrocities of hate and retribution (and the factional power struggles) bisected the countries of Italy and Yugoslavia. Countless cases of murder, child genocide, even the disappearance of whole families were reported, but as there was no law and order, nothing was done and rather than become involved, people would shut up instead of running the risk of jeopardising their own or their family's safety. Distrust and betrayal, constant fear and hunger were our bedfellows, before the post-war mass migration program that the International Refugee Organisation (IRO) started. And of course the Mafia had its extortionist tentacles everywhere. For a fee, a family name will move quicker up the list of evacuees.

They say a very young child cannot remember events of a global scale. But if one experiences horrors that touch you personally, then those horrors will remain with you and haunt you forever. By the time I was around three years of age, I was in the care of my paternal grandmother who had not left the Adriatic town of the Naval Institute, though by then Grandfather had died. His pension was quite adequate to support me and another one of her grandchildren as well as herself. My cousin was a boy just a couple of years older than me, who was sporting a 'short back and sides' haircut. While this insignificant detail may seem irrelevant when whole families were now short of food, and scrounging for roots and berries in the country, it may well have saved my life in the months and years to follow, because on his next visit home, father shaved my head to make sure that I too looked like a boy, and instructed his mother that I must be dressed like one at all times as well.

Many years later, by means now forgotten, I came across a photograph of me playing on the beach alongside Grandmother. And how I hated my father then, for cutting away my beautiful, titian curls. Angrily, I confronted my mother. How could she possibly allow such sacrilege, the visual de-sexing of her only daughter? What she told me sent shivers down my spine and goose bumps throughout my body. It was the only time ever that she spoke in detail of some of the unimaginable horrors of war.

Two Epic Films

Angelina Jolie made a film that included some of the atrocities committed during another, a later warring period. I have not seen it, but I imagine she would have had to tone it down some, to appease some 'delicate' viewers.

After WWII, as a part of the peace treaty, the Allies (US, Britain and the USSR) took Istria away from Italy and incorporated it into a new country that they formed and called it Yugoslavia. This Peace Treaty had the opposite effect and peace did not return to Italy. A civil war between the three major political factions and the new Yugoslavia continued for another two years. The fighting was so vicious that friends and neighbours, and sometimes even family members, fought each other to the death. And then there was retribution!

There was also internal fighting between the 'new rulers' representing Yugoslavia and the original inhabitants, who now understandably feared genocide. Some ethnic groups became so depraved and vengeful that they would snatch little girls and babies and literally rip them apart.

Around that time, one of my uncles, the youngest brother that my mother had, was betrayed and killed. It was said that his body was weighted down and thrown in the *Canale di Leme* (the Lem Canal), a bottomless canyon washed at high tide by the Adriatic Sea. In any event, his body was never found. He was only one of the many hundreds of thousands, some say up to two million, people who have never been accounted for. I have read recently in one of the publications issued by a group of the remaining survivors from the times of the massacre in Istria, that the number of people missing and unaccounted could well top two million.

The site of this bottomless cemetery later became infamous when the film 'The Vikings' was filmed in that location in 1949, starring Kirk Douglas. It is a terrain so inaccessible, naturally rugged, and untamed that it would spell certain death for the unwary. It is a truly awe-inspiring section of the coastline and one that holds many secrets never to be revealed, though there have been many concerted efforts to unveil these mysteries over the decades that followed.

With this new information it became abundantly clear why my hair was cut off, and why I was left with Grandmother so often. Mother had joined the guerrilla warfare, and with whatever weapons they could muster, they roamed the hills and valleys in search of the Communists (partisans, what a misnomer that was). In other words, they hunted the enemy, and those who betrayed, killed and ousted the rightful landowners who were working the land for centuries past. The executions of so called 'collaborators' were on public display in the town square. The hate, I am told, was etched on people's faces.

Father was working without pause at the Naval Academy where they were supplying the Italian Navy with torpedoes, but once the city fell, he joined Mother in hand-to-hand combat and guerrilla warfare. This information came to me many years later, because neither one of my parents ever spoke about that period.

"You Are Under Interrogation"

At the time we were living in what I remember as an impressive white, two-storey house, and I had the bedroom upstairs. Again, Grandmother and my older cousin were with us. As clear as in a picture, I can even now see the huge loquat tree with the gnarled branches that we called American apricots because we never knew its correct name. It was laden with fruit, growing just outside our bedroom window. The moon was shining brightly on the orange coloured fruit.

It was a full moon, and the temptation was too great. We should have been asleep, but my cousin dared me to climb out of the window with him. I was never one to ignore a challenge, so we crawled along the roof tiles right up to the edge to pull the delicious fruit from the overhanging branches. We stuffed ourselves full of as much fruit as we could, spitting out the large pips over the roof, and had barely climbed back inside when there was a tremendous noise at the front door. Loud banging with the butts of rifles in the middle of the night. The lock gave way and a group of men forced their way inside. They had come looking for Father. They took him away, and it was some time before we saw him again. Naturally, I was frightened, but both my parents seemed to be always coming and going, so I was not too worried. But when some time later he finally did return, he had horrific injuries consistent with torture. I was told he fell!

The bombings became more frequent and destructive, and as soon as the air raid sirens shrieked, we all raced to the shelters. This particular morning in winter, Mother managed to grab her coat, and with me in her arms, she raced out amongst the bombs and the fires that they had started. Houses were exploding all around us and craters opened up at our feet as the roads caved under. To avoid falling into one of these holes, Mother sidestepped just as a beam from the roof of someone's house flew upward and came to rest at her feet. With the momentum of her flight, she was unable to avoid it, and her foot landed on a huge, rusty nail that pierced her shoe, went through her foot and out the top of it, impaling her. As she toppled over, one of the older ladies grabbed me from her arms, and continued running on to the large rock shelter carved out into a hillside. It was a tunnel-like structure, with seats carved out in the rock face interior and it was there that I learnt to finger crochet. All the ladies did their utmost to distract us children, by teaching us different skills that required some degree of concentration, to keep the crippling fear that gripped us all at bay, at least temporarily.

Not very long after, I woke up early one Sunday morning to the sound of mourning bells. Everyone was still in bed so I dressed and wandered up the hill toward the church not too far away. The sun was just rising over the hill so I had it in my eyes. But as I approached the hill, I could see the silhouettes of three structures of what appeared to be crosses. Intrigued, because it was not Easter time, I continued uphill. As I got closer, I could see that something was attached to each cross. Suddenly, as the sun burst over the trees on the horizon, I could see three men nailed to the crosses. They were naked, and they had been hung first because the ropes were still around their necks, and nailed later.

I got back inside the house just as Grandma was coming to look for me. Distraught, I told my story only to have it vehemently denied. However, no one left the house that day. No one took me up that hill to disprove what I had seen. It was just a bad dream, I was told.

Well! Tell me why then, I can still clearly, in my mind, see that scene now? Despite all claims to the contrary, no young child dreams of seeing three men hung and nailed to three crosses, and then clearly remembers the incident for the rest of her life! Of course, I do not have a clear time frame that I can check on, because once my parents migrated, they never spoke again of the atrocities of war, nor would they answer any questions, saying instead that it was a period of their lives they wanted to leave behind them. What nightmares they must have been having! They could not possibly ever forget their ordeals, but I understand them for not wanting to relive that period, over and over again, as so many other migrants did. Unfortunately for me, I am left with many unanswered questions and doubts in my mind, time lapses that I cannot fill because now there is no one left alive that I can ask. But, best let the dead rest in peace.

Whooping Cough

Memories of my parents and our relatives during the 40's are very sketchy and fragmented. It must have been during my mother's guerrilla fighting days that she became pregnant. Certainly it was at a time when I didn't get to see much of either her or Father. At that time I must have been around four years old, because another photograph had surfaced portraying me like a lost waif, and dressed in practically dowdy rags. No one knows who took that photo or where, as it seemed so uncharacteristic and I wondered if it was taken while I was in a convent or an orphanage. Next to me was a gorgeous child in a white, full-length, lapin (rabbit) fur coat, with matching fur bonnet. Rabbits were a good source of food, were easy to breed and their fur was used for winter clothing. The pathetic look on my face would make anybody want to cry. I seemed to be gazing longingly at this other unknown child.

Worse, much, much worse, was to come.

The other child was in the initial stages of whooping cough and highly contagious. She passed her disease on to me at a time when mother was close to giving birth, and I suddenly found myself in a convent in Padova, with no clear idea of how I got there, but apparently I had to be distanced from Mother immediately. Alas, it was too late, as by then, she too had contracted whooping cough, and the physical exertion of the continual coughing brought on an early parturition. Much to my Father's delight, he now had a son.

The joy was short lived. The new baby wasn't strong enough to survive the onslaught of the disease that his mother passed on to him at such a tender age, and at just under three weeks of age, he drew his last feeble breath. I never knew his name.

Needless to say, Father was devastated. With a wife still in a convent hospital, and in isolation, he sought solace with his fighting mates. He drank whatever raw alcohol was available, until he collapsed in a heap. For nine days he maintained this state of stupor until someone slapped him sober because he was becoming a danger, not only to himself, but to the whole platoon, and this could have unforeseen repercussions in that combatant environment.

Finally he was coherent enough to face his wife, the mother of his boy child. The person who carried in her womb for nine months, the child that died in her arms. For a mother, a baby is her baby, be it a boy or a girl, her baby is blood of her blood, and equally precious. For a European man, a male child is the reincarnation of himself. The one who will carry forth his name. Thus, the first wedge was driven between them. Each had an intolerable pain that they could not communicate to the other. And the first chink in the armour of their love appeared.

Eventually, both mother and I left the convent, but at a different time, and in my mind there is a huge blank for the next couple of years. I simply cannot piece anything together in a coherent time frame. However, we must have gone back to my and Father's birth city at some stage, because I very clearly remember the episode (seeing the three naked men nailed to crosses, described earlier), that they would never confirm (nor categorically deny).

The fighting continued. Families became fragmented. Siblings lost touch with each other. We were continually moving around and every adult we met seemed to be holding his or her index finger to their lips and telling us children, "Shhh, don't say anything", so we children withdrew into our own private world of 'make believe' where everything was fine, safe and we had plenty to eat.

What Are We Now?

Overnight, my father, mother, and I had 'changed' nationality. We suddenly found ourselves stripped and discredited of our proud Italian citizenship. We were now Yugoslavs, who couldn't even speak the language and who would not have survived had we stayed on, because under the self-proclaimed Communist leader, Marshal Tito, the massacres continued for another two years, and the fear of betrayal was constantly with us.

The secret police, so strong and active, with tentacles throughout Europe, excelled in their dedication to have dissenters exterminated, especially if they were Italian landholders, so they could steal their lands.

Strangers would take us into their homes for days and weeks, and finally, with the help of friends, and of friends of friends, we made it to the new border and Trieste. As we were escaping from Yugoslavia, we had to destroy the new documents that the regime had issued to us, because once we got over the border they became dangerous to have with us and if these documents had been found upon us by our Italian compatriots, we would have been shot as traitors. No one trusted anyone in or out of uniform any more, even if they appeared to be friendly, as there were traitors all around. Many people died by execution for no valid reason.

Many others became great actors and were able to change their stories to suit the changing situation simply to survive. But these people became a threat to the other citizens who had been their friends so recently. They were the much-hated traitors, suspected of spying for the authorities. People could not be trusted. There was still much fighting all around Trieste, with no one being sure who was friend or foe. There were those who would have turned us in to the authorities of the day, because without papers and documents, we were nothing, neither Italian, nor the hated Yugoslavs. We were in limbo and it was a struggle just to stay alive. This period is sketchy in my mind. We left the town of my birth and I did not return until 1984, when I felt it was time to visit my native country that was no longer the country of my birth.

By No Means Alone

Just recently, I met an older person who lived in Trieste at the time of our exile and we started to talk about that period. Naturally I queried some of my memories. He did not for one moment think that what I had described as having seen and lived through during my early childhood was in any way exaggerated, or imagined. In fact it was only a small part of what was happening all around us. The war seemed to be more clear cut elsewhere but in Italy and across the now newly formed country called Yugoslavia, there were many factions who wanted to claim a piece of the booty and the internal fighting was as vicious as it had ever been before the official Armistice Day. Now it was personal. Neighbour against neighbour. If that were possible, some of the recollections that he related were even worse than my own nightmares.

He recalled times when normal, decent, law-abiding neighbours would morph into bands of rabid animals. The hate within a human being that has suffered extreme mental anguish, like that caused by the violent death of a child or children, would fester and explode into unnatural acts of violence, of premeditated retribution.

He recalled an instance when an injured person threw a homemade bomb into a van of German soldiers, killing five of them, then he died himself. But to teach the citizens a lesson, fifty citizens were taken randomly from their homes by the Germans, stripped and hung in the city's public square, as an example of the revenge that was common in those times. That is a ratio of ten to one.

I understand that in 1943 there was a massive revolt by the Italian population that never wanted to be involved with the war at all, nor had wanted to side up with Germany. The catalyst for this revolt was the Nazi invasion of Italy across the northern border and the persecution of all dissenters. Their ruthlessness in the well-documented attempted extermination of the Jews did not stop with the Jewish population but also involved anyone who was a friend or sympathiser, or even a neighbour or client of a Jewish person.

Civil war has always been the most destructive of wars. It turns father against son, brother against brother. It is a truly insidious and reprehensible form of conquest, with no winner and each side eventually is left to 'lick their wounds'—my father's words. Land is of paramount importance in Europe. In fact, everywhere in the old continent land is power. A power to be used immediately, and within a few months of the Communist takeover, Polaris, the fertile lands and pastures of my mother's family ancestral farm was turned into the new Jadran Youth Camp. These beautiful shores and the pristine waters so clear that one could see oneself reflected in the smooth surface of the bay; where the small silvery fishes flash past white rocks and pebbles with the bigger fish fast on their tail. Waters that were transparent all the way down to the bottom quickly became the playground of Communist youths, who were still being indoctrinated along party lines. Many became the Yugoslav version of the Nazis—The Ustaše. As long as they did as they were told, they could enjoy the fruits of the labours of others.

And to make sure that they did not lose their advantage, many preyed on the weak, old, and tired. These youths were the product of the times. They had seen countless atrocities in their short lives and were so hardened of heart and spirit as to want to impart even more fear and grief.

No wonder Grandfather died of a broken heart! He had lost his beloved Polaris where he was born, the farm that had been in the family for generations and should have been the inheritance of his off-spring. He had nothing left to live for.

After the breakdown of Communism in Yugoslavia in the early 1990's, the country was separated into seven regions, comprising of the new republics of Serbia, Slovenia, Croatia, Montenegro, Macedonia, Bosnia-Herzegovina, and the autonomous landlocked region of Kosovo.

Another Life

My aunt Lucia was a classic titian beauty, a Veronese of distinction. When she married a '*de Costantini*' of the Venetian aristocracy, her social status was indisputable. Somehow with the onset of war and throughout, they remained uninvolved and refused to take sides. Perhaps they saw through all the lies, or history had taught them the futility of conflict. Some referred to them as cowards. Or perhaps they felt that they had nothing to lose. Whatever their reasoning, they managed to come through the official five years of WWII relatively unscathed, and refused to believe that there was another war in progress across the Adriatic. A war where my mother's family stood to lose everything that many generations before her had built up.

At some time during this final period, I must have been entrusted to the care of '*Zia Lucia*' and by then she also had a son, not much older than me, a precocious seven year old, destined to become Mayor of Venice. Lucia, like my father, was a perfectionist, always perfectly groomed. She was a patron of the Arts and the Theatre, so when the perceived 'peace' returned to Italy, she immediately became involved with the Classic Operas and the Theatre.

It was my first experience with the stage, though Mother sung many of the operatic arias whenever she had the opportunity. She seemed to know them all. It was said that Gilda's voice was the nectar that soothed and healed the soul, and those who were sick or injured lived just to hear her sing. Father was intensely jealous. He certainly admired her voice, but he couldn't handle the attention she was getting from other males, and it drove him insane. How typical to believe that his wife's beautiful voice should be only for him. Not only that her classic beauty should be kept behind doors, also her healing hands and spirit that had helped and soothed so many should now lie idle. He forbade her to sing in public, and in the end she had to stop. 'The Lord has spoken!' (It was another sign of the times)

Aunt Lucia took me to see *'Lucia di Lammermoor'*, and maybe it was just a coincidence that the opera had the same first name as hers, but I was not impressed to sit through a play where a mad woman goes shrieking around the stage with a huge knife in her hand, kills her new husband on their wedding night, and ultimately ends up plunging it into herself. I had seen blood and killings close to home and in real life, and I didn't need to sit through this again in the name of entertainment.

By contrast, when Mother returned from wherever she had vanished to and listened to my critique, she took me to the *'Arena di Verona'* for a performance of the immortal 'Aida'. The Coliseum that had been so badly damaged in the U.S. air raids now had a complete fanfare of animals, white war horses, lumbering pack camels, and a train of live elephants, hundreds of slaves, and sensational sets. It was a spectacle to be remembered—and I still do. There were plenty of holes in the walls, so that those immense beasts could be herded in and out, as required. The people now wanted to be entertained and our senses absorbed the feel of timelessness that the shepherds imparted while tending their flock to the accompaniment of twelve violins. The eeriness of the blue Nile in the moonlight, complemented with the intonation of the flutes and the harp; the trumpets of the 'Triumphal March' is a memory that even so early in my life touched me deeply, and I can still almost hear its riveting pathos now. But the eternal love triangle, in a world so grounded in the conquests of war, escaped my sensibilities at so tender an age, so it wasn't until much later that I truly came to appreciate the grandeur of Aida and the genius of Verdi. Though I have been generally disappointed by the modern versions, the grandeur and pathos have been watered down—diminished.

Just like in those other literary epics, 'War and Peace', 'Gone With the Wind', 'Doctor Zhivago', and many, many others, no matter how often we read and discuss the stupidity of war, or witness the resulting agony of the conflicts on humanity, the world has learnt nothing. History repeats itself, as the greed of nations prevail. Those in power have always been excellent orators and able to persuade or threaten the masses into believing that fighting brings glory. Fighting only brings death and misery, starvation and hardships. How can we be so naive?

There Is Hope for a Better Life

Somehow, after the war and our move to the south of Italy, Father found work as a Naval engineer in the industrial port city of Taranto. It was now 1948 and it was here that my little sister was born on the last day of the year just before midnight. There was finally some semblance of order and stability in our lives, and I went to the local school where the dialect was Tarantino.

It was quite a walk home and on the way we picked fat *'asparagi'* for dinner. The juicy, fat spears grew among the rocks where poisonous vipers also nested. We were lucky that these vipers were as timid as they were deadly, but we did see plenty, slithering away from us as we scrambled among the rocks. It was around this time that I started to have nightmares about snakes. Not the thin vipers that I could see live almost daily, but big, fat constricting snakes that one sees on church murals wrapped around 'sinners' on their way to purgatory, or hell. The boa constrictors with gaping mouths and forked tongues squeezing the life out of fat men and women, who had obviously indulged in a life of gluttony, probably with no thought about the starving multitudes, were now being punished. Their grotesquely depicted faces with bulging eyes and swollen tongues protruding out of discoloured, distorted faces. They were horrible, screaming nightmares that plagued me throughout my life and I often wondered what I had done to offend the priests, who preached about damnation, and the ever-consuming fires of hell. I also wondered if those who had vanquished and survived, went to church to confess their sins to some priest hiding behind a grate and got away scot-free, with the traces of blood still wet on their hands. To me that seemed hypocritical.

With the war now behind us, there was time for the finer aspects of life, and Father was able to locate the works of Dante Alighieri, the philosopher and poet from Verona that he had been studying years back in his student days. Re-energised with the intense passion and admiration he felt for his works, Father would now spend every spare minute he had learning and reciting some passage from 'Il Paradiso', or 'Purgatorio', or 'Inferno', and driving Mum crazy in the process. He would carry on, "Abandon all hope those who enter these gates."

I thought now we could start hoping for a better life! No wonder I was having nightmares about snakes!

Food was no longer a problem and most essentials were available now for a price, but when Mother wanted fresh eggs for us, Dad built a chook pen out of slabs of rock. It was his pride and joy and neighbours would come to admire his handiwork, laughing and saying that it would have withstood air raids and bombs, as it was much sturdier than the hastily built houses we all lived in currently.

We children were discovering numerous unexploded bombs on our way to and from school, and some of us did some really stupid things like pelting rocks onto the casing to see if we could make them explode, and trying to see how many could sit astride them as on a horse smacking its 'rump' to make it go faster. There were no play parks with safety fences around them and children made their own entertainment. If we climbed a tree and fell off, breaking a limb, or fell off a bike and scraped our knees and got a bleeding nose, it was regarded as part of growing up.

Once when I attempted to climb onto a swing that had been commandeered by some older children, they unceremoniously pushed me off, causing me to scrape my chin, nose, and forehead on the gravel beneath. I had to nurse my own wounds and stop my own bleeding as no one else around cared. When I got home, I was chastised for intruding in the games of older children.

Going Around the Long Way

Eventually, we made some progress in the never-ending line of refugees waiting to find their promised land—the land of milk and honey, where we were told money grew on trees. Did we really believe it? Hope springs eternal after so much chaos, and it was energising to have something positive to look forward to. I remember Mother furiously sewing so we would all have new clothes for the long trip. Hers was a bright yellow embossed cotton dress with raised black poppies and it had a sweetheart neckline, as usual very stylish, but then, that was Mother!

Ours was a very long and slow queue made up of people with no documents, and when it looked like we were getting closer, it was discovered that I was missing my birth certificate. I am not sure how they eventually discovered that I was ever born, but amongst all the rubble and devastation of the long war years some evidence must have survived, because eventually an extract arrived on the 10th of January 1950, when I was nine and a half and by then, the only available passage to Australia would be on a U.S. war ship leaving from Germany. I believe we could have gone to the Americas or Canada if we were willing to wait until the following year, when Chile and Argentina would also be opened up for an intake of refugees, but Mother and Father had enough of the uncertainty and wanted to take the first available passage out.

I shudder to think what that period might have been like. Getting from the south of Italy to the north of Germany would have been a logistical nightmare in those days. With the continual disruptions of timetables, the breakdowns of hastily-repaired train tracks all over Europe and the chaos of the displaced multitudes, speaking in a babble of languages, all travelling together, conditions must have been unspeakably difficult.

Today, we would find it difficult to comprehend what it would feel like—what it could have been like without public facilities—crowds moving in all directions, carrying their scanty luggage, losing sight of their loved ones, and the screaming and shouting of names and instructions that no one could hear. Finally, the ear-piercing train whistle again and again, and we found ourselves packed like cattle on rattling old, dirty train carriages, chug-chugging out of the musty, damp, old station, because by this time everything in sight was old and neglected, or broken down.

Again, we had left our meagre possessions behind and taking the absolute bare necessities, we were making our way from the port in south of Italy to the port in north of Germany. It was a crazy existence! The first train stopped in Venice, where we changed platform, got on a different train and waved a final good-bye to *Zia* Lucia, her husband, and the future Mayor of Venice, my cousin. By this time they had another child and this second young cousin made his first appearance to us in St Mark's Square during the short break we had between changing trains on our way to the unknown north. It was the one and only time that any of us have seen him and I can't say that I have any recollection.

Going Nowhere

We could not think of anything more senseless than having to travel so far north when those refugees from the northern countries were travelling south to embark on their ships, from the very same port-city in Italy that we were now leaving to travel by train northbound. Our ship was leaving from Bremerhaven, but problems were found with the damaged hull in the bowels of the old U.S. war ship, so it wasn't ready for boarding when we got there. Perhaps we should have taken the other options and waited for the shorter journey to the other 'promised land'. In effect the people who waited got to their 'promised land' much sooner than we did. There were recriminations: "You wanted to…"and "I wanted to…"

Father was reading a lot of books by Jack London and I remember a few excerpts he used to read from the area of 'The Yukon', maybe he too expected to find gold paving the streets of the Klondike. I did enjoy 'Call of the Wild', the close dependence and understanding between wolf-dog and man, and the desperation driving explorers to find and open up the new frontiers. Perhaps it would have been an easier life for us, but I doubt it. Anyway, I hate the cold!

But right then to me it meant nothing. I had no idea where Australia was or how we would get there. Seeing we had boarded a train I expected to eventually arrive by train and I wasn't sure why we had to wait for a ship to be repaired. I was just as fed up as the rest. We languished there, in a foreign speaking country that had lost the war and the last thing Germany wanted was another horde of refugees, many of whom had fought against Hitler and were still regarded as the enemy. I have no idea how we passed the time of day, or even where we lived during the long and bitterly cold northern winter with no suitable clothing. We were just another family of refugees who probably stayed in some hastily erected camp to wait out our time until we could board our vessel.

Chaos and Corruption

Years passed and bit by bit the odd photograph surfaced. Mother had been writing to her younger sister who had remained in Istria to care for their elderly father. He eventually died, apparently from a broken heart when the Allies, in their collective wisdom, handed the beautiful, triangular-shaped Italian peninsula of Istria to the newly created country they called Yugoslavia. Under the self-proclaimed ruler, Marshall Tito, the Communists exiled all residents and landowners who did not fall under the banner of the new regime, and whole-heartedly adopted their creed and philosophy. From those that he banished, he then confiscated all their lands and properties to be used as seen fit by the new regime.

Today, officially in the Archives in the City Hall at Rovigno, there are documents that claim these properties are 'abandoned goods and chattels', not 'confiscated goods and chattels'. It would never do to show up the Government of the day as the corrupt, land-hungry mongrels that they were. However, when enquiries were made by the descendants of the original owners, new owners came forward, who swore in the Magistrate's Court, that they had legally bought these properties through proper legal channels from the Government of the day. Someone was and still is lying! A few of the heirs who were better off financially, and are now affluent citizens living in America, contested these findings, and in the minority of cases had some compensation paid to them, but, as is always the case, it takes a lot of money to obtain a little justice. Whereas for the greater majority, including one of my still living cousins, the legal contesting has now been in progress since before my mother's death in 2001, with an inordinate amount of money having been paid to Magistrate Courts, and numerous lawyers, without any definitive outcome.

Corruption of those in power still rules the masses. I for one have abandoned all hope of obtaining any satisfaction, or any entitlement from what should have been my inheritance, because for me it is quite obvious that the current Government is no better than the previous one, and is simply waiting until all descendants die, as no one has any intention of surrendering anything, or compensating anyone, and in the meantime these legal eagles get richer as everyone procrastinates.

New Kids on the Block

With Mother earning good money, but wasting so much time in travelling to and from work, it was time to move onto larger premises, and in a better locality. I was ready to start high school, and I wanted to start sewing my own clothes, so during the Christmas holidays we started looking for a conventional but modest home. We looked close to Mother's work, and soon found a place we could afford, giving the land and the shack where we had been living for nearly three years as a deposit.

It was a steal but we were the victims, because we ended up with a mortgage for the twenty-seven years that my parents lived there, but we didn't know any better then. Even if anyone had bothered to warn us, I doubt that my parents would have listened. Mother was happy because she had a lounge room where she could sew, and the house had two bedrooms and a kitchen. It had a small bathroom, with a dangerous, rusting gas-fired heater but we learnt to be cautious, and a toilet under a breezeway. Bloody cold in winter, but an improvement on the outdoor thunderbox we were used to. On the plus side, there was a living room (that boasted an open fireplace) connecting to a compact dining room. The house had been built in the pre-war years of bricks and tiles, and it had a problem with rising damp. But of course, this did not become evident until winter set in. Then we felt and smelled the mould. We children who were sleeping in the back bedroom started to become sick with recurring colds. The southern wall had no window, but there was a lovely row of silvery ferns that looked truly magnificent in summer as they were protected from the sun, but in winter they absorbed the moisture, and the wall was being slowly but surely undermined by dampness so the ferns had to go! Sadly, we watched them being torn down to be replaced with a rock garden that didn't require watering, but not much grew there anyway.

This was 1954. No television yet! In fact our house did not have TV until several years after it became available in Melbourne in 1956, but we did have a small radio on the mantelpiece where we tuned in for the daily news and serial stories when Father was away. When he came home, we could not listen as it interfered with his sleep, his nerves were so taut and strained that any noise upset him. It is a sad fact that the more he worked to improve the living standards of his family the more he became alienated from us. Once the downhill spiral had started, it was impossible to arrest it. And with shame I concede that Mother and I did little to slow it down because we were impatient with him and his moods. We tried to tell him that he should leave his bad moods outside the door but it only made him angrier. We never played any games at home or listened to music any more. It was Ondina, the gentle one, who took the time to listen and give him some moral encouragement.

We immediately became known as the odd ones in the area.

We were the only non-English speaking migrant family in South Caulfield. Mother could now walk to work in Glenhuntly Road, eliminating the need for two long train trips, and a tram ride, and she commenced work immediately after we relocated, because she wanted to be mixing and talking with the other ladies she had met only briefly earlier, when she was taking work home.

In no time at all, she made friends with her work colleagues, and now that she had more time to spend in the company of others, she settled in nicely. But that meant that I was alone with my sister in a quiet house because it was still school holidays.

Mother and Father went to work, while our days were filled with walks in the park at the end of the street where there were several tennis courts, and we spent hours watching the players, both adults and children who would sometimes talk to us, then we would go to the swings and sea-saws, but we were essentially on our own. When it rained, I would use the sewing machine, but there was little money to buy the material, nevertheless I made some 'pinnies' for Ondina by sewing together off-cuts that Mother sometimes could bring home.

A New and Expensive Interest

Most of the high couture dresses that Madam Bazaar designed were rather frivolous and appealed to the theatre-going socialites who competed with each other for the most showy, colourful or flamboyant styles—clothes that could never be worn by the general public going about its daily routine. They were made of diaphanous silks of a myriad of hues, dyed in rainbow colours, and with many flounces, and ribbons for the after five, or cocktail dresses. Then there were the very fine linens with many pintucks, and corded embroidery, and many had an array of self-covered buttons and eyelets, sometime in rows of dozens, and often, in contrasting cloth covered buttons and buckles. For the idle rich, some of these adornments were substituted by tiny, fake diamante, or pearl buttons, on outfits they wore to the lunches or dinners they seemed to continually indulge in, or for the race meetings, parties and soirees for which Caulfield was and still is famous.

But even the Caulfield races have changed and lost some of their class and appeal. The grounds have been completely changed. The precinct has been landscaped and refurbished for the purpose of taking in more punters and ostensibly to make it safer. Though for my part, give me back the good old days when everything was so much simpler and more accessible for families. We loved to walk to the track on a Saturday morning, with a picnic lunch packed. We would arrive early and sit on the grass to watch the horses going through their paces with their trainers. Sometimes the jockeys would come out before the races, already dressed in their silks and colours and it was a feast for the eyes to see them so close and personal, bonding with their glossy mounts. All our senses were alerted. The smell of the newly mowed grass, and even the droppings of the horses held a certain sensory appeal that enhanced the atmosphere. The excitement as the starting times approached and the odds changed on the betting boards above sent ripples of anticipation through the lively crowd. The tables of the bookmakers on the 'flat' had hopelessly long queues of gamblers, mostly males, with noses glued to the daily papers and anxious to leave their hard earned cash behind in the hope that some of their bets would find a winner, or a double, or even a trifecta!

Then came the excitement of the pre-race, the cheering and shouting, the encouragements and cursing as the horses are led to their cages. And nervous fillies baulk at the sight of their enclosures at the starting line.

Now they are in and the starters' gun startles them into that initial jump out, as the gates fly open—and they are off! The horses stretch out to their fullest length as each one strives to get a pace ahead early in the race. Ten, twenty or more shining, sweating animals bunch up thundering around the turn on the inside of the track to gain a nose length, and then they're on the straight again. The whips come into full view as those bright jockey-shirts flash past. Some would pound the flanks of their steeds with their whips in hand, others rise in their stirrups for the home run as the finishing line nears at lightning speed. It's a frenzy of glistening, sweaty muscles and hoofs kicking up sods of earth and then, it's over. Silence.

One can almost tangibly feel the suspense. The breath of the spectators being held back in anticipation! And the winner is announced. Then the anti-climax of the post-race, when the greatest majority of punters come to terms with their losses and already consider the prospects of better luck at the next race.

Both Mother and Father became hooked. We kids enjoyed walking around the two small lakes to look at the ducks and the little spray fountain shooting water upwards into the air where the wind catches the mist. There were tents and marquees with seats where refreshments were served, and I remember the excitement of my very first bet when Father jokingly asked me which horse I fancied would win the next race. Looking down at the racing guide, the names meant nothing to me so I gingerly pointed to an appealing name, 'Wild Cherry'. In consternation, Father looked at the odds that gave some indication of the likelihood of a win. He shook his head, the odds were sky high, but just to humour me and to illustrate the foolishness of not following the form guide, he gave me the money for an each way bet. This being the first time that I had a stake in a race, I got as excited as everyone else when my little 'Wild Cherry' started to pull away from the bunched up horses. It was a young and relatively small field of chestnuts. A fill-in race really, but when this filly pulled out ahead of the others at the finish line, I was as proud of her as if she had belonged to me—and for a moment she did! With the odds being so high, the payout for the outsider was quite considerable for my each way bet. I didn't collect my winnings until the end because I didn't want to be tempted to take another bet and risk losing what was now mine. This initial success did nothing to tempt me to become a regular gambler. Not with horses, dogs, nor anything else. The odd fling might be acceptable but I could see the direction my father was heading with Mother not far behind, and for me, money was too hard to come by to risk losing it.

For a long time my 'luck with the horses' was brought up in conversations as if I was a veteran gambler who had won the jackpot, but I refused to be drawn into 'picking the winner' again or giving anyone the often asked for 'tip'. Whether they would have taken any notice of me was debateable anyway.

Doing It the Hard Way

At times, Mum and I would laugh when we would go to the local stores for provisions, with me still sometimes interpreting, but Mum would take corrections on board, seldom making the same mistake a second time. Some of her gaffes were classic. She would laugh at herself later when reminded of the time she blissfully asked the drapery assistant to be shown some nice embroidered 'shits'. The flustered attendant would try to direct Mum to the toilet, much to Mum's indignation, who kept repeating, "No, no. I want a shit for the bed, you know?"

Or we would wander into the butcher and ask for some muscle meat (gravy beef). At least that was an improvement on the earlier attempts of 'muuskl for the gullash.' That time we were sent to the boot maker for ankle galoshes after we had pointed to our calves to indicate the muscles on the hindquarters of a beast to the puzzled butcher. And then she would say to the good guy, "No, we don't like to eat ships, thank you," meaning 'sheep' or 'lamb'.

We always managed to do things the hard way, I guess that was because no one was there to help us, or guide us, and we would have been too proud to ask anyway. I knew that Father had been tricked into paying more than the going price for some articles he had purchased because he was told by the assistant who came to 'help' that the quality was superior. In hindsight though, we should not have been left to our own devices to such an extent, to struggle with language, money and advice, because even in the 50's there were migrant services to help individuals and families. I guess we fell off the radar when we started doing things for ourselves in the very early days, instead of asking for help and handouts, as the greatest majority seemed to do, and still do today.

Even more so today actually, because it is easier now to get someone to listen to a sob story—whether it's genuine hardship or sheer laziness, doesn't seem to matter much. And one's success in getting the most out others and for themselves, for the least possible effort, depends on how well one can act out a sob story.

The new school year was about to begin, but where should my sister and I go to school now? She was of kindergarten age, and I needed to start high school. We were not enrolled anywhere because we had simply left the western suburbs to relocate, thinking that we could simply walk into the nearest school and we would be taken in. We were so glad to see the last of that God-forsaken place that we hadn't considered our future education. Class sizes were huge in the western suburbs, so we assumed that we would be accepted regardless of their class numbers' limits on the other side of the city.

Ondina had to be settled first, and it had to be somewhere close to home so she could walk alone, and preferably without her having to cross major roads with tram tracks, but the only vacancy for her that I could find was too far. In the meantime, the days and the weeks were passing, because walking was time-consuming and all the searching had to be done on foot. I was not confident enough for us to take the bus that stopped at the bottom of our street, as I had no idea where it was going or the route it would take. In the end she found her own solution by befriending another little girl who had just started pre-school not far from us. Class sizes were smaller in the eastern suburbs, and all the schools nearby had already fulfilled their quotas, but somehow, one morning we found ourselves walking along with this young girl to her school. It was one of the schools that I had already approached earlier without any satisfaction I may add, and now, lo and behold, a place was suddenly found for her! I left her there and took off fast, afraid that they would change their minds if I looked back.

Then I began my own thankless search of the district alone. At least I could now cover more territory, quicker. The construction of McKinnon High School should have been completed for the beginning of the school year, but I was already learning that work in the public sector progressed at a slower pace than in private enterprise. The school opened its doors for the first intake of students in 1954, and I was enrolled on April Fools' Day. Once again I found myself among the oldest students in the entire school—the second oldest, in fact. The oldest was a Lithuanian boy who shared both Christian name and country of origin with the man I married 5 years later.

How do you get to a school which is situated over a kilometre from the railway station, and one's residence on the other side is almost two kilometres from the other train station? The bicycle is the only other option. So for my fourteenth birthday in July, I was promised a bicycle, but that was more than two months away, what do I do in the meantime? We discussed the options and everyone agreed that I should get home as quickly as possible because Little Sister still needed supervision, so I got my independent means of transport, before my birthday, but for my birthday. From then on I gained a little bit of freedom and a lot of leg muscle from my daily pedalling to and from school.

High school was a new experience that to this day I remember with a mixture of pleasure and disbelief. The new, totally Australian school was located in what was at the time also one of the newer outer suburbs of Melbourne, which had better housing and schools. There seemed to be also a greater number of people with an open mind and a healthy, non-judgemental curiosity. A society that was generally more affluent and professional. Living in Caulfield in the fifties was practically unheard of for a family of Italian immigrants so we were a bit of an oddity. It was a pleasant neighbourhood that would most probably have appreciated the newcomer in me, and welcomed me in their midst had we both been given the opportunity to assimilate. The very first adult I met was Mr Wall, our next-door neighbour. He would have been in his seventies at the time and lonely, since his wife had recently died. My shyness and insecurity prevented me from being open and receptive of his friendship, and I regretted not having spent more time with him as he was a true gentleman, and tried to be helpful too, but it is ironic that at this stage of my life, my father was still over-protective and forbade me to spend time alone with a male. That was one time that I should have disobeyed him and spent some quality time with our neighbour, when our parents were at work.

When he also died not long after we moved in, both sister and I felt the loss, but one thing he taught me, and in turn I have often repeated to others, "No matter how bad things may appear, if you smile, the whole world smiles with you," and he would encourage me by saying, "What a lovely smile you have." He was such nice, kind elderly gentleman.

In the following few years I only made two friends that I retained for many years to come, and only one of those was from high school. The other girl, Teresa, was from a typical Australian family that lived two or three streets away. Later, I learnt that she was not so typical, and that she carried with her, throughout her life, deep-seated hang-ups that could never be resolved; an unfathomable, dark blight on her subconscious that surfaced at unpredictable moments and in unpredictable circumstances, without warning. This in time caused me to want to distance myself from her. It may have been cowardice on my part, but the last episode that I witnessed and became involved in one of her 'dark moments', as she called them, I had no forewarning other than her little Pomeranian dog whimpering with his tail dragging on the floor and wanting to hide behind any piece of furniture that would give him shelter from the wild demon his mistress had suddenly become. I stared at her in horror immediately noticing the change in posture and demeanour, but it was the look of pure evil on her grotesquely distorted facial features that frightened the daylights out of both her little dog and me. But that took place some twenty or more years later. In her middle age, Teresa needed the kind of help and understanding that I was not in a position to give her because by then I too was subjected to continual mental, psychological, and emotional abuse that I could barely handle – and in the end didn't

Rebellion

School life took me on a life-changing course, though not necessarily an easier course, as it was still mandatory that I cycle directly home after classes. No sport. No social interaction. No friends' gatherings away from school and I was always apprehensive to bring anyone home. Father was still incredibly suspicious, yet at the same time he was a uniquely gullible and trusting person with strangers and his own work acquaintances. Even when he was let down, as often happened, he would make excuses for these relative strangers, but he would never forgive his own family the slightest misjudgement. He was a hard taskmaster and was used to being not just obeyed but pampered and cossetted. I started to rebel at his unfairness, and he started to beat me. We were probably as stubborn as each other. Mother often had to step between us and just as often ended up receiving a blow that was meant for me. Her patience was tried many a time, until one day she had enough. Using her strong, long, and painted nails, she raked them down the side of Father's face, gouging it deeply and drawing blood. Mum didn't lose her temper easily or often, but when she did, look out! Father, who had been a very good-looking man in his young days and vain too, was often considered a double for Rudolf Valentino, tall, with his black, well-groomed pencil moustache and glossy hair, held in place with brilliantine, so he took his disfiguration rather badly and refused to go to work until his face had healed.

On his first day back at work, he didn't stop at the Young & Jackson as was the norm, so he was home in time for a rare family meal but didn't have any wine to go with the pasta and salad that Mum had prepared. The only way I can describe his reaction to that meal is that he built up so much steam and pressure, like a volcano, that he eventually exploded—blew his top. The three of us looked in amazement as Father picked up the plate of pasta and meat, and hurled it onto the masonry wall of the dining room. Pasta, meat, and tomato sauce stuck to the white wall and then dribbled down onto the carpet.

Ondina started to cry and wanted to get up to start cleaning. Mother stopped her and very matter-of-factly announced that she had cooked the meal for all of us to enjoy, and if my father didn't want to eat it then that was his choice. It was also his choice to clean up the wall and carpet or to spend the rest of his life looking at the mess he had made because no one else was going to clean it up for him. She really put up with a lot. For a while I was left alone if I kept out of the way. I missed the only friend I had but not the place where we had lived. Even so, overall, things were not much better. I felt supressed at every turn. Given too much responsibility but not enough freedom to be myself. I didn't know who I was, halfway between a child and an adult, confusion and rebellion churned inside me.

Sometimes I felt that like Father, I too was ready to explode. The catalyst event happened one Saturday morning when I was in the lounge room trying to cut some material on the bias for a skirt that I was making and Little Sister rushed in to say that Father was cooking on the barbeque and he wanted me to come immediately with the plates to serve up the meat. And was the salad ready?

Can't imagine where Mother was, but when Father speaks, we all jump. No one can remember how it happened, but somehow the opened scissors that I was holding slipped out of my hand with one of the points piercing the wrist of my little sister's outstretched hand. Thankfully it missed the artery but she carried the scar of the deep wound right through adulthood. I don't remember bandaging it but I must have done so before fainting. That night we all went to bed at the usual time. Father had gone out and I couldn't sleep. I couldn't continue living like this, I decided. Quietly getting out of bed and into the clothes of that day, I found a sheet of paper and a pencil, and sneaked stealthily out of the bedroom, into the passage, opened the front door and quiet as a mouse, I went out to where my brand new bicycle was stored on the porch. Carefully wheeling it down the few steps onto the front lawn and then holding my breath as I opened the squeaky iron front gate hoping that no one would hear me. Made it, so far. Now I must write a note to my parents so they would not worry. How crazy is that? I remember telling them not to come looking for me. Haa. What was I thinking?

I wrote that note by the light of the lamppost, without realising that I was being watched by my little sister. Then I slipped it under the front door and continued quietly up the street. Obviously she had woken up while I was dressing. Pedalling to the train station I wondered if I would be in time for the last train into town. I was, but it does not take very long to get into the city from Caulfield, and there were no more trains going west tonight, so I had to wait several hours on the cold city platform until the early morning for the first train to St. Albans. That one got to its destination too early for a Sunday morning visit to my friend Tonia, so riding around the countryside for a while, I was making plans for my future. I could see myself going to work preferably in Footscray and living with my friend and her family. Of course they would welcome me with open arms! They were surprised to see me, to say the least. We spent a pleasant enough day together and the day bed was made up for me for that night. In the morning, I would take the train to McKinnon and go to school as usual, but I would take all my belongings with me and return to my friend. I don't know why they went along with whatever I said. I was making all the plans for everybody knowing that they would fall in and agree with me. It was too easy.

Monday morning I did just that, and walked right into the arms of my worried parents who were waiting with the police in the headmaster's office. So much for my escape to freedom! My rebellion backfired.

We did talk a bit about the way my parents were taking me so much for granted and we all promised to change our ways, but the police had done their duty and they took off. The headmaster had done his duty and showed us to the door and I was left exactly where I had been the previous Friday, in school. For maybe a month everything seemed a little better. We went out together as a family, to see the old, green steam locomotives at Ferntree Gully. We took a trip on 'Puffing Billy.' It was interesting to watch the steam trains chug-chugging along with puffs of black smoke and white steam announcing their arrival from a long way off. We could not imagine then that they would be phased out by 1975 to be replaced by diesel locomotives. But 'Puffing Billy' became a national icon that still takes tourists for memorable runs along the forests of Victoria. It has become a treasure for the state. Father was entitled to two free train trips a year for himself and his dependent family so we made plans to go on a trip—all the way to the beach at Mount Martha. Well that was to the end of the line, a whole hour out and a bus ferrying us from the station to the beach. But sarcasm aside, I enjoyed the beach, though swimming was not my forte.

Unfortunately, Little Sister burnt to a crisp, with her fair skin exposed for most of the day in the relentless sunshine. Because we hardly went anywhere, I clearly remember that beach, as it was back then. The big flat rock that burnt to the touch at midday; the lone tree with the sparse foliage where Ondina tried to find some shade; the sandwiches and water that we brought with us, that we tried to have on the hot rock and they too, were hot. We ate them anyway. We may not have gone far, but we did go somewhere and that was better than nowhere. Sadly, it was just a passing phase, too soon over.

I thought that things might improve at home if we didn't see each other so often, if I could take up some sport. I met Teresa one Sunday morning after church when she asked if I played tennis, if not, would I like to learn, and be her partner. She was very helpful and soon we became friends, and shared meals at each other's homes. Much to my surprise, and Mother's too, Father actually liked her, so he relaxed a bit when she was around. She spoke slowly to him, and really tried to understand him, and his reasoning, which wasn't always lucid—that always depended on how much he had imbibed during the day. But she was tolerant, perhaps even more than we were. Mother was ambivalent about our friendship. She felt that my friend was a bit rough, uncouth, and had something to hide. I had to remind her that she was kind enough to teach me how to play tennis when we met after church on Sundays and on the tennis court, I was the uncouth one.

Academically I went from strength to strength, without really trying too hard. My love for reading and literature helped both me and Mother also, as she was an avid reader too, but I regularly got into trouble in class for reading novels under cover of the lid of my desk, instead of paying attention to lessons. My response once had been, "I can always study at home, but cannot read just for pleasure". Giggles from some of the girls made me realise that I was being more than cheeky, I was being unfair to our form teacher who was a great guy.

Those from my era would remember that back in the 50's and 60's we had a form teacher, and that teacher was responsible for us throughout our high school life. Early in my first year, when subject teachers realised that I was falling behind in maths and science, but was great in logic, social sciences, and literature, I was placed under the care and tutelage of a young male teacher who brought history and geography vividly to life. He had just recently married his sweetheart from Western Australia and what I particularly liked about them both was their down-to-earth approach to problems, their passion for travel, and the interesting narrative skills that they shared enabled them to bring a faraway land almost within reach. They took every opportunity to discover outback Australia and then would describe the deserts and Lake Eyre, the native fauna and flora, the seasonal changes in the rivers, the hardships faced by farmers when in droughts cattle would only have spinifex to eat, and the constant threat of fire. We found it hard to understand the necessity of fire in this arid country and to understand that many seeds will only crack open under intense heat to be able to germinate. The Aborigines knew it all before us in this ancient land.

Their travels also took them to exotic places most of us only read about. One could almost smell the herbs and spices from the bazaars of Marrakesh and hear the hauntingly moving music of a faraway lute on a balmy, moonlit night as countless stars shone brightly on the sand and the Bedouins with their trains of camels slowly advanced carrying their cargoes of silks, carpet, and trinkets. We shook our heads in disbelief when told that Australia sold camels to the Arab countries. I could almost see the circle of light where the snake charmer sat with his flute, or the belly dancer performing her mesmerising gyrations to the totally enthralled audiences. I can't remember how our relationship started. Perhaps he was doing some post-graduate course involving a thesis on immigrant children. If that was the case, then he only had two to choose from at that particular high school and presumably I looked the more vulnerable. When we worked back in class we were exposed to many inquisitive eyes and idle tongues. I was, after all, the eldest girl in the entire school, tall and not bad looking. No one knew much at all about me, or my family in those early days. I didn't join in any of the social activities unless I was kept back after school, and that caused its own problems because I still had to start preparing for dinner—or go shopping for it! So I was not generally visible out of school hours. Perhaps the headmaster, or even Mr C.'s young wife, may have suggested he meet my parents. They had never attended a parent-teacher interview. One evening after dinner he came knocking on our door. We were expecting him, but still I was extremely anxious and apprehensive about the form of greeting he would receive from Father, as that invariably depended on the sort of day he had at work, how much he had had to drink before he came home, and if dinner was ready and to his liking when he got home. Luckily Mum took over and charmed Mr C., emphasizing how delighted we would all be if he undertook to help me with my studies. It never, ever in the two years that followed, occurred to us that coaching was usually given for a fee. And as far as I know, not a shilling ever exchanged hands. Perhaps there was a Government grant for post-graduate work. I don't know. Mr C. alternated after-school lessons between his home and mine, so I got to know his wife very well, and we even played the occasional game of tennis at their lovely home. I was still as uncouth as ever on the court, but at least I got away from home for a while, and sometime they also had other students that I could associate with outside the classroom environment.

The other girl I befriended at school was a quiet redhead who didn't seem to join in lunchtime activities either, so we spent most of the time talking and eventually we got to invite each other to our homes for Sunday lunch. As usual Mother made her special pasta and meat sauce, with the crisp green salad accompaniment in which she tossed the tangy homemade Mediterranean dressing, and Father brought out his flagon of claret. Lorraine liked the pasta and salad, but we all laughed at the faces she pulled each time she sipped on her glass of claret—obviously not a hit with her. But she was a hit with Father. He would sometimes make a special effort and turn on the charm, of which he had plenty when he chose to display it. Earlier that week at school, we had been rehearsing for a play and one of the songs that we were singing began with the words, "Do you ken John Peel?" [1]

We started singing this catchy tune there at home while we were helping Mother clear the table and wash the dishes. Father would be there listening to us with his amused smile, not able to make any sense of the words. From that day onward Father always referred to her as 'Little John Peel'. The hospitality of the South Europeans soon became the topic of conversation at school, both in and out of class and only much later did we understand the disapproval of the girls' parents when they discovered that dinner at Number 28 was always followed by a glass of red wine, and their daughters were not averse to experimenting with this new piquant drink. Sometime we would have a very sweet wine, like mead, that we would drink from small, delicate crystal glasses following another one of Mother's delicacies, an exotic, tangy apple strudel like nothing else my new friends had tasted before. Other times, delicate fine china cups about half the size of teacups were offered to my guests. The thick, bitter liquid we called espresso was another new taste and the girls had to put copious amounts of sugar in the tiny cups to make it

---

[1] A Scottish song that lent itself to singing in rounds. 'Ken' translates to 'know'.

palatable to their unaccustomed taste. We were a bit of a rarity and we knew we were being discussed in private. Our lifestyle was also an education for the parents and neighbours, as they were still not exposed to many immigrants in Caulfield. All that people knew was what they read in the papers or heard on the radio and later what they saw on the television, unless they lived in a densely populated migrant area. In many cases, what they had heard and believed did not correspond with what they were now witnessing. We didn't seem to fit into the universal mould.

Home from the Dance

Today it would seem totally unthinkable, but my parents were overprotective, where it suited them—Father mostly! One Saturday morning, the sixteen year old boy from across the street came over to me as I was working in the front yard and asked, "Would you like to go to the movies with me?"

I looked at him blankly, "What are the movies?"

Mother gave me the money for the matinee and for an ice cream saying, "Under no circumstances are you to let him pay for anything. You must not let him think that he owns you or that you owe him anything."

I can't remember what we saw because the tension was palpable in the dark theatre, and he never asked me out again. He probably thought that I wasn't worth the effort.

My first dance was just before graduation and it was on the way home from that illicit dance that I understood what she meant. I could never speak to anyone about it, and I blush even now thinking about it. How naive I was! At the time I had two quite close friends at high school. One of them liked dancing and went to the Caulfield Town Hall quite regularly. One day I begged her to ask her parents to pick me up on their way, as they would be practically passing my home, then I could go along with her. Under normal circumstances there would be no opportunity for me to lie, but this time, just before graduation, I told my parents that everyone had to attend rehearsals, so the lie seemed legitimate, and it rolled off the tongue very easily, as I excitedly prepared for my first, unsanctioned, and illicit night of pleasure.

Of course, my dancing was pathetic, not having much opportunity to practice, but I never refused a dance, and when a young Dutch man took a shine to me, bought me a can of soft drink, and sat next to me to talk, I was happy to rest a while, and soak up the compliments which were a welcome novelty. We danced to the last tune, and then he asked to take me home. It was only a short distance so I must have said something like, "yes," or "okay".

With an embarrassed smile, I apologised to my friend and told her that I would not be going home with them because my parents would probably ask them all to come in to share a bottle of wine, and that I had lied to them about going to the dance in the first place, so if they found out I would be punished severely and would not be able to go to the graduation after all, and it would all be very embarrassing. How very clever of me, I thought, especially since wine was not the preferred drink of that time, and to let someone think they would be forced to drink a bottle of wine at midnight! We all walked out together and went to the respective cars.

After driving a few minutes, my escort stopped the car at the bottom of my street, and quite politely started to put the hard word on me. We talked for a while but when he took my hand and placed it on his grossly enlarged member that he had surreptitiously extracted, I recoiled in horror; my hand burning as hotly as my face, as another vision appeared before my eyes.

Sometime earlier, one morning on my way to school, I was riding my bike along North Road where there is a slight incline, and I had to pedal uphill slowly. A car passed me and then stopped. The driver's door opened. An older man with a hat and a ruddy complexion had taken his huge, blood-red, engorged penis out of his trousers and was frantically masturbating, and calling for me to stop. I pedalled up that hill as fast as my legs would carry me and never once looked back. I never mentioned a word to anyone either, as I was so embarrassed and ashamed, and for some unexplainable reason, a guilty feeling enveloped me, as though it was somehow my fault. What could I have done to that poor man to bring on such a reaction? It must have been my fault for showing too much flesh while I was riding. My skirt must have crept up. The mentality of that time, especially amongst immigrants was that if you expose yourself in any way, you are a slut, and you deserve whatever happens to you. That was the mindset of an innocent child who has been brainwashed into thinking that whatever happens, it must somehow be brought about by some action or reaction or inaction on her part. But I was not so young anymore and I should not have reacted with guilt!

Not having any brothers, I had very little knowledge, or understanding of the male body. We didn't even have a dog! I realise that today, my story may seem farfetched and many may snigger and doubt my words—I would probably doubt my own words but at the end of my high school days, at the age of seventeen and a half, and this was 1957, I still had no clear concept of the mechanisms of the healthy, young, male body. I had seen mutilated and deformed bodies, some naked dead bodies, much blood and gore at a very early age.

The only other display of a healthy penis happened to me in Taranto, on the roof of the barracks where we lived with many other families, while awaiting placement either in the U.S.A., or Canada, or Australia, under the I.R.O. scheme for displaced persons. It was at the time of my sister's birth, when I was left in the care of a young couple, just newly married, and obviously not too concerned with the comings and goings of an eight year old kid. There, I had befriended a girl with the most beautiful golden hair I had ever seen. Plump waves of silk cascaded past her shoulders, and she had cute ringlets framing a delicate, if knowing and cheeky face. She also had an older brother, who delighted in teasing and chasing us around. There wasn't a great deal to do to keep us children occupied, so one sunny afternoon, when the adults would indulge in their habitual afternoon siesta, he dared me to climb on the roof with him and play hide and seek. With all the racket we were making on that roof, laughing and carrying on, skidding on our bottoms and tramping up again, it is a wonder that we were left to our pranks for such a long time. Suddenly, he was nowhere to be found. So, okay. Finally he was really hiding now and I was supposed to find him.

When I did, he was reclining behind a wide brick chimney, with his member in his hand and a smile on his face. Fleeting impressions can last a lifetime, and though in this case, my memory is of a pale, shiny, almost opalescent and rather pleasant appendage, in my mind he was pitifully deformed and as I was running away, I remember feeling sorry for him having to carry that monstrosity around everywhere with him, and having to shamefully hide it in his trousers. How come I had never noticed his deformity before? From then on I kept my distance.

Now, dealing with the earlier visions, and the current situation in which I found myself, I was gripped by a choking fury. Why was this happening to me? In anger, I swung towards the car door ready to jump out, when my eyes turned to a figure on the opposite kerb. It was my father's silhouette caught under the streetlight and he was looking up and down the street, ready to cross over. Luckily, he could not see the occupants inside the car. In a horrified whisper, I demanded that the Dutch guy take off post-haste. His reflexes were excellent and I must say that in his haste to be gone, he almost ran my father down as he was crossing the street. When I looked out the rear windscreen, Father was in the middle of the road shaking his fists, and swearing loudly. Home was only a couple hundred yards away, so I didn't have much time to get into the house, and into bed. My insistent, loud-knocking brought Mother immediately to the door and when she opened it, she was almost overcome by this whirling dervish that flew past her. She asked no questions, went to her own bed and pretended to be asleep when moments later Father barged in, full of accusations and anger, shouting.

"That young slut of yours is staying out past midnight."

"What are you talking about? Your daughter has been in bed, sleeping for ages!"

Doubting Tomas, as Father was sometimes called after his own father, he insisted on barging into our room, as if the devil was chasing him, yelling and screaming, and waking little sister, who in turn also started to scream, but she was screaming in fear, knowing full well how a frenzy of Father's could end. Yes, we were an interesting family.

Towards Independence

Towards the end of 1957, I became really restless. At seventeen and a half, I was becoming annoyed and impatient with everyone and everything. It was time for me to earn some money and become more independent. Pocket money was unheard of in our home. I was given what I needed for necessities, but I had to justify every penny spent.

Mother and Father tried everything in their power to encourage me to continue with my education, and Mr C. kept saying that I would make an excellent teacher and that he would help me to stay on at school and continue with my studies. Mum must have told him that it had been her ambition to become a teacher before she met Father, but his studies took precedence and she had to forego her own education. They had a long betrothal, of eight years I believe, and it might have gone on for longer, but had married because of the impending war threat. Actually in my mind's eye I can almost see Father in his most appealing demeanour, pleading with Mother, probably after he recited some love poem to her, that he may have to go to war, possibly be killed and their love never consummated. I don't doubt for a moment that they loved each other deeply but Mother had been too busy with illness in the family, then her years in Algiers had kept her away. Now she was in her late twenties and it was time to make a decision. My thoughts have always been that the decision was made for her and that is why they never celebrated their wedding anniversary.

I was adamant. I couldn't stay in the house any longer. Ondina had made her own friends, and she was quite capable of looking after herself now. I felt that I wasn't really needed and I didn't want to be used anymore, so it was time to think of me. Home had become a jail, it was claustrophobic and I felt like I was being smothered and in the end everyone realised there was no stopping me. I would be looking for work as soon as exams ended.

After final exams, we had our graduation ball, for which I had been frantically sewing a glamorous dress, 'a la Ava Gardner' style, from a film of hers I had seen, I think it was 'The Barefoot Contessa'. Mother had bought a length of exotic material in midnight blue, embossed, silk brocade simply because she liked the feel and texture, so I begged her to let me have it. I designed, cut, and sewed an unusual two-piece outfit. It was a slim fitting sheath that could be worn alone, as a glamorous cocktail dress, for all those dates I envisaged would come my way, one day really soon now! Then there was an overskirt that was shorter, fuller, opened in the front, and was lined in shimmering white satin, with a very wide waist band held together with a large self-covered buckle under the bust. This overskirt had a row of tiny buttons and eyelets sewn on the edge from waist to hem as understated decoration for an otherwise unfussy classic line. Both pieces could be worn separately for different occasions and they were timeless, 'avant-garde' and got worn to death! It was a very grown up looking dress that not only made me look five years older, but also set me apart from my younger peers in their soft pastel colours, and debutante style dresses. It got me a lot of admiring and envious looks from both daughters, and mothers present. But not many dances as the boys, and their fathers, felt too intimidated and hesitant. The evening cemented my decision to leave school.

Not much later, with my better than average report card, I fronted up to a randomly chosen insurance company in the city, and walked up to the reception desk. The young girl behind the desk looked at me doubtfully when I asked to see the manager about working there. They had not advertised any positions and she didn't think there were any vacancies. Nevertheless I persisted, stood my ground, asked for an interview, and waited.

With my heart in my mouth, I approached the office of a kindly older gentlemen, a war veteran whom everyone called Uncle Wal, who politely invited me to take a seat. He interviewed me, checked my report, asked me a few questions, then he rose, shook my hand and introduced me to the others in the office as the newest member of the staff of the Legal and General Insurance Company. Just like that!

My time there was short. Four months in all, I think. Shorthand and typing was not my forte, and I was ambitious. So, when Uncle Wal opened a new branch of the Zurich Life Insurance Office, together with a younger man, a representative from Swizerland, I was asked to join them, I think because of my pretty good marks in French. There was some translation work involved, but I quickly found out that my schoolgirl French didn't quite measure up to the legal requirements, so I had to hire an older French lady to help me out. I was given carte blanche in that fledgling institution, and the company grew, and grew. I loved the job, and I worked very hard, often staying late to help with interviews, and soon, from the original three of us, the office had a staff of thirty-three, with just two females.

During this time, I slowly, patiently but systematically worked out with my parents a plan that would allow me to stay out late one night a week for my own pleasure, to either go to a show or just window shop. Working in the city made it easy for me to meet up with my two older, erstwhile, guardian angels from primary school, and I organised for someone to be always available to cover for me at work during my lunch hour as I insisted on leaving the premises. That was *my* hour. We, old school friends, worked in the same industry, within a couple of blocks of each other in fact, and we met almost daily. Now it was my turn to do a bit of bragging. Though both the other girls could touch type better than me, the language let them down. Spelling and grammar I mastered well, and it was I who now had a cushy and responsible job. But responsibility was not something they wanted. They already had what they wanted, and these young ladies, being competitive females, gloated about their entourage of boyfriends, and the presents they were receiving from them. They both had mastered the art of playing one against the other, so that each boy came-a-courting with bigger and better presents. Tonia, in particular, could play the coquette to perfection. I have no idea where she could have learnt this bewitching art, unless, being the ultimate mimic, she used every look, word and intonation, walk, and motion she picked up from her almost daily outings to the movies, because one thing I knew for sure, she didn't read, in fact she considered books a waste of time, and money. Her dancing technique though I admired and so did everyone else. The way she moved her body, it was so liquid, and provocative, I thought she was every bit as good looking as the two sexy sirens of the day Marilyn Monroe and Jane Russell, and she too should have been on stage. She knew how to wear clothes that suited her, and usually favoured slim skirts with deep slits at the back, or sides to show her shapely legs. One almost failed to notice that her legs were a bit on the short side, because her shoes had the highest of high heels, and she was a good actress in her own right at the time, she called all the shots. We used to say, not in a mean or nasty way, that she always got what she wanted by wriggling her bum. But then there were those who got personal and nasty, both male and females, old and young, and when walking behind Tonia, they would whisper, "If you stuck a broom handle up her arse, she would sweep the pavement!" She knew that she was being mocked, but she shrugged, laughed, and took it in her stride, bearing no malice, while strutting along her way like a good-natured peacock. It worked for her. By comparison, I felt that I looked awkward and clumsy, the shy, ugly duckling that was always ungainly. At least that's what I thought at the time, but my height was my asset, though I may not have been as voluptuous, or sexy looking.

The Catwalk

For my eighteenth birthday I got the ultimate gift, and just like Cinderella I was transformed from the cinder maid to someone who could hold up her head with pride. Mother made me a dusky rose, woollen-crepe dress with a dropped waist, finely fluid pleated skirt, and three-quarter sleeves finished at the edge, and also at the neck, with a narrow edging of cream lapin fur. It was so classic, and simply elegant that it needed no other adornment. It was simply stunning. To keep her gift a surprise she had to sew during her lunch hour at work and so all the ladies there, including Madam Bazaar, were able to see her progress. There was a lovely card from all of them, and they helped mum to place my gift in a box with scented tissue paper and with a personal request from the boss to me, to come into work so all could see how well I looked in it. The following week, wearing my new, ridiculously high, taupe, patent leather plain court shoes and small, matching shoulder bag, I paraded before a factory full of dressmakers.

Madam Bazaar was beside herself, always quite chatty and effusive, she had a natural bubbly personality but this day she was effervescent! She absolutely forbade me to wear the complete outfit again until the following month when the Spring Fashion Parade was to take place at the Royal Exhibition Building, in Melbourne. It was the kind of dress that was absolutely *me*. The colour was just right, the cut was perfect and smoothly skimmed my blossoming curves, the soft, creamy fur softened the deceptively unfussy look, and there was no need for any jewellery. In fact jewellery would have detracted from its overall effect of elegant simplicity. And of course, being tall, and at that stage very slim, I was to model it.

I tried to copy the models' walk with the swinging hips and the sultry, haughty expressions of the professionals, but failed dismally, at least I felt that I failed. I couldn't tell which of the models on the catwalk were being applauded more or longer and louder, by the sophisticated audience. But to me it seemed that those patrons in the audience were wearing nicer clothes than the models themselves. Later I was told I made quite an impression, but I still think it was the dress I was wearing that was impressive, rather than me and my obviously contrived demeanour. In any case, I was quite proud of my one and only claim to fame on that catwalk! The Fashion Parade that year was a turning point for Madam Bazaar.

My simple, elegant, obviously expensive dress in just one solid colour, and with the minimalistic adornment of rabbit fur was a screaming success, and as a result her establishment received so many orders, that she varied her usual range quite considerably, and opened another boutique outlet in South Yarra.

In all fairness, I didn't miss out. Madam Bazaar gave Mother a very fine piece of wool mixture material to make me another dress, and the time to make it, for me to wear in the interim. The dusky rose beauty was back nestling in tissue paper. This second dress had a very subtle weave, and Mum decided to make it into a high waisted bodice, with a gently flared skirt, and a band on the bias under the bust line. A decorative diamante buckle that accentuated the slightly different shading of the material when it was cut on the cross, was stitched neatly under the bust. This was also courtesy of Madam Bazaar. Once again the sole decoration and highlight being the diamante buckle. There was no need to wear any other jewellery. Just as well, because other than the gold heart-shaped locket with the small red ruby, I only possessed the new rose gold watch, and they didn't go together anyway, each being of a different shade of gold. Mother didn't buy much but what she did buy was of the best quality. Her motto was, "Not quantity but quality."

Again this dress was cut in a very simple line and this time the soft powder blue fabric contrasted with my skin and hair, and I loved it just as much as the dusky-rose beauty. Feeling like a princess for the first time in my life, I needed to show off my new treasures, which also included the dainty rose-gold watch—my second piece of jewellery that was only to be worn for special occasions. Now going to the matinee was not enough. What I needed was to go dancing! But dancing was something I could not face going alone, I was still too shy, and there was no one to take me. I never knew how to bewitch a young man into asking me out and how could I meet anyone anyhow, if I never went out. I have always been a bit of a contradiction, I was too shy, and yet I'm told that I could be forbidding and intimidating. I could work with thirty-odd males, but I didn't know how to flirt.

And I never did master the art of playing the coquette with a guy. Maybe my friends were right and I was too down-to-earth and matter-of-fact.

Going Dancing

During one of our frequent lunchtime meetings, I had to appeal to my best friend from primary school days to come my rescue. Her parents were working as well, but as an only child she was given a pretty free rein, not that there was much else that the parents could do if they wanted to hold a job, but trust and hope that she behave responsibly. As she was fifteen months older, once in a while I was reluctantly entrusted into her care or allowed to go out with her. She was rather well liked by Mother but not so by Father—he may have felt that she could lead me astray. She certainly was a siren.

Once again though we had a problem, she lived quite far from Caulfield, but Tonia was not only very beautiful, she was also very resourceful and she knew how to use her considerable attributes. She was popular with the boys and she chose those with cars to go out with in the evenings. So we worked on a plan where I could join them, when I was able. I would catch the train to town, and they would meet me in the city. We would then all go to whatever venue they had decided on for dancing, and at the end she would be taken home, with me in tow. I don't think that the boys were ever told that there would be a third party present for the trip home, but I suspect that Tonia planned it that way so she would not have to fight them off when they invariably would put the hard word on her. I would go with them to her home and stay overnight. Her mother would kindly make up a cot for me in the lounge, and on Sunday morning I would catch the train back home.

I liked her mother, she was not forceful, and did not appear to be a very confident woman. She felt intimidated by her husband, who was also an alcoholic, just as my father was fast becoming, but I never knew of her talking back, or standing up for herself. On the other hand, I don't think he was ever violent. If he had been a violent man I am sure that I would have heard of it, as I often complained about my father's rages.

Actually, this arrangement with me staying over only worked a few times because soon Tonia met a special guy, and then—well, three was a crowd!

In any case, I found that Caulfield Town Hall was much more convenient for me, and I could go there with Teresa any time she was going, and even better, her father was always ready to drive us in his new pride and joy, a new, light blue FH Holden, that he cherished to the end of his days. Undoubtedly he felt as privileged to be taking two young ladies out in his car, as we felt to be chauffeur-driven to the dances in it. He had a wide circle of friends and acquaintances because he was an SP bookie, and he attended all the race meetings at Caulfield and elsewhere. But we were not supposed to say what kind of work he was involved with, because in those days, bookies were frowned upon by all except those people who followed horse racing. Anyhow, my father was becoming very interested in the horses and sometime later, Mother too.

It wasn't long before someone noticed me one evening. I must confess I don't really remember how it happened, but we were dancing together for the third time when Teresa noticed that this guy was a pretty good dancer, and we were whirling around the dance floor, looking very professional while the other couples kept out of our way. "Me, looking like a professional dancer? You've got to be kidding, kiddo!"

But he was a good dancer, and easy to follow, even for me. It turned out that he and his younger sister had been folk dancing with a troupe for a number of years, and were chosen to represent the 'Baltic States Folkloric Dancers' whenever there was a festival in Canberra, Melbourne or Adelaide, or wherever there was a large congregation of migrants from the Baltics.

As I found out much later, the Government facilitated cultural festivities of this kind, and the costumes, as well as the dancers told tales of their homeland, which kept that community engaged and cohesive with the parents teaching the children the dances, telling the stories and music of their old culture.

We seemed to get along well, he was polite, and didn't come on strong. In fact it wasn't until we met for the third or fourth time that he asked to take me home. In trepidation, I said, "Next time, not tonight because I have to go home with my friend, her father is picking us up."

During the week I confided with Mum. I dare say she was expecting it, because she had her speech ready. She would approach Father when the timing was right, and she would explain that I was a young lady now, "As if he wouldn't have noticed!"

I had, after all, been working for the best part of a year, even he couldn't fail to see that there were new things around the house that Mum didn't buy! But I guess ignorance is bliss. If he chose to ignore the fact that I was getting older, I guess he could hope that I wouldn't want to leave home too soon.

Little did he know that I was counting the days, and little did I know that I would be jumping from the frying pan into the fire.

There was never any doubt that Father loved me, but he couldn't control his temper, which seemed to flare at the slightest provocation, and I was still getting slapped around and getting sick of it.

The first time I was escorted home, we were both nervous, because by then I had explained that my father's idiosyncrasies were not always easy to cope with, and how protective he was, wanting to know that anyone taking me out had honourable intentions, etc. What impressed Mother was the brand new Vauxhall Velox in which we arrived. She was probably more taken in by the car than I was, because I already knew the story behind its acquisition. I had noticed a limp, a favouring of the left leg during the time we had spent together, the way he sat, and the way he walked, not noticeable when we danced though. He carried himself well, and was always well-groomed and polite, so one did not notice anything wrong immediately. It was not a pretty story, and it was a while before I told Mum, and asked her to convey it to Dad. It made them both more receptive and friendly towards my suitor, though I daresay that Father always had reservations, and he never really opened up and accepted Allan fully, whereas Mother did. Little Sister liked him too and hung on to his every word! Finally, I too had something to tell my guardian angel.

Only one was left now.

Marriages

The older girl, Vera, had been missing from a lot of our lunches, and the next thing we heard was that her marriage had been arranged, and was to take place soon. Neither Tonia nor I was invited. It was to be a big Hungarian affair that would last for a few days and, as it turned out, it was the end of our friendship, for a while at least. But by then I realised that Tonia wasn't really interested in what I had to tell her either, because she also had news for me. She too had met someone. So, we each went our own way, and the weeks and the months passed with each of us committed to our own plans for the future. My engagement was an understatement, with the only notable feature being the design of my ring and then finding someone who could make the small diamond look like I wanted it to look. The marriage was arranged for three month later.

Tonia and I still kept meeting, but not as often and she was becoming unreliable. What really set the fuse alight was one Saturday morning when we had made arrangements to meet, and she didn't turn up. Knowing that trains could sometime run late or even be cancelled, I waited and waited in the foyer of Flinders Street Station for the arrival of three trains, scanning the faces of all arrivals and pacing around trying not to look too conspicuous or unduly interested while I was feeling prominent and exposed. It was a shopping trip we had planned for shortly before my wedding and I had intended to ask her to be my bridesmaid that morning, so

I felt that she had let me down badly and vowed that I would not be making the first contact after that disappointing day. Contacting each other had always been a problem as neither one of us had home telephones so we usually rang each other from work to arrange meetings, but the next week I didn't ring, and nor did she.

I spent a lot of time examining our relationship eventually realising that in the last year it had always been me who made the first approach, and now that she had a significant other person in her life that she fancied, her energies were channelled elsewhere. She had met a German man ten years her senior who, she was quite certain, would take care of her and look after her forever. He did, but not in the way she expected. That marriage was to be the exact opposite to the one organised for Vera, our Hungarian school friend. Tonia's wedding was quiet, quick, unpretentious, and I wasn't invited. In fact I didn't even know that it was taking place. I never did ask her the date. When much later I asked her why she had married him when she could have had the pick of her numerous besotted suitors, she answered that they all seemed so immature by comparison, so keen to do whatever she wanted and they were always at her beck and call, whereas her husband had a distant allure, 'a catch me if you can' attitude. My private thoughts were that he simply thought of himself first and foremost, had always intended to return to Germany but with the flush of success, a beautiful and devoted wife, a son who bore his name and a cute little miniature of Tonia. Later she was sent a formal wedding invitation to my church wedding in Caulfield, which she didn't even bother to RSVP. We saw each other on and off over the years, but that strong bond we had was gone. We each blamed our spouses for the rift. It is a fact that though we went out together from time to time, our guys never got too friendly.

Tonia was not the kind of girl to fall head over heels in love with anyone. With her, I am sure it was a calculated coupling that in the end went wrong. There is no doubt that she was promised the world on a platter by her suitor and I have no hesitation in saying that if her expectations had not been so high, she would not have been so disappointed. Probably the same could be said for him. In any case I can't ever remember either one saying he, or she loved the other.

After we were married, the favourite haunt was the German Club because the music was better there. But I suspect it was because Tonia's husband was German and he had friends there. He didn't dance but didn't mind his wife dancing with others, but I minded when I had to sit it out because she liked dancing with my husband who could dance very well, whereas most of the other club patrons were loud, overweight and danced the way they would have marched in the German Army, with precision but no flair. We lost touch for a little while until we each had two children. Both of hers were a year older than my two boys, but distance kept us apart and it was only rarely that we met now, and then I proceeded to have number three, my own little doll that I could dress up like a little princess.

Ironically the age difference between Allan and I was the same as the difference between Tonia and her spouse, and they both lived to the same advanced old age.

A Gift from the Heart

During my working career, I made a point of keeping in touch with my form teacher from McKinnon High, who had helped me so much and had become my friend, Mr C. and his wife, and rejoiced with them at the news of their impending parenthood. In turn, they were just as happy for me when I told them I was about to become engaged. True to form, my partner and I were invited to dinner at their home, and a tennis afternoon was arranged for the following weekend. Mrs C. and I got along very well and we could talk about most things, as she was really not much older than me, apart from coming from a totally different background, so we were quite comfortable talking about sex, and she took this opportunity to talk about the darker side of wedded bliss.

"What do you know of marital relationships?"

"Not much," I had to admit. And she proceeded to educate me, not only on the physical aspects, but also the psychological requirements, and the emotional differences between male and female. I was starting to understand my mother and father, and their differing needs that had changed over the years, and thinking that they didn't really have much in common any more. They talked but didn't communicate! Big difference!

How I wished that teachers were as committed to their vocation when my children went through school. Mr and Mrs C. were dedicated and involved with every student. They both went far beyond the call of duty—they actually loved us and they loved their work, but it is with special thanks and gratitude that I remember their contribution to my 'special day'.

Mrs C. was married in an expensive, limited edition, imported, Italian dress. Designed by a well-known, world-class designer of the time, it was made of the finest embroidered silk with a short train. The skirt opened from the waist to reveal a finely sunray pleated semi-transparent crystal organza panel that came to the floor. The bodice was plain but well-fitted and with a low neckline. To complete the outfit, a short bolero with just below the elbow sleeves and a small catch under the bust was worn for the ceremony but it could be taken off for the reception and for dancing. Overall, the outfit was not fussy or tizzy. The beautifully patterned embroidery in the silk with the contrasting crystal organza front panel made the ensemble quite unique. Mrs C. offered this prize to me for my wedding. Not on loan as I would have expected, but as a gift, to alter and to fit as required, and Mr C. said he would be honoured to act as 'The Master of Ceremony'. I was truly blessed!

My circle of friends was very restricted at that time, because my work colleagues were, with the exception of one, all males, and while I enjoyed their company, a respectable distance had to be maintained, though we certainly chatted and joked throughout the day, there was no time to socialise. One of the younger men who had recently joined us made it clear that he was attracted to me and always went out of his way to help, but he was a whole month younger than me, and that would never do! I wanted someone more mature than a nineteen year old, even if he did look older, and was quite presentable and sophisticated, the extent of our friendship was to share a lunch occasionally and discuss our weekends. His were much more interesting than mine, but we remained good friends for a number of years after my marriage, and at a time when I was getting to the end of my tether living with the in-laws, he helped me find a lovely flat on the beach at Seaford, near the water.

Shortly after we moved into our new abode and finally away from relations, I became pregnant and he had also married. We remained friends.

My 'Special Day'

Once I was married there was no time for anything that did not involve my newly adopted family. Not that they embraced me to their bosom, more that I was expected to drop everything including my own personality and become one of them. There was only one that I could tolerate throughout my marriage, and she only barely, even though she was a kind soul, but I valiantly tried like a good, devoted wife in love with her husband to fit in the Lithuanian-speaking family, the folk dancing and singing, the card playing and the drinking till all hours. Really the marriage was doomed before it started, but I wasn't to know that initially, and by the time it sunk in, I was too proud and stubborn to admit it, and still forever hopeful.

My 'special day' day started out as a miserable, wet September morning. We all went to the hairdresser where I asked for a sophisticated hairstyle similar to the style that Teresa, my only bridesmaid, had chosen and we both ended up looking older rather than sophisticated. The look didn't suit either of us. It was not starting out well. It was raining, the photographer was late and no one thought of taking an umbrella. The only person not having a fit or a heart attack, for a change, was my father, who was impeccably groomed, looking quite debonair and for once in control, as I walked out the door on his arm. He opened the car door for me before walking around to sit beside me being touchingly careful not to crush the silk, or the tulle of my veil. It only took a few minutes to drive to the church where, to my horror, the groom's car was nowhere to be seen—they had not yet arrived. Why not? He didn't have far to come either, as their family home was just on the other side of the train line, in Malvern.

"No, no, don't stop. Drive around the block", I frantically whispered to the driver. A few minutes later, we were back. Still no groom! What on Earth is going on? Isn't the bride the one who is supposed to be late?

"No, don't stop. Drive around again, slower this time."

Third time lucky. The marine blue Vauxhall is now standing in front of the church. And groom, groomsman, and the obese old lady were fumbling with umbrellas in the wind and rain. They made it up the stairs and inside the foyer and then my future brother-in-law had the decency to come back with the umbrella to escort my bridesmaid, and then me in the now pelting rain to the front foyer of the old church where we could reassemble into some semblance of dignity. Was it an omen? Probably!

I can't remember the service, the only thing I remember was having to hang on to my veil on the way out, now as Mrs K., or it would have taken off in the gale force wind that had sprung up. Teresa was holding up my train so the dress wouldn't get too wet and muddy, but my beautiful, white Italian leather shoes with the '*intaglio*' pattern were squelching rudely on the steps and all the way down to the waiting car. Somehow we got to the reception and it was cold—cold in more ways than one. Suddenly, to me it seemed like a hostile environment! With my friends and family, consisting of Mother, Father, and Little Sister, who was looking so sweet in the white felt hat and gloves to match the sensible dress, also white, that Mother had made for her to protect her from the bitterly cold day, sitting awkwardly on one side of the RSL Hall. Allan's family was sitting just as awkwardly on the other side. In the middle of the room was the sparsely decorated bridal table. Nothing noteworthy there either, except for the valiantly delivered speech by the Master of Ceremony, my ex-form teacher. How sorry I felt for him! It was so obvious that what he was saying went straight over the heads of the majority of the wedding guests, and that included all my new in-laws and their friends, as it was they who made up the numbers. My new mother-in-law never stopped talking to those around her in Lithuanian. She was one of those immigrants who never made the effort to learn English, simply because she never had to. She always managed to have a captive audience of her own. Somehow we all sat through the mediocre meal.

How appropriate were the songs that the orchestra played at our reception, 'September in the Rain' and then Johnny Rae sang, 'Singing in the Rain'. I certainly didn't feel like singing that night, nor dancing, but the bridal waltz was an ordeal that we had to get through before the other guests joined in and lightened the mood a bit. In the days when the Rock 'n Roll craze took young people by storm, it was amusing to watch them trip and stumble in their effort to conform to the more sedate dances played tonight for the benefit of the older generation. Had they played 'Too Young to be Married', I might have been warned of things to come.

The Honeymoon

What was noteworthy was our first night of wedded bliss. We couldn't find the door of the hotel in the rain because it was in an area that was not familiar to us. We had forgotten to book it until the very last minute but had decided that it had to be on the way to Bright and Mount Buffalo so we wouldn't be wasting so much time driving in the morning. So where was it? Where else but next to His Majesty's Prison.

When we finally found our way in, and fell into bed with sheer exhaustion, we had the lullaby of the night trams outside the window, not to mention the cars skidding on the wet road. And the police sirens! At some stage we must have fallen asleep, at least until 4:30 a.m., when the alarm went off in the backyard next door—time and time again. I didn't know Pentridge housed crowing roosters as well as criminals. The cacophony went on and on until we couldn't stand it any longer. How many roosters did they have in that goal?

We got dressed and headed off for our honeymoon, still in the rain. It had been a bad start but it couldn't get any worse. Or could it?

Soon we stopped for breakfast at a friendly looking café and enjoyed a mountain of savoury and sweet pancakes followed by hot chocolate—lovely. It revived us. And made up for the meal we were too nervous to finish the previous night. Picking up our jackets, we turned to go and guess what? We both realised simultaneously that we had forgotten to bring our pillows with us. The lovely, new, fluffy, goose-feather, plump pillows we had just bought for the occasion. We can't go on our honeymoon without our feather pillows. So back we turned, still driving in the rain and an hour or so later we are back in Malvern—to pick up our special pillows. Mother-in-law was ecstatic, 'her favourite son has decided not to leave his mother after all, but has decided to come back home already!'

Of course we had to stay for another breakfast. Oh well, we won't need to stop for lunch, I thought to myself as I witnessed the excessively emotional parting of mother and son. I guess she won't be number one lady any more, I consoled myself.

Finally we got on our way and arrived in Bright for the first week of our long awaited honeymoon. The fire was burning in the hearth, and it was nice and cosy. It was time to start unwinding, with a drink, beer I think because that was all we had taken with us, and we realised it was a while since we had eaten. So where should we go for dinner? This is a Chalet, there's no food around here, it was getting dark, snowing, and if we were going to find a restaurant we had better go soon, so we grabbed our coats and dashed out. No problem, as dusk settled we saw a welcoming door with well-lit windows where from the outside we could see the friendly flames of the obligatory burning fireplace. We chose a table close to the fire so I could defrost and get the blood circulating again in my fingers. I needed to get some feelings back and unstiffen them to be able to hold my fork and knife. The Aussie food was quite appetising and plentiful, so we lingered for a while until our hunger was appeased. Well-sated, we started back to the car and found it covered in snow, but it soon warmed up inside, the snow melted and slid down the windscreen so we could see where to go—by the headlights now, because there didn't seem to be any street lights around. After a few false turns, we found our street and our Chalet. Feeling finally at peace with the world, we opened the door to our home for the next week to find that the fire had gone out! I hate the cold. I can't even think clearly when it's cold. My brain as well as my body goes into hibernation, and we have one week here, and another in Mount Buffalo in the real high country!

Somehow I survived that first week, but I was convinced I wouldn't survive the next. We arrived at the old Victorian Railway Resort and it didn't look too bad from the outside—it was certainly a lot bigger than the last place. A good thick covering of powdery snow was on the ski slopes, and it all looked lovely, white, and clean just like in a picture postcard. There were not many people inside but there was a lovely great fire blazing that even I couldn't deny was very inviting. Having booked in, we ventured into our room, which was nowhere near as pleasant as the hall downstairs. Okay, so we will spend more time in the lounge in the company of the other guests who were just starting to come in from the ski slopes. A motley crowd, happy, loud and tired, they dropped off skis, boots, jackets, helmets, and all their odd items of clothing on all available surfaces, and soon the whole place looked a mess and smelled even worse. Smoke from the fire, smoke from an assortment of cigars, cigarettes, and the alternative grasses, spilt beer, sweating bodies, and everyone talking louder and louder the more intoxicated they became. We had only been there a couple of hours and already I was wondering why we had come. I can't, and never could (nor wanted to) ski. Allan could ski when he lived in the mostly frozen Baltic States, but that was before his accident. With his left leg not able to bend fully now, and being shorter than the other, he was not even going to attempt it. So we headed for the dining room, which was still relatively civilised and quiet, as the hordes had not yet arrived there. Dinner was good and plentiful, and we took our time eating and drinking. I had a Scotch with dry ginger, with Allan sticking to his favourite—beer. Thankfully, he was not a huge drinker. Too soon, we were joined by the other guests who were, by then, in various stages of intoxication. Their loud and coarse language flowed as freely as the alcohol. One thing I have never been able to understand is the need to use foul language and swear words in conversation. The occasional 'b' one I have used myself in times of extreme frustration, but when it comes to the continual use of the 'b', 'c' and 'f' words, to me it signifies that a person is not the master his or her own language, who has a very limited vocabulary, and little or no imagination. It was time to leave the noisy, and now unfriendly dining room, so we headed upstairs to relax and unwind the way honeymooners do.

New Name – New Abode

It was a very long week with lousy weather, even when the sun came out, it turned the snow into dirty slush. We were both glad to be heading home.

Home was a single bedroom that Allan's brother and his wife had kindly offered to us as a temporary measure until we sorted ourselves out, and of course we had the run of the rest of the house. At the end of our honeymoon, we were left with ten pounds in cash, and a double divan bed we had just purchased, plus our wedding gifts. I had my work and was very glad to go back to it, but my new husband had no work. He had been helping his father out, who was a house painter, and that was okay while he was single but would not do now that he had a wife. I had visions of owning a house of our own someday but we needed two wages before we could even start planning. Back at work, my charges, as I liked to call the thirty-odd life insurance salesmen, were without exception, happy to see me return and the old routine restored. Except for my new name, which was unpronounceable by most.

I didn't particularly like my new name either, so the next morning when we all met for our daily conference, I announced that I would be shortening the name to make it sound friendlier. Unanimously they concurred. So that night I made the announcement at home as well—and was met with a stony silence. I asked Allan why the shocked silence when he had done the same thing himself many years earlier, when he was in hospital and he found that most doctors and nurses could not pronounce his Christian name, and so he had Anglicised it and shortened it. His older brother had done the same. Why did they all frown at me when I had done the same thing with the surname, shortening it only by deleting several letters from the middle section?

For the rest of the year I kept the peace by not saying anything about the work situation and the fact that we were living on my wage alone. We were not paying rent, just contributing to the cost of the food and the utilities, but after the Christmas holidays I suggested that the 'positions vacant' section in the daily papers should be explored in more detail, so together we circled some entries that might return a result. Allan did not like getting paint under his nails anyway so he was quite amenable to start looking for something that would not spoil his manicured fingers, but wouldn't you know it, he met his future employer at the same hotel that my father frequented regularly on the corner of Flinders and Swanston Streets—the Young and Jackson. They must all have been admiring the 'Buxom Nude', the full life painting of 'Chloe', on the wall that's been there for more than a hundred years.

The New Chloe

On a recent visit to Melbourne, I could not go past the ultra-modern Federation Square without checking out the corner building diagonally across Flinders and Swanston Streets to see if 'Chloe' was still there. She was not where I had last seen her, on the main sidewall of the ground floor lounge peering out onto the smoke haze of a thousand smokers both past and present. Undeterred, I wandered through this well-known watering hole that obviously had recently been remodelled and restored. It even smelled fresh. I climbed the carpeted steps to the next floor of this edifice. The boutique hotel now catered for a multitude of functions and on this day groups of ladies sat at tables engrossed in an assortment of games, mah-jong, bridge, etc., and some were just conversing. So I deduced that this institution is as popular now as ever because 'Chloe' had gravitated upstairs, had taken up another wall that was surrounded by mirrors, where not only the guests could admire her attributes, but she could also admire herself in their many reflections. She had been professionally cleaned and restored to her former beauty, sans smoke and grime. She now stood proudly in her pose of the young and alluring courtesan that many would find even more appealing than the Mona Lisa. Certainly she was so much bigger than the painting by Leonardo da Vinci.

'Chloe' was not the buxom lady that I expected to see hanging on the wall, but a youngish and well-formed seductress.

In the course of lunchtime and hasty after-work drinks when men were downing their last pots before the six o'clock closing time, Allan must have made it known to all and sundry that he was looking for work. Much to my surprise and pride, he soon landed a job with The Victorian Printing Works Pty Ltd, a private company that printed for the Victorian Government, and that not only paid him a good, regular wage but also employed him for the next eighteen years. He often said that all or at least most of the work contracts were negotiated in pubs. We got our home within three and a half years with the help of a personally guaranteed loan from his employer.

Just like school life in the fifties and sixties, when one could build a rapport with and become quite close and friendly with dedicated teachers, so in employment one could become close friends with one's employer. In Allan's case, he befriended the whole family of three generations, as their children came along. It was a win-win situation, with benefits to both sides. They were fully aware of his limitations. I shudder to think of how many times he would have repeated the details of his near-death experience to them, but in his case it paid off because it made them aware that he was not a bludger, but a very dependable person who needed to take time off, if he was truly unable to work. When I had to ring his work, I could speak to anyone in the family business, they all understood the situation, so I made a point that whenever I could, I would visit the interesting set-up they had going and we could all put a face to the voice on the telephone. They were a sociable lot. It was only a short walking distance from my own office in the city, and at times we would go home together, though generally Allan finished work earlier.

The Seduction

We lived for almost a year with his brother and his family. The kitchen was crowded but we managed not to get in each other's way by cooking at different times. We needed a bit of privacy, so we converted the garage into a temporary bedroom/sitting room and just shared the bathroom facilities. The single toilet tended to stretch friendships to the limit, especially when the 'Truth' racing guide was draped over the paper roll holder, and carpeted most of the floor. Notebooks and pens were nailed to the walls, and it was obvious that this private and restricted space was conducive to illuminating reasoning for backing the 'winner'. It was also a handy hiding place where one could hope not to be disturbed for a while. On what little floor space was left, a neat pile of 'Awake' magazines, and the New Testament Bible of the Jehovah's Witnesses rested, hopeful of converting sinners who dared to turn its pages. In all honesty, I did pick up many useful bits of knowledge and handy hints that have served me in good stead over the years, whereas the articles in the 'Truth' were anything but the truth. It was interesting to find such conflicting reading material side by side in such a confined area. But the two individuals in this unlikely union were as diverse as day from night. One was a dashing rogue who could and often did charm the ladies and fancied himself irresistible. The other had been a very trusting young girl of sixteen who fell hopelessly in love with my husband's older brother when they had first met eight years earlier. It was Allan who had escorted her to a dance and then introduced her to his 'irresistible' brother, two years his senior. He did confess to me on one occasion that he actually felt guilty and responsible for much of her later sufferings. This is their story.

Galina was a young child who was brought up by her much older sister. They were White Russian refugees who migrated from Harbin, China but had been permanently separated from the rest of the family. Much later, when I eventually met her sister, I understood why there had been so much speculation about their relationship within the brothers' family. Were they really sisters, or mother and daughter? No matter. Both were wonderful persons in their own right. The seduction was swift. Security at the hospital where the two sisters worked must have been very slack and the girls were working different shifts. One fine, full-moon night Vic, my brother-in-law to-be, scaled the wall to the first floor window where the young nurses' dormitories were located. How he managed to persuade the other room residents to clear out is open to conjecture, but the outcome was obvious. Galina gave birth to a baby boy shortly after her seventeenth birthday. Eleven months later, and shortly before her eighteenth, another child, a very delicate and beautiful baby doll was born to them, belying yet again the commonly held belief that a woman cannot conceive while she is breastfeeding. The following years saw the young mother spend more and more time alone. To supplement his income now that he had a family, Vic took a job as a night time taxi driver, and this was how he came into contact with the underworld of gambling and prostitution. He spent more and more of his free time at the gambling tables, and it seemed that Lady Luck was on his side, but his successes did not go unnoticed. He was headhunted by 'the mob'.

Plans were drawn up to build their family home and during the daylight hours work would proceed with tremendous impetus. Periodically though, the work would come to a standstill. This was when money ran out and it became necessary to bolster income with night work. At least there were no more babies for the next five years. I remember one night, shortly after we moved in with them, when his personal winnings were very substantial, while the loser had already lost all. The loser just happened to be the manager of an electrical store, and next morning my brother-in-law took delivery of the latest model, family-size refrigerator. There was one major problem with that fridge though. It was great to look at, it was the latest model and the object of much admiration, but it was utterly useless when there was no food to put in it. Because money had a habit of coming in and going out, with devastating regularity, either feasts or famines ruled their lives. During the feast times, nothing but the best was good enough. Firstly came the gourmet foods, then the theatre performances, and the ballet shows. Bills were paid but they had to wait their turn. And then the cycle would begin again—the gambling, the losses, and the recriminations, the stress and the long absences often lasting several days at a time, and the utter loneliness for mother and babes.

It was around this time that a popular British actress named Sheila from ABC TV became an immensely beneficial influence in the life and future direction of this strikingly beautiful, Russian lady that was my sister-in-law by marriage. They met through my brother-in-law, Vic, who was also working for the same television and radio station. The beguiling, doll-like child with the name of a Russian flower was enrolled in a ballet school, thanks to Sheila's stage connections. The exquisite grace and natural talent of this endearing love-child made both mother and daughter favourites in the theatre circles. Sheila's intervention when the going got tough for the young mother extended to mentoring her, as well as often paying for the ballet lessons for the child. Through her new theatrical friends, Galina, a committed great thinker, became exposed to another group. A group that was becoming more and more vocal about the excesses of this world—the Jehovah Witnesses. It was she who became an enigma with her clear, deep blue eyes that were seemingly able to reach right into the soul, searching, penetrating, understanding, and she was very forgiving, but she never forgot. Her beauty became legendary as she matured, her heavy hair was always plaited and coiled around her lovely face, free of any make up. The high cheekbones and the long, thick, honey-coloured hair were typically Russian in both mother and child. Her grooming was impeccable, and she was talented too, taking much pleasure in creating unique theatrical outfits for her daughter. Without the support and company of a husband, whom she would always love deeply in spite of all his faults, she took on new commitments. In her desperate need to make a statement and give her life a new direction and meaning, she embraced the new faith with all the intensity of a drowning waif, never sparing herself, she led by example and dedication, devoting a great deal of time to this religious doctrine. I admired the silent inner strength and tenacity of my sister-in-law, and though I liked her immensely, I was never able to penetrate that loving reserve that she presented to everyone. It was almost as though her fear of being hurt yet again prevented her from being able to get too close to anyone. Vic, who no doubt loved her in his own way, tended to be flighty and self-indulgent. He never seemed to be around when he was needed, and always had an excuse if he let his family down so they learnt not to rely on him. He was a persuasive talker, with a forceful personality who took pride in his lovely and gifted daughter, but on many occasions it was Sheila who paid for her classes and the entry fees for the competitions in which the child invariably topped her age group. He never failed to praise and encourage her or let her know how proud he was to be her dad. And she idolised him. But the pain that his wife had endured, and the scars caused by the continuing emotional turmoil eventually took their toll. She suffered an aneurism in the early stages of her third pregnancy. Sheer determination helped her recovery and she went on to produce a fourth, fifth, and a sixth child. But Sheila could not continue to pay for the ballet classes for the delightful Petal, and now there were another three girls at home. The family was growing too fast.

This time in her husband's life had many peaks and valleys, and the stress that he subjected himself to with his erratic lifestyle culminated in a heart attack at forty-seven and a fatal cardiac arrest at the age of fifty-two. Sad to say, but I think she was able to cope better in life without him. During our time with them, I learnt a lot about the vagaries of self-indulgence and a lot about loyalty in spite of all odds, but I was not able to achieve that never failing, inner tranquillity in the face of adversity. My personality is more volatile.

In our time of living with them, Allan and I used the train to go to work. We started work at different times and I treasured that travel time on my own as it gave me the opportunity to think clearly. Then his old mother (people were old at the age of sixty-two back then) became really ill and we were asked (more like ordered) to return to the family home. I could not object, because by that time we had probably outstayed our welcome with his brother's family. His wife was also expecting their third child, so we moved back, taking our few possessions to the already overcrowded parents' house.

Back Home

Without a doubt, it was the worst year of my life. Even if it didn't last the full year, our time there felt like an eternity. I had a demanding full-time job that paid very well, but I had to put in the time and the effort to justify the rewards, which was something that Allan's family could not or did not want to understand. I was a woman, and a woman's place is in the home to pander to the whims and wants of the males in the household, including Alan's younger brother who was exactly one month older than I was. I still had to do the filthy washing for the men and the sick mother, housework on weekends, cooking the nightly meals for everyone, and then copping a lot of complaints because I didn't know how to cook the way of the 'old country'. Lots of pork and potatoes, and fat floating on top of the gravy—Yuk, I didn't always want to eat that in any case. They didn't like my Italian cooking, I didn't like to cook their way, but at least I tried to reach a compromise.

Everything came to a head one evening when everyone was sitting at the table and I had forgotten to place a spoon by the young brother's plate. It was one of those rare times when the mother had come out of her bedroom for a meal. We were all seated at the table ready to start our dinner, when the young upstart complained that he was missing a spoon. His attitude of spoilt brat, who always gets what he wants when he wants it from everyone, had always rubbed me the wrong way, so I just glared at him and told him he had two perfectly good legs of his own, and to find his own way to the kitchen drawers, which were only a few paces behind him. We sat there glaring at each other until the mother pushed herself up with the aid of her walking stick to shuffle her way along the table, past her young son, to get him his spoon. That was the last straw, I got up from the table and left the room in disgust at the male behaviour in this household—and I thought my father was bad!

That night I told Allan that I had enough of the situation and that I needed my sleep at night if I was going to be able to keep on working, because by that time the mother was in a great deal of pain with her aggressive cancer. According to doctors, it was supposed to have killed her before the previous Christmas, now it was almost July of the following year, and who knew how long she would still hang on to her miserable existence? She could not sleep at night, and was crying and screaming most of the night, keeping everyone awake but she would not go into a hospital. I informed my husband that I would be moving out the coming weekend and that if he wanted to keep his marriage, he was welcome to come with me. At that stage I didn't know where I was intending to go. Returning to my home was not an option because the first words I would hear would be, "I told you so."

The next morning at work, it was obvious that I hadn't slept well, and when my young colleague asked the reason, I had to tell him my dilemma and that I didn't know where to go. In the last year, Eric had matured and filled out, and he had also recently got engaged to a lass a bit older than him. I was genuinely happy for him and expressed a desire to meet his girl. As we returned to our work he said to leave the accommodation problem to him and he would have a proposition for me before the end of the week. I trusted him implicitly and gratefully accepted his help. That night I brought Allan up to date with my plans which were unchanged in spite of all the pleadings, cries, and screams in the night—I was leaving at the end of June, the coming weekend. Again I told him that his mother should be in hospital. In spite of all the problems I had faced in my young life, I was very resilient and also blessed with a few good friends. Eric was one of them.

The following morning he was at work before me, and waiting to give me the good news. His family had one adopted son, Anthony. He was an older boy whom they had taken in to care for after his parents were killed in a road accident. He was at that time thirty-one years old, the same age as my husband, though I didn't know it then, and in fact not for a while. Our landlord-to-be was working away in the country, with what was then the Victorian Forestry Commission and only came home for short periods. Eric's family had the key to a new apartment that Anthony had recently purchased and everyone was concerned that the flat remained unoccupied for so long while he was working away. What a perfect solution to my woes! I came with 'triple A' recommendations from his adopted family so he knew that I would look after his home. I would be paying minimal rent for a two-bedroom unit that was fully-furnished, except for the second bedroom, which Anthony was using as a study. We had his permission to move in immediately instead of waiting until he returned from the country. So we cleared his desk and chair from the second bedroom, put them in his bedroom where they fitted quite comfortably for when he would be using them while he was home, and we had the second bedroom to ourselves. Even Allan couldn't fault this scenario except that he was understandably concerned about his mother.

The following weekend, we moved our scanty belongings into a new, light, and breezy home in a wonderful location fronting the beach. What a pleasant change this was from the dark, musty, smelly, old house that I had to put so much effort just to keep reasonably clean and tidy. I was beside myself with happiness at my newly found independence and started thinking about my approaching twenty-first birthday in two weeks' time. Now I could actually have some friends over for a small celebration. Encountering no resistance, I immediately set about inviting a few friends that included my ex-form teacher, classmates, and a few of my work friends. No sooner had I posted my twenty-first birthday invitations out, Allan got a phone call at work from his brother saying that their mother was in hospital, and not expected to last the night. She died on the 2nd of July, the week before my twenty-first birthday celebrations, which of course had to be cancelled. So I was being punished for forcing her son to move out of the family home, where they had all been so 'very happy together' before I married him and took him away. The incident was referred to on a number of occasions.

We continued with our work in the city in spite of the longer travelling times and we were able to save really hard to build a home for ourselves, so the low rent I was paying was immensely helpful. When we eventually got to meet our landlord from the next bedroom, we all felt very much at ease with each other. He was glad to have someone there to keep an eye on things while he was away, and obviously we were happy to pay for the utilities that we were mostly using. My love for the sun and sea saw me walking, swimming, and sunbaking any time I had to spare, and while my husband saw fit to pass the weekends with one or another of his relations, and used the car to drive over, I invited my family of three to come and share with me my happy sea escape. They occasionally did come by train as no one had a car or a driving licence in those days, not even me. The months passed very quickly, and for the Christmas holidays we decided to visit Adelaide and the ex-husband of Allan's younger sister who was living with his own sister in an inner suburb of the 'City of Churches'. He and Allan had been great mates since migrating to Australia, and the divorce did not come between them and their friendship, though he told Allan he did have to move away from his ex-wife and daughter because the proximity was too traumatic for him.

We started out on our journey straight from work, and followed the Great Ocean Road to Warrnambool, where we stopped for the night in some nondescript motel. The beautiful winding road continued on, but we detoured to view the extinct volcanic crater of the blue lake of Mount Gambier. The trip itself was pleasant enough but uneventful, except for the fact that I conceived for the second time in my life. I don't remember a great deal about the first time except that it was immediately after we were married and no way in the world was I going to have a child with nothing behind me, other than in-laws I couldn't stand. I wasn't that good of a practising Catholic, so I had an abortion, with no regrets or everlasting traumas to follow. Often, since that very personal period in my life, I wondered at some of the claims of guilt and depression made by other women following an abortion, whether all were actually genuine, or simply a cry for attention, because that was in vogue at the time. 'Oh, poor me, I had an abortion, a cataclysmic life-changing experience, and now my conscience is punishing me'.

Just as Germaine Greer was the champion of the next era with her book, 'The Female Eunuch', I firmly believe that a foetus in the early stages is not yet a baby, and I have never felt any guilt or depression over the incident. I made a conscious decision because I was simply not ready to be a mother as I had only recently stopped being a pseudo-mother to my younger sister. Full stop. End of story. I had to put myself first in this instance and moved on with life.

Once we returned from the trip to Adelaide, we felt it was time to knuckle down and start planning for our new home. We had the land, as everyone said, 'in the never-never', now we needed to put a house on it. I designed a simple, unpretentious, three-bedroom home with a flexible plan that could be extended at a later date when we required more room.

With my pregnancy confirmed, several things had to be taken into consideration, with the first and most significant being the loss of a wage. Would we be able to repay a mortgage? How would I get around once we moved to Ringwood? How would my husband get to work? Sensibly, we decided to look at the most pressing of our concerns. Pay the land off. And stay a while longer in our most amiable, and for me very pleasant, if temporary, accommodation. Sell the car and buy a smaller, cheaper vehicle, and most importantly, since I needed to be mobile, I had to learn to drive before the baby arrived. I can see Allan, imagining me dinting and damaging his beautiful car so he decided to sell it to a friend who had coveted it for a long time and he bought an almost-new, green Volkswagen that we christened 'the pregnant pasty'—appropriately!

Getting My Driver's Licence – 1962

Time galloped merrily on and I found that my driving lessons were not making me proficient fast enough. I could only practise on weekends and most of that time was taken up with household chores, but I had no better plan while I was still working. It was with mixed feelings that I left the job that I loved. The long travelling time by train was starting to get to me, and I guess that I wasn't as fit as I should have been for my age. I was putting on weight too quickly. What had happened to my twenty-one-inch waist? My pregnancy was not so advanced as to appear obscene, but working with an almost all male crew, I felt out of place and clumsy. As part of my work I was expected to convene on our daily meetings, and I guess I felt a bit uncomfortable to be 'on show'. In any case, I knew that they would all be well looked after professionally after I left. My right hand lady, the only other female on the whole of the sixth floor had been with us for nearly eighteen months, and I felt confident that I had trained her well enough to take over from me. I had made sure that each and every one of the thirty odd reps had some firsthand experience with her one-to-one with work-contracts requirements. And though her English was not quite up to the standard required to conduct the daily presentations, I knew that it would not take her long to fit into that role. Her native French more than made up for any shortfalls and her translation skills were excellent. She would continue to translate the French contracts from the Swiss home office, and 'Uncle Wal' would compose them into a workable English version.

One of the newer arrivals at work was a young chap who had recently married, and his young wife was also, as we used to say then, 'in the family way'. It turned out that we lived not far from each other, which was quite a coincidence, seeing that home was a one-hour train trip from the city and the office. Marlene's pregnancy was only a couple of weeks further advanced than mine, and we soon became friends. She had already stopped working and often came to the office following a visit to her doctor, or shopping trips into town, to wait for her husband so that they could go home together. Sometimes I would go with them if they were going straight home so it was natural that we should continue to get together once we both became 'Ladies-in-waiting' at home. We had a car sitting in the garage that didn't get much of a workout, as it seemed easier for both my husband and me to travel to work by train. We were starting and finishing at different times. But now with the baby on the way, I needed to get my driver's licence and become independently mobile.

Actually, what I needed was someone to sit with me while I clocked up some driving time and gained more practical experience. If I was going to sit for a test before the baby's arrival, I had to have some serious and consistent daily driving lessons, so Marlene undertook to become my instructor.

Soon I was ready to sit for the written test, and the next day I booked for the practical driving test to take place as soon as possible, because my companion was becoming huge too. On the set day, we drove to the police station at Seaford, which was in a semi-rural area. Not at all a developed suburb in the early 60's. The police officer that was to come with us was young and unmarried, and it was so blatantly obvious that he felt uneasy to have two ladies, both in the advanced stages of pregnancy, sitting with him in the compact, green Volkswagen that we had christened 'The Pregnant Pasty', because it looked bloated just like us. We proceeded to drive around the designated circuit as required for as long as it was stipulated in his manual, without any mishaps or mistakes on my part. I felt very confident, but starting to get a little uncomfortable. My belly was rubbing against the steering wheel, and I was a bit concerned about Marlene having to sit for so long in the confined space at the back. A Volkswagen is not the roomiest of cars. First part done, now it's time to head back to do some parking.

As the road in front of the police station had no car-space markings, the young cop indicated a tree, then paced out the regular length of a car space, stood there and directed me to park the car in the area between him and the tree. Crikey! This was a new one. I looked in the rear vision mirror, and Marlene's head, with the bird's nest hairdo, was in the way. Wouldn't you think that a tree would be big enough to be seen, even out of the smallish window of a Volkswagen? I took a deep breath, looked at the policeman, and tried to judge the distance. The last thing that I needed now was to knock him down. It didn't even occur to me that he could have jumped out of the way if I got too close, so I gingerly started to back the car keeping a close eye on him. Crunch! The tree got in the way! Almost in tears, I clumsily got out of the car knowing full well that at the very last minute I had definitely flunked my driving test. We were all quiet and subdued as we walked inside. "Just fill in these forms, and pay the cashier," he said, "And make sure that you stick to angle parking until you become more confident"

I could have kissed his feet! Elated, I drove to the train station to pick up my husband, stopping on the way to pick up something appetising for dinner to celebrate the occasion.

My family had reasons to celebrate another occasion and asked me to join them. They had applied for Australian Citizenship. It never even occurred to me that I wasn't legally Australian until someone handed me a certificate that said so. As far as I was concerned, I was as Australian as the next person. The ceremony was held at the Caulfield Town Hall, where I had danced at night and met my husband. Now I was very pregnant and I was back here to swear allegiance to the Queen. In return I would get a piece of paper that confirmed what I already knew, that Australia was my country and that the Queen had little to do with it!

Labour Is Just Hard Work

My delivery date was approaching, and then passed. Two, three, four days, on the fifth I was starting to wonder why junior hadn't yet arrived. The other young mums in the small complex where we lived were fussing around me, full of well-meaning advice, but that didn't help with my feelings of frustration.

The next morning I went shopping, paid the gas and electricity bills, driving the car, independent as ever, then later we all went out to lunch. I found myself starting to fidget and feel uncomfortable. Thinking that I had probably over exerted myself earlier, I should now take a rest and got up from the table as a contraction gripped me. Before I was fully aware of what they had in mind, my new friends had gone upstairs to pick up my ready and waiting hospital case, put it in the car and now were waiting to take me to Chelsea Hospital.

Getting into the car was becoming a challenge these days. Why all the fuss? Surely I can manage, but they were adamant that I should go now and that they knew better, as they had two and three children respectively already. Once inside the hospital, the midwife announced to us all that nothing much was happening. I smiled at them, "I told you so." With a hug and a smile they turned to go and I was left waiting on a trolley in the passageway, on my own, until I knew that something was definitely happening. Sure enough when it did, it happened quickly, before the doctor could even get there. At four o'clock I was given a telephone so that I could ring my husband and announce that he had a son, and I didn't even forego the afternoon tea they brought to me. I chomped away with great gusto, to everyone's amusement. It was hard work, I told them and I had to regain my energy quickly. After all, doesn't labour mean just strenuous work?

Life was good and I was happy. It was hard to tell if Allan was happy or not. He was not one to show emotion. My first baby was in every way as perfect as could be. Five days later, I was home and everything I had learnt about being a mum I tried valiantly to put into practice, but soon discovered that in reality, life is not quite the same as the text books like to portray it and certain shortcuts are necessary, if all that's important is to get done in a day. My son, Robert, suffered from colic, not unusual but nevertheless distressing to both mum and babe, and wouldn't you know it, he was always at his worst in the late afternoon when I needed to prepare dinner for his father. I had an abundance of milk so feeding him was never a problem and we both got used to him resting on my left hip as I went about the daily chores.

We spent quite a bit of time on the beach too, mainly in the mornings with the other mums and their babes, and one day the fragility of life was brought home to us in a most unexpected and unpleasant way. While we were sitting on our towels, sunning ourselves and chatting about everything and nothing in particular, we always kept an eye on their three toddlers who played happily each day with their buckets and spades, building sandcastles and digging swimming pools in the wet sand, when a bigger wave washed up on the beach and swept the sandcastles away. Angrily the two year old dashed after the offending wave and met up with the next one that swept him off his feet and dragged him into the ocean. The tide was coming in fast but the undertow treacherously swept the toddler out just as fast as the tide was bringing him in. The two mums rushed out and between them they dragged the unconscious boy to shore and applied CPR while I dashed to call the ambulance. Not having far to come, the paramedics quickly took over and thankfully, after three days in hospital, the child fully recovered. This potentially fatal accident happened right in front of all our eyes so quickly and unexpectedly, shocking us into abandoning the beach, unless we could follow the young children right into the water and stay with them at all times. Summer was over and the waters were cooling anyway, so we would go for long walks and picnics instead, letting the children race ahead, play and tumble with their new puppy that was a present to the toddler who nearly drowned, and delighting Robert who was too young to join in the tumbles with them just yet.

About that time, I realised that instead of losing the post-natal weight a woman often carries while she is breast-feeding, in my case I was putting more on. By now Robert was seven and a half months old, and I had foolishly believed the old wives' tales that while breastfeeding one doesn't get pregnant. A visit to the doctor confirmed what I suspected and our second son was on his way. Neither one of us was particularly overjoyed to hear the news, but we consoled ourselves with the belief that the siblings would grow up companionably together. Immediately though, we realised that there would be a problem with the shortage of space in the flat once the second baby arrived. We got on well and happily with our landlord but we could hardly stretch the friendship by overcrowding him. He had a laid back, relaxed personality and I don't ever recall him complaining about anything. He was pleased to have someone in the flat to welcome him with a homemade meal when he came back from the bush. He was besotted with Robert and often spent time playing with him on the floor when he was home from his country work. He would ask about his health and wellbeing as soon as he got back after an absence. When we decided to baptise our first born, we both felt that we would be hard pressed to find anyone more suitable and caring than Anthony, and so Robert's baptism name is Anthony, in honour of his Godfather. We knew that there was a common bond, a sense of belonging, of having the next best thing to a blood tie for Anthony, who really had no one on earth except for an adopted family that he had outgrown.

Planning Our Modest Home

We had already toyed with the idea of building our first home but had not progressed much further than a rough plan or outline of what we wanted. We now realised that our 'wants' and what we could afford were miles apart. I imagine most young couples like to build castles in the air until reality strikes home, then have to come down to earth with wishes versus needs. So I went to see a local builder mainly to get some ideas. He was a young man with a family who understood our dilemma. We spent quite some time with him and in the end decided that he could build a basic house to the lock-up stage. Once we were in, we would do the finishing work in our own time. In effect this worked really well for us. I could do some things during the day when Allan was at work, and things like the painting we could do together in the evenings when the children were in bed.

My pregnancy was progressing well but as I was approaching the ninth month, I started to have what the doctor called 'false contractions'. Nevertheless they were debilitating and drained me of much strength. During one of the weeks that our landlord Anthony was stationed at the home office, I was scheduled to visit the Women's Hospital in the city. I was pretty huge by then and with a thirteen month old baby tagging along it would have been quite challenging to get myself into town by train and then over to the hospital, so Anthony offered to drive me there. Half a century later and I still remember that drive, how caring and calm he was, yet amusingly comic and teasing as he managed to keep Robert engaged for the whole duration of the long drive into Melbourne.

Daniel was born that day but not without drama. My phantom contractions had been bothering me for close to a month and on that day when I was to see the gynaecologist. I was several days past my due date so I figured the event was well and truly overdue. But when the doctor examined me, he shook his head, "No, I don't think anything will happen soon," he said to me, so out I waddled ungainly towards the tram that was to take me to Allan's work near the Flagstaff Gardens. When the tram stopped, I attempted to get in with the pram containing a healthy and squirming Robert. The conductor, whose proper interest is the safety of his passengers, tried valiantly to help me with the pram just as another contraction gripped me. No way could I climb up that tram, and later negotiate the steps down again, so I held up my hand to stay the worried conductor and told him to go on his way and not to worry, that I understood he could not take responsibility for me. In the middle of Swanston St, Carlton, I now had to negotiate traffic to get to the other side of the road, and slowly make my way on foot along the four or so blocks separating me from my husband's work. Common sense should have told me to go back to the hospital but the words of the gynaecologist were still ringing in my ears. I should have asked him to define the word, "soon", but young and trusting as I was at the time, I believed him and persevered on foot while pushing the pram that was in effect supporting me, to the front door of Victorian Printing Works, where I collapsed on a bench with relief once I was inside. It was late afternoon when Allan finally got me back to the Mater Hospital, then took Robert to my mother in Caulfield and left him there. Mother had to take time off work to look after her grandson. That was the accepted practice in those days—kids are a woman's problem and responsibility. She certainly didn't mind having her first grandchild there, though she would have preferred to have had some notice beforehand, but no one had even thought to ring her from the office to inform her before we left. Back at the hospital shifts were changing when I was left there. The outgoing shift couldn't have cared less about someone who had been having contractions for over a week already. I can almost hear them thinking. "It may be another week before she's ready to give birth."

The new shift didn't know that I even existed, so once again I was left languishing in the corridor. Until I screamed with the pain of a contraction and someone came over to look at my chart,

"Oh don't worry about her, she's another Aytalian"

"They all scream the roof down at the slightest twinge!" was the reply she gave the young nurse who came to help. Stupidly, I clamped my jaws shut. What I should have done was scream some abuse back at the senior nurse, thus I would have got the attention that I so urgently needed. Instead, I meekly groaned and whimpered until the baby decided he wouldn't wait any longer and I practically delivered him myself before some doctors who were passing by realised what was happening. As it turned out, this wasn't the easiest of births, because by then I was really and truly exhausted. Regardless, I was sent home after three days.

This time I told Allan not to bother to take time off work, but to just stop somewhere to have something to eat so I wouldn't have to worry about cooking for him initially. I knew that I could ask my neighbours to do some shopping for me and that I could also rely on them to pop in from time to time to see if I needed anything. They would take Robert to play with their own children so I could have some rest. For that first month, I even stopped ironing Allan's shirts. I washed them, but if he wanted them pressed he had to do it himself as he did before we were married. Only he didn't have a job back then and the one shirt he had to press was his dress shirt. Not that he didn't hopefully look in the wardrobe first, just in case during the day I had nothing better or more important to do. I thank God, on behalf of all the young mums of today, for the wash and wear clothes that are widely available from any department store now.

We had signed all the contracts for our new home and work was about to start. When I regained my strength and looked around the cluttered small unit, I realised that we were not being fair to Anthony who had been so good to us so I gave in to Allan's nagging to return to the family home in Malvern while we were waiting for our own to be completed. His father had recently died of alcohol abuse, leaving the youngest son the entire property. That was the Eastern European way—the last one who remains home 'to look after the parents' ends up with all the loot. So that was another punishment for us. We had left the family home therefore we had no claim to it, and Allan could (and did) blame me for his father's revenge. What I couldn't understand was, why move back now? Surely at twenty-three years of age, his spoilt younger brother, who inherited the house and everything in it, could take care of himself? But by moving back, he explained, his travelling time to work would be halved.

History Repeats Itself

I took my leave of Seaford, Anthony, and all of my friends, and we took our still-scanty belongings to Malvern the following weekend. In the week that followed, I begged the builder to get the house to the lock-up stage as soon as possible, and somehow managed to get through the rest of the week. On our first full weekend back in Malvern, we were planning to take a car ride to Ringwood to check on the building progress. We were all sitting around the table having Sunday breakfast and at 8 a.m. the telephone rang, as I was the closest, I picked it up. The caller identified himself as the Chief Inspector of police, Road Accidents Division. Was I the person whose name and telephone number he had just rung?

"Yes," I answered perplexed.

"Do you know who Anthony's next of kin is?" The Inspector asked, after confirming the full name and address.

"Both his parents were killed in a road accident when he was a child, and he is my son's Godfather," I started to worry. "Why?"

"Does he have any brothers or sisters?" he persisted.

"No. But he was adopted later in life. Can you tell me what this is all about?"

"I am sorry to tell you that Anthony was killed early this morning in a collision with a milk tanker."

My knees gave way, and I had to sit down quickly. Immediately my thoughts went to his parents who had died the same way. Does history repeat itself? Everything points to it. "Please tell me how it happened."

"He was coming home after finishing work near Benalla."

"We don't know yet if he fell asleep at the wheel, or if he had a tyre blowout."

"Anything else you can tell me?" I asked as Anthony's pleasant, smiling face flashed before my eyes, and I added, "He was not the type of person who would fall asleep at the wheel."

"He veered into the path of the milk tanker," the police inspector replied.

I took a moment to think about that. "He was not a drinker, he was a very careful driver," I said softly, and then asked him, "How long before help arrived?"

In my mind I could see him all broken up and bleeding for an eternity before anyone came to help him. "The driver of the milk tanker was with him and talking to him until the ambulance arrived. He assured us that he was in no pain and he was talking back when the other driver spoke to him."

"How long before help arrived?" I repeated the question.

"The ambulance had to come from Benalla, but when it arrived, there was nothing they could do for him. But he was in no pain," he answered, still avoiding my question.

Yeah, right! He was in no pain because his entire nervous system was so smashed up there was nothing left to feel the pain. I realised that he wasn't going to tell me how long it was before the ambulance had arrived on the scene because it wouldn't have mattered anyway.

I couldn't swallow that last mouthful of my breakfast that I had taken just before the phone call came through. The food was stuck halfway, but I just couldn't get it down. I put the phone down and made it to the toilet just in time to bring everything up again, then sat on the floor for a long time, not crying, just sitting there with an aching heart. Why is it that this sort of thing happens to the nicest of human beings, while the bastards of this world live on and on?

It's just not fair. We didn't go anywhere that day. And my young brother-in-law knew better than to rub me the wrong way. In fact, for the whole day, I was thankfully left alone by both brothers.

Allan did take some interest in the progress of our home but only after I had something concrete to show him. He never had an opinion unless it was a negative one after the event, but with our limited finances he conceded that we had done quite well to be able to move into our new home by the time Danny was four months old. To me it meant that I had to put up with his arrogant brother for only three months.

Now that I had moved to outback Ringwood and far away from my friends, I had a lot to do to keep me busy. The kitchen had an expensive double bowl sink, a luxury I wanted at the time because the other fittings we could get as finances allowed, but the basics had to be good to start with. I also wanted a good brand washing machine that would last me forever, and it did. As for the rest, we made do with the little we had until we saved up enough for the next project. Going into debt was not something either of us wanted, so we worked initially to get the allotment cleared and it took quite a while to remove the many hazards lying around to make the yard safer for the children to play. It was still a jungle, with blackberry bushes growing with gay abandon, but at least it was still berry season and the boys liked the purple, juicy berries, especially when they squashed them between their fingers. It didn't take them long to have faces, hands, and clothes a mottled shade of purple while they squealed with delight as they popped the mushed up berries in their mouths, the juices dribbling down their chins. We sat around bonfires at night with our new neighbours who had gone through the same building process only the year before.

Spontaneous Combustion

One of the things we requested from the builder was for him to include in the house price the perimeter fencing, because in my mind's eye I could already see the boys wandering off to explore the vast countryside. That year we had a very hot summer, with temperatures consistently around forty degrees, and weeks without rain. Everything around was tinder dry. Clouds would gather and we would hopefully look up at the sky, but it was only the thunder and lightning that roared and clapped all around us.

One late afternoon the children were playing naked outside after their afternoon nap, I hadn't even bothered to put a nappy on them because it was so hot. I was pottering around my seedlings in the sheltered patch under the bedroom window, making sure that they had enough water, and didn't dry out and die in this drought, when I thought I could smell the acrid tang of smoke in my nostrils. "Some idiot is burning off in these dry conditions," I mumbled to myself.

"Mommy, look, fire," said Robert a few minutes later, pointing to the fence. I turned and my heart jumped in my mouth. Grabbing the boys, one under each arm, I put them in the car and backed it out of our very steep drive, leaving it level with our boundary but pointing up the street which was a dead end street with only one way out. If the situation became really threatening and I had to make a quick getaway, I could do so quickly.

It is amazing that children, even as young as mine were at the time, could sense the urgency of danger and understand my need to protect our home. They both sat in the green Volkswagen and watched me quietly as I raced back for the hose that was already attached to the tap and aimed it at the roof gutters that were closest to the fence. I tried to wet the fence going towards the fire that was raging now, having taken hold in the dry timber fence palings. I knew I wasn't going to make any impression on that fire with just one garden hose, and looking back at the car with the kids in it, I also knew that I would have to make a decision very soon. If the fire reached the fascia boards of the guttering, the house was gone for sure.

Never one to follow the norm, I had planned the siting of the house so that it angled slightly diagonally, and also with the slope of the land, but it had to be excavated on one corner. It was that corner that was closest to the burning fence now, and the timber fascia boards were not much higher than the fence palings so the flames didn't have to reach very far to set the house alight. Once the fascia caught fire, the timber roof trusses would be next, and the roof would collapse.

As I looked up the road, hope and relief flooded my being, because our neighbour was coming home. He stopped his van behind the Volkswagen and raced to get his hose and attached it to our rear tap. Between us, we kept the fence wet and also the side of the house nearest the fire.

As he later said, it was very important for both of us not to let the fire take hold of our house because if ours went up in smoke, so would his timber home. It was all over in under an hour. Then there was the post-fire investigation. How did the fire get started? Looking over the remains of the burnt-out fence in front, we could see glass amongst the shrivelled up, burnt bushes. Was it spontaneous combustion? Had the glass overheated and started the fire? Possibly. What other explanation could there be?

We were still discussing the close call we all had when I looked at the time and realised I was going to be late to pick Allan up from the station. He didn't like to be kept waiting at the end of the day and sure enough he was in a foul mood when I stopped the car in front of him. "Can't you be on time? Do you know how hot it is in the train in the afternoon?"

"Daddy, fire at home!" Robert tried to tell his father, but characteristically, he thought that I was watching the news on TV.

He still had the problem with his suppurating leg, the poliomyelitis that would fester every few months and be very sensitive to the touch, so that if he was bumped on the train it was terribly painful and the travel time to his work was taking its toll, especially on his humour, which wasn't great at the best of times. At home now, he glanced at the fence that the children were pointing to and made the comment that some ratbag had probably flicked a cigarette butt out of a car window. It just didn't seem worth the effort to point out to him that ours was a dead end street and the only people driving by were the neighbours, and that the road was some five or more feet below the level of the land so anyone hoping to set alight the dry shrubs would need a sling shot to catapult a fiery torch so high up and into the bushes.

At that stage we didn't know about the plans that were already being executed right then by his employers. The price of real estate was going through the roof in the city, with more and more tall buildings going up as Melbourne expanded. The central location of the Victorian Printing Works site in the city was much coveted by investors, and eventually the family sold the property. The company was relocated to a much bigger and more modern building in Blackburn where they could expand operations. This move cut Allan's travelling time by about three quarters, but if I needed the car, I still had to drive him to and from the train station or even directly to work.

With two young children, a car is a necessity, especially if one lives away from all the amenities. It was lucky that I had it on the day when Danny decided he wanted to get out of the high chair that I had placed in the still wild yard, near where I was working. He didn't say anything, he just stood up and stepped out—falling flat on his face onto the earth under him. Not only was he accident-prone, at times I felt he was obtuse or dull-witted, as well as stubborn.

He wouldn't listen or accept help, and sometimes I could get really impatient with him. But he was "Nonna's golden boy", and for her he could do no wrong!

Danny's hair and skin was as fair as Robert's was dark, so I had to be very careful that the sunscreen was always by my side when I had the children with me in the garden that I was trying to establish. Of course they wanted to help me plant things and they had their own little patch of dirt that was good for experimenting. One day they would plant a cutting and the next week they would pull it out to see if there were any roots growing. Bean seeds were great entertainers. The beans would go into the soil and be regularly watered a couple of times a day, then if leaves did not appear within two or three days, the earth would be cleared away to see why they were not bearing fruit yet!

Everything that I put in the earth grew; cuttings from other people's gardens, seeds, anything would grow as long as I could keep them moist. Water came from the sky and it was free. It still comes from the sky without any effort from mankind, so why do we have to pay for it so dearly now? Back then we could use as much as we wanted. When we were building the house, we had to wait a while for the water pipes to be laid because it was still a very recently opened up area and work was allocated on a priority basis. We paid for the water pipes to come into our property and there was a yearly fee for the Victorian Water Board to maintain the infrastructure, but water was God's gift to humanity, and as long as we didn't abuse that gift, it was free to us to use as needed. And my fledgling plants needed plenty right now, until at least they became more established in the next season.

In my enthusiasm to get the garden established, I overdid it with the pick and shovel, and one day I tore some ligaments in my lower back. The pain was excruciating and I could not move from the ground where I was working while the children were having their afternoon sleep. Eventually they started to cry for attention but there was no way to get to them, other than crawl painfully around to the back of the house where there were no steps, but even when bit by bit I made it to their room, there was nothing I could do for them. I couldn't stand up, so we sang songs and told each other nursery rhymes until their father, who luckily had the car on that day, arrived home. The doctor was called and after he administered a pethidine injection, he and Allan rolled me over onto a couple of blankets on the floor with instructions not to move for a couple of days. Yeah, right! With two babies underfoot?

It was a long time before my back healed enough for me to resume my normal routine and with manipulation, therapy, and a lot of medication, I should have been totally healed, but that wasn't the case, probably because I still had a normal family to look after and little time to rest. However that didn't stop me from getting pregnant again. I was twenty-six and healthy, except for my back problem that everyone said was only temporary. So, why not hope for the delightful little girl that every woman, who already has two sons, wants. I could already imagine us promenading along the street with the boys walking on either side of her, protecting their sweet baby sister and feeling so important, as little boys would.

My Precious Princess

Backaches hounded me right through my pregnancy and it was a repeat of my ninth month with Danny when it came to 'phantom contractions'. It was quite debilitating and though the hospital was a lot closer this time, I didn't know how I would get there if I went into labour during the day. Luckily, my precious little girl decided to start making a nuisance of herself around four o'clock in the morning and she couldn't have planned it any better. Allan dropped me off at the hospital, took the boys to my mother, who this time was expecting them, then he came back in time to commence work—right on time!

Regina was the size of a doll for a very long time. She was not premature but she had congenital heart problems that caused me a lot of anxiety, mainly because she wasn't growing normally and her body weight remained static for what seemed forever. Had she been my first child, she probably would not have survived, but by the time she arrived, three years after the boys, I was confident enough to tell the doctors to go and take a running jump when each one gave me conflicting advice. I even stopped going to the surgery altogether when she started to come out in rashes each time doctors put her on some medication, which they kept changing in their efforts to 'try something that works'.

I also stopped listening to the nurses after their well-meaning advice caused an almost catastrophic turn of events that nearly starved my baby. Those were the days of regular four hourly feeds. Probably great for the average baby, but it didn't work for us!

Regina was taken away from me at birth. It was a rather difficult birth, the most difficult of the three, and it was longer too. She was going into trauma and her heartbeat was weakening so the delivery doctors had to use instruments to help the birth along, but bruising her in the process. Other new mums had their babies next to them but I didn't see mine for many hours, no one came to see me to tell me why, and none of the day nurses could, or would give me any information.

It never fails to amaze me that doctors and nurses can be so thoughtless at times. How can they be so oblivious to a new mother's feelings, and not think of the worry and anxiety they cause, simply because they don't stop and exchange a few words at the appropriate time? It would have taken just a few minutes to stop by and casually say, "Your baby is not so strong at the moment and we are monitoring her, but we will keep you informed."

When she was eventually brought to me for a feed, I immediately knew there was another problem apart from the bruising, when she vomited all the milk she had taken from me. She didn't keep much down the next day either so I insisted that my baby remain close to me, as I didn't want to be treated any different to the other mums, even though she cried most of the time. The only time she was consoled was when she was at the breast, but she would only take a few sucks and fall asleep. Soon I figured that she was exhausted, so I let her sleep and when she woke, whenever it was, I would feed her again. After a couple of days, we settled into our own routine, much to the horror of the nurses and doctors who wanted me to follow their four hourly routine, more for their own convenience than my baby's benefit, I'm sure. We were discharged with a plethora of instructions that simply did not gel with me, and that I never could follow—and a cloud hanging over our heads.

We were now living in Ringwood, 'in the middle of nowhere' as all our relations kept saying, and much to the consternation of my parents (Allan's were long-departed), so there was no chance of me getting any help with the children from anyone and I managed quite well anyway, all things considered.

Our one and only neighbouring house belonged to a Dutch family who had only one daughter, Heidi, but later a second daughter arrived early the same year that my Regina was born. Rita became more than a neighbour, she was a friend I could rely on when she was home. Unfortunately that wasn't often enough as her husband was a busy tiler and she went to work with him, taking their baby daughter with them which wasn't a problem, as Rita had weened her within weeks of birthing her. Rita was a bit older than me and of bigger stature, she had large breasts that never changed during her pregnancy, but they did not produce the milk the infant required either. Whereas I was the opposite, I had small breasts normally, but like a Jersey cow, I produced enough milk that could have fed the babies of an entire hospital, and I certainly did keep a few infants nourished, while I was in there.

At home now with two small boys, the going got a bit tough. They had to be looked after as well. Allan took a week off his three week annual leave, presumably to help with the babies, but he was as glad as I was when the week was over. I was happy to do whatever had to be done at my own pace.

I learnt to get by on very little sleep and at night I kept my baby close to me in bed. Logically, I would agree that sleeping with your newborn beside you is a dangerous practice and can be fatal. However, I also maintain that each set of circumstances are different, and in my case having become a very light sleeper and always attuned to my baby's needs, it became the only way we could all survive. Regina took the breast whenever she felt the need. Her tiny, frequent feeds is what kept her alive, as she could not tolerate a normal quantity of milk. Her birth weight was just below seven pounds. Her weight on her first birthday was just over eleven pounds.

However, this lifestyle was taking its toll on me, and I was losing a lot of weight which I could ill afford as my baby was totally dependent on breast milk. Not only was I eternally tired and had to push myself to function normally, but my back was still troubling me and I had to remain consciously on guard not to move suddenly. By the time Regina was three months old, the advice frequently given was, "Give her the bottle, and put her on solids. She will put weight on when she has more nourishment!"

That was all sensible advice, and given with the best of intentions. Certainly it would have freed me up a bit if I could make it work.

"But she won't take the bottle, not even for orange or apple juice," would be my reply, "Not even water," I would wail in desperation.

"When she is hungry enough, she will eat."

That made a lot of sense, and I desperately wished I could take that advice given by doctors, midwives, nurses, and anyone who wanted to buy into the argument but I kept putting it off. However by the time she reached six months, even I accepted the need for a bit of normalcy in my life, and under the urging of our family doctor and the paediatric nurse, I persevered with half hourly offerings of different foods and liquids while withholding the breast from her. It was winter now, so I was well wrapped up and she presumably couldn't smell the milk. But she was born stubborn. Like her mother, I guess. For two days, that child refused to ingest anything. With growing concern, I noticed that the continual crying was getting weaker, and she was becoming dehydrated. And guess what? My love for my baby made me take her into my arms and do what I should never have stopped doing, which was continue to nurture her. I was the one to give in. And how sorry I was that I had finally succumbed to 'expert advice'. The experts who go by the book, rather than by the feelings and instincts of a mother, should realise that not everyone fits into a slot of someone else's making, aren't we all individuals? With personal needs and feelings? Unfortunately the damage was already done. The stress and anxiety that I had subjected myself to proved too much, and in those two days I had lost the ability to produce milk from one breast.

So now we were in the unenviable situation where I still had two small boys, an unsympathetic husband, and a difficult and demanding baby, and only enough milk to feed her from one breast.

Can anyone imagine the challenges involved when one tries to feed and dress a three and a four year old? Do the household chores, the ones that can't be ignored like the washing, and in those days we had to iron our husbands' shirts for work. Do the cooking from scratch because there were no prepared meals in the shop aisles that one could simply pick up and pay for at the checkout, then reheat in a microwave—there were no microwave ovens. Getting the shopping done with two toddlers in tow proved to be a huge challenge and doing all this, while at the same time holding on to a small baby whom I was nursing most of the time. We still only had the one car and with the small children I needed to have it home with me, but this meant that I could not even get my husband to do any of the shopping. Back then there was no weekend shopping or extended hours—trading hours were 9 a.m. to 5 or 6 p.m.

I was starting to realise that I was making excuses for him that most of the time were unwarranted. He could have done a lot more to help! Other husbands helped a lot more around the house than mine did. Little things like hanging out the washing, setting the table, starting the fire in winter, or cleaning out the fireplace—small and practical things that would not have been too stressful for him, but would have been very helpful to me. Other husbands in our neighbourhood took much more interest in their children than mine did too. Coming from a large family I would have thought he would be more adept with his own children, but I soon realised that his traumatic, near fatal accident must have changed his character as well as his personality. Made him more dependent, and prone to wallowing in self-pity. In all the time I knew him, he could never cope with stress. Whereas I was born into stressful times and my life has always been surrounded by stressful situations.

Almost overnight, Regina started to pull herself up on her feet. She was eleven months old and wanted to join in the play with her brothers. In two weeks, she started to walk and then she wanted nothing more to do with me. She was reaching over for her brothers' food and they gave it to her. When I offered her a cup of milk, she took it. When I put a spoon and a plate with food in it in front of her, she ate it. The complete turnaround was almost eerie, and it took me by surprise—it was as though she had skipped the learning stage, by-passed it completely. Suddenly she knew how to drink from a cup, how to eat with a spoon. And she was clean—no spills, no runs, no dirty dresses or hands, no messes. She never had a bottle. She never had baby food. She went straight on to eat what her brothers were eating. She never was and still isn't a big eater, but once she started walking, it was like turning a page. No looking back. Her growth pattern stabilised almost into normality, though she always was small for her age, and we called her Mini or Mini Mouse. Of course we would always have to keep monitoring her heart, especially at times when she needed dental work, but generally everyone coped well and with few limitations. With the extra time I now had, I wanted to make my beautiful, little, live doll cute dresses that would set her apart, and have passers-by stop and admire her. She had survived, and so had I. It was a time to celebrate. From the tiny scrap pieces of material her aunt passed on to me, I made multi-coloured, frilly, feminine doll-like dresses. My sister-in-law was also a seamstress, with two grown-up boys, so she took a lot of pride in her miniature niece as well, and I kept the great stock of materials that she had passed on to me for many years and I continued to sew Regina's clothes right up to the time she graduated.

Though the doctors maintained that there was nothing wrong with my back that they could detect, I was still having considerable, intermittent pain. The strong prescription painkiller and anti-inflammatories that they prescribed helped but I didn't want to become too reliant on them for too long a period. It was Rita, my next-door neighbour, who suggested that we try a yoga program to see if that would strengthen my muscles. We both enrolled for the course because there was a baby sitter on the premises and our girls would be supervised while we practised our postures and did our mantras. We continued with the exercises, both at home and with the yoga teacher for three terms and by the end of the year, I felt better not only physically but mentally too. In fact the psychological part of the discipline, the meditation, was even more useful and kept me on a balanced mental course that helped me to cope better with the needs of my daily life.

My Green Thumb

Confined to the house with three young children, there was little I could do but tend to the garden, not just the flowers to embellish the house from the front, or road aspect. It seemed such a waste to me to have the traditional quarter acre block of land and just have grass grow on it, as ultimately it has to be mown.

My belief was that if one has to work in the garden, it might just as well be for a purpose like growing vegetables or fruit trees, and grape vines of the eating variety, passion fruit and climbing beans. Guess that's my Italian background talking! But in no time, I had such a crop of cucumbers, tomatoes, peas, and beans that I didn't know what to do with them all. Sister-in-law Jane came to the rescue by passing on her ancient preserving kit and a multitude of jars that had been stored for a thousand years in some dark corner of her garage. Those I could clean I used, and particularly the big ones were just perfect for pickling cucumbers for the winter. A delicacy that my husband and his family did appreciate, and I learnt to make them well and in abundance for everyone.

Tomatoes seemed to ripen by the tonne, and Mum was still making a memorable pasta sauce, so I made literally hundreds of preserved tomato paste jars that we could both use for years to come because Mum's pasta with the famous gravy beef and tomato sauce was not only legendary, but I could reproduce it just as well—not that it was well liked or appreciated by any member of my husband's family. Their taste was for sauerkraut and sausages, potatoes and pork with sour cream—the Baltic traditions.

So potatoes were another crop that I added to the garden, but they spread out messily and took up a lot of space, and seeing I was the one doing all the work in the vegie patch, I refused to dig up the ground to plant them and then dig it up again to harvest them, so after the second season, that patch was left fallow. Potatoes were cheap anyway. The peas and beans went on for a long time because my children were fussy eaters, and like their father refused to eat vegetables—unless they thought they were doing something naughty, like picking the pods off the climbing plants! I didn't care how they ate them, as long as they ate their vegies, and raw was always best anyway. What we couldn't consume or pass on to friends and family was frozen for the off seasons.

I just couldn't keep still. Contrary to what many thought, my back problem was more troublesome if I sat and rested. I had to keep moving, but I also had to wear a stiff back brace that prevented much movement of the spine between the lumbar and the thoracic regions, so I used my knees a lot in the garden.

The children grew and it was time for the boys to start school. They had been to kindergarten and enjoyed the friendship and social interaction with other children of similar age, and they were now ready and looking forward to being 'big boys' in a school uniform. I had to spread my time and myself in several directions now but it was a good, happy time and the kids thrived. Several of the neighbouring families became friends and remained friends for many years, but thinking back it was I who held those friendships together. Though Allan was cordial and friendly, he never went out of his way to make my friends feel at ease and welcome. It was a different matter when his friends came to visit. They were invariably welcomed literally with open arms by him and they tended to remain through dinner and afterwards for one, two or more games of cards and copious amounts of alcohol. But I always felt the same aloofness, the cool reception and subtle holding back that I had felt with my own father when I was young and had invited someone over to our home, as though my friends were somehow encroaching on his space.

All In a Day's Work

Years passed and the boys needed to become more involved with outdoor activities and other children who were with the Scout Movement or Sporting Clubs. No objection was raised so I, the eternal optimist, enrolled both boys in Cubs. The Club House was very close as the crow flies and in summer, when it was light for longer, the boys could easily walk across the creek at the bottom of our street where some of the fathers had felled a large tree and manoeuvred the thick trunk to form a bridge across the creek, that under normal conditions held only a little water. But in the evening, at the end of the Cubs' sessions, someone had to pick them up for safety reasons. That someone always turned out to be me. The same could be said for any other activity or sports meetings.

Parent-teacher nights were always mother-teacher nights in our case. The husband was working and providing for the family, everything else was up to the wife. That was then, and in some cases still is, the continental attitude! In all fairness, his health, as the result of the earlier accident that he was involved in, years even before we met, was now somewhat affected by the full-time employment and the long periods of standing on his feet because he was still suffering from poliomyelitis of the left femur. Luckily his employers were very understanding, and if he had to take a few days off work from time to time, to attend hospital or to recuperate, they knew that his work would not suffer in the long run. But after the first couple of years, I had learnt enough about his recurring condition to be able to sterilise and lance the affected area at the appropriate time, then apply a tampon to collect the infection fluids, firmly bandage the leg and change the dressings daily, as well as any doctor could do. The advantage for Allan was that he didn't have to wait for hours at the hospital and he could lie down at home without the long car trip to the hospital and back. All he needed was antibiotics, but he was on those most of the time anyway and there was a prescription always available for him. What he mainly needed after one of his flare-ups was rest. He had a continual long list of medication that was worrying for me as he was not always careful to put things away, out of the children's reach.

Initially, these attacks flared up every three or four months but sometimes the antibiotics would prevent a full eruption and he would go for longer periods without any problems. Still, at the back of our minds the fear was always present that his 'bum leg', as he called it, would erupt when we least expected. This meant that it was quite difficult for us to plan for any outings in advance. In between these episodes, I found that he was quite good with woodworking and he enjoyed his newly found creative ability to construct useful articles which were much appreciated because money now was scarce with the demands of a growing family. Not only because we needed one, but also because I felt it was important for him to have something to occupy his mind as well as his hands, one of my first requests was for a day bed and matching table, and I was pleased that he didn't baulk at the thought of such an onerous task. In fact, he accepted the request as a worthy challenge. But furniture grade timber costs a lot of money. Money that we didn't have to spare.

An Enterprising Duo

Allan was able to bring home some really good quality timber lengths that came with the packaging crates that were holding together the large bales of paper for the printing industry. The soft wood would be easy to work with and light, both in colour and texture. These crates arrived at his place of work on a regular basis, but the timber was not always salvageable so we had to be patient and wait until we could pick the good pieces as they arrived. I gave the design for the frame for the day bed considerable thought. It had to be strong enough to take the tumbles of two boisterous boys and the miniature tornado that used to be my delicate baby doll.

To my great pleasure and surprise, in record time, a very presentable and sturdy frame was built, and then it was up to me to do it justice by covering the dense foam rubber seat in a decorative fabric that would tone in well with our scanty furnishings. My time was always at a premium, but I loved shopping and going into the city, especially to stores like George's on Burke. This used to be a good quality department store, in my opinion superior to Myer—more like David Jones used to be before it too lowered its standards to compete with other department stores over the last few years. Taking my Mini Mouse in the pram we headed to the train station and one hour later we were happily browsing in the materials' section, which was on the lower basement level, for some sturdy, practical but pleasant material I could use to cover our new day bed.

There was nothing much that appealed to me in the furnishings department so we wondered into the winter materials section and after much to-ing and fro-ing, right in the corner, near the store rooms, I spied some thick rolls of material leaning upright against the wall. Excitement welled up in my chest. I had seen nothing like it before, and I always had an eye for the unusual—'kinky,' my friends used to amicably call me. In front of me stood a roll of wool and acrylic material in the most unusual wide stripes of three different shades of purple broken up by a narrower band of gold. I didn't have to look any further—that was exactly what I wanted. Now, how do I haggle for the price I could pay?

Cheap, I knew, it wasn't going to be! Hesitantly I walked up to the most senior looking sales lady to make enquiries. When she told me the price by the meter you could have picked me up from the floor. Not that expensive surely! I told her what I wanted it for and we chatted for a while. She then confided that the pattern was too bold and unusual to be popular and they had had absolutely no sales off that particular roll for the whole season. Hope springs eternal!

"So, what are you going to do with that roll?" I asked her, and then held my breath.

"We will have to send it back to the supplier." She replied. I walked around this upright column of material, thinking, looking at the yardage—the metric system had just recently been introduced, but most people were still thinking Imperial.

It was a lot of material, could I use it?

Taking a deep breath, I whispered, "If I took the complete roll, would you be able to make it a special price? It would save you having to send it back?"

"Let me check," she disappeared for what seemed an eternity. Beaming, she came back. And again I held my breath. "You can have it at our cost price and I will deduct return delivery costs as well."

"I'll take it,' I almost screamed at her, "I will get some money from my husband and be right back. I have to walk to his work, which is on the corner of La Trobe Street, so it may take a while." I knew I was overexcited and talking too much and too quickly, but she was older and she understood.

"Dearie," she says, "It's late afternoon already, why don't you go home and talk to your husband, get the money from him tonight, and come back tomorrow," logically, she added, "You can't take the roll with you now any way. Someone will have to pick it up for you."

"But I don't want to lose that material, I really love it!" I wailed.

"Don't worry, dear. I'll make sure you get it, and no one else." And she asked all the relevant questions, like name, address, etc.

I couldn't believe my luck, and blissfully Regina and I made our way back to the station for the return trip home. I was in seventh heaven and in my mind's eye, I could already see the completed day bed, and then it struck me that the complete job would maybe take up one tenth of the amount of fabric I had just committed to buy. The logical question I would be asked that night would be, "And what are you going to do with the rest?"

I had to come up with an answer, and soon. Another thought struck me; Allan would hate both the colour and the pattern, and seeing he would have to pick it up, I could hardly surprise him with it. I had to come up with a plausible story because no way was I going to lose such a striking statement for our home. But that's it—it was our home. Okay, so it was a lot of material for one day bed, but what if he also built a table and chairs and they were upholstered in the same fabric? That would make up a complete suite. And that would take up perhaps another two tenths of the material—still a lot to go to make the purchase worthwhile. Think!

And I did. By the time the train stopped at Ringwood Station, I had worked out my argument. Dinner that night was Allan's favourite, pork fillet, sauerkraut, boiled potatoes with sour cream, and when we sat down I smiled happily and told him that I had found the perfect material for our lounge room drapes and that I was going to get enough material so I could cover the day bed to match. We had a very large window for the times, a landscape picture window, so he knew a lot of material would be needed for the drapes, which was the reason we didn't have any yet. The perfect solution!

The next day he would ask to borrow the work delivery van overnight. I would meet him at the back door of George's delivery area with the wrapped up roll of material for which he would pay on pick up, and he would not see the pattern until I had the material cut and draped over the timber curtain rods at the window. It was easy to find an excuse not to unwrap the roll that night, and by the end of the next day I had already cut the lengths for the drapes and provisionally draped them over the existing rods under the pelmet. The gold stripes caught the light from the recessed continuous strip lighting we had installed under the pelmets, and the effect in the evening was every bit as striking as I would have hoped, and I knew I was on a winner. No one could possibly object to the exotic effect that the wide purple stripes and the gold had created in an otherwise uninspiring, plain lounge room. At least so I thought! Evening came, and Allan arrives home, obviously in pain from another impending flare up of his chronic leg problem. Dinner, and early night in bed is the usual ritual because he won't be able to take time off until the inflammation is really bad, so he doesn't even notice the curtains. That will give me more time to work on the cover for the day bed, but getting the long zipper sewn into the rear edge of the foam seat turned out to be more difficult than I expected, and eventually I have to ring mother for advice. What she suggested made a lot of sense in the light of all the material I would have left over. Make two covers because the day bed would get a lot more wear and tear than the curtains and it would look shabby sooner, so I could just change the covering for the foam insert whenever I needed. To buy me more time for now, I could just hand stich the first cover and put the zipper in the second cover when I had more time. Mother ended up doing it for me anyway.

Eventually Allan notices what a blind man would see, but he is unimpressed. He is much more concerned with his wellbeing which is understandable. What wasn't so easy for me to understand was the blame that he keeps heaping on me. My demands for the day bed and the exertions he was subjected to while he was working on it (with help from me, I might add) is what's made him feel so unwell now. What a lot of hogwash!

So much for my idea of asking him to make a table and chairs to match, I wouldn't dare even suggest it now. In any case I had my own work cut out just to complete the drapes, as that large quantity of material was hard to manipulate, and my little domestic sewing machine was barely up to the demands I was putting on it. So the dining setting was put to rest for a while.

The Legacy

I am very good at making excuses for the shortcomings of others (a trait that I picked up from my father, though he didn't apply it to me) but eventually these excuses start to wear thin if overused, and I was starting to see things differently.

Allan was involved in a near fatal accident when he was twenty-one years old. He was having a test run on a motorbike that a friend of his had just purchased and while he was approaching the corner of a major intersection, he failed to see a bus that was turning in the opposite direction. Maybe someone cut a corner, but the result was a head on collision of such force of impact that the motorbike went under the bus and was crushed, while Allan flew over the top of the bus. When he landed, probably hitting his head with considerable force, the skin on his face was shredded and he was unconscious, but the most serious injuries were to his left leg, which had numerous compound fractures both in the femur and the tibia. His lower leg was broken in three places and all his life he carried a silver plate with many screws to hold the pieces of broken bone together until they bonded. However it was the femur that was even more severely damaged with the bone badly shattered.

Apparently it was a while before the ambulance arrived, and when they did come, they declared that he was not expected to live (probably to prepare the relatives for the worst possible outcome). But he was a fit and healthy young person, and after being in a coma for three days, he opened his eyes to find his mother holding his hand and weeping beside him.

She was extremely dedicated and sensitive to his needs, and she was there every day with freshly made, clear soup that he could suck through a straw, because his face and head were entirely bandaged. An even stronger bond was forged between mother and son. It was three months before his constant request for a mirror to view the injuries to his face was granted, and by then he had captured the heart of a young nurse who would give him daily assurances that his good looks would soon return. She was the person who regularly came to the house to tend to his wounds and apparently they became quite close but she was Australian. The mother was grateful for the help but the rest of the family looked on with disapproval. But then I don't think anyone would have been good enough for the prodigal son who came back from the brink of death to continue dancing with his young sister the folkloric dances that brought fond memories of 'home' to the elderly parents.

The major injury to his femur did not heal as well as his face. He underwent seven operations to try to remove floating pieces of bone, and after six months flat on his back on traction, he was provisionally sent home to lie on his back in the familiar surroundings of his own room to allow some of his injuries the time to heal. It was two years before he was declared 'fit for work', as well as could be expected under the circumstances.

Of course he was still in a lot of pain, and his left leg was two inches shorter than the other after all the operations he went through that had, bit by bit, destroyed healthy tissues as well, but he was continually improving. In the meantime an enquiry was under way but as Allan could not remember anything about that day, nothing could be proven and he may or may not have been at fault. The coroner only had the police reports to go by and the statement from the bus driver to help him form some composite picture of the place, the events and the conditions on that fateful day.

The bus driver was exonerated as the brake marks from the vehicle he was driving were apparently in accordance with the required response. The maintenance log kept for the vehicle did not highlight any defects and the brakes were in good condition. In time, a trial was held and the judge ruled that the insurance company for the bus and transport company pay the very substantial hospital costs, as well as an amount to allow him to provide his own transport for the ongoing outpatient's visits he would require at the hospital for quite some time yet to come.

All this took a long time to transpire, several years in fact, after he was discharged as an in-patient from hospital. He was convalescing at home for a further two years (the wheels of justice move slowly).

By the time we met, Allan was twenty-eight and I was eighteen. He finally had been paid some compensation to enable him to buy his new means of transport, the new marine blue Vauxhall Velox that he had purchased just before we met.

I imagine he had regrets when our marriage and his growing family forced him to part with his prestigious car in favour of a more practical vehicle.

TRAIN TO AUSTRALIA

Some lesser known waterways in Venice.

Ermenegilda Tromba (mother) in mourning after hearing of the murder of her younger brother, Bruno.

Family reunion before departure from Italy.

Final goodbyes from train heading to Bremerhaven, Germany.

153

Me dressed as a boy—which probably saved my life.

Zia Anna and grandfather Domenico on his farm, 'Polaris'.

The mule and cart taking family members to work on the farm.

Mother and Father bathing near the family's farm. Gilda and Egidio Caenazzo.

*'I Bagni Nuovi', the new baths in front of Polaris.
They were demolished after WWII.*

Mending the fishing nets.

Fishermen on the pier at Rovigno.

TRAIN TO AUSTRALIA

The town of Rovigno.

Street named in honour of the martyrs.

Passport photo of Mother, 1949–50.

Father.

Me.   Ondina.

An entry to the catacombs under my cousin's home in via Mezzaterra, Feltre.

Tonia at the flooded mill.

Restored cars belonging to my sons and used for weddings.

Goody-Goody/Baddy-Baddy

The boys were starting to branch out with their activities as they progressed from Cubs to Scouts and more time, supervision, and parental involvement was required when outings were planned. The fathers of other boys were always there to support and cheer their sons on, and to give them encouragement in their new endeavours and I was there to cheer my sons on as well. What they were missing was their father. What was making me very sad, and sometimes furious was the fact that the boys were never encouraged in any aspect of their lives. When they ran home excited about some personal achievement and they went to their father for approval or encouragement, he was either busy or watching television, or not feeling well. It would not have taken very much effort to listen to, and give some praise to his sons. They were not getting the nurturing boys depend on for a balanced view of the world around them, and soon they started to get into mischief.

The chastising, punishing or smacking of our children was exclusively my domain. Any discipline had to be handled by me. So naturally I became the 'baddy-baddy' and Allan was the 'goody-goody'.

Bit by bit, resentment built up between my husband and myself. More and more we entered into arguments that were triggered by the most trivial disagreement. Many of these disagreements could have been resolved quite easily, simply by talking through them, and taking the appropriate action, preferably together. Two quite serious incidents come to mind involving the boys, when I thought that their father had let them down while at the same time piling the blame on to me.

The first one actually endangered their lives, though it was not of his doing. But that always seemed to be the problem. Nothing that ever went wrong was ever his doing because he never put himself in a situation where any blame could be apportioned to him.

An overnight camp was arranged for all the younger boy scouts and a proportionate number of parents were required to supervise them. Part of the program was a canoe trip down the Warrandyte River. For anyone who doesn't know what that river was like back in those days, let me tell you it was wild! The rocks, and the rapids are what made it exciting, but for young, inexperienced boys it was downright dangerous and not recommended for weak swimmers. Knowing from past experience that their father would not become involved with any such activities, I arranged for a neighbour to take Regina for a sleepover at the home of her little friend, and I volunteered to accompany a group of boys on this excursion.

Amid much commotion, laughter and yelling, we were all sooner or later successful in erecting a tent and lighting a campfire to cook some damper for the evening meal and the BBQ. Boiling the billy was the next hurdle, but we got that under control too. What we hadn't expected was the fear some young boys had of spiders. They imagined daddy long-legs crawling all over them all night long, and keeping the rest of us awake with their shrieks and whimpers. The weak rays of an early autumn morning sun finally ended their paranoia, and we started getting breakfast under way. It was so funny to watch how disorganised the group would become as each child made a bewildered dash in different directions while excitedly preparing for the first big event—the canoe race!

The canoes were already loaded on to the vehicles that some of the fathers had brought over. The boys were instructed to put on their waterproof safety vests and whatever floating devices were needed. Helmets were not required back then and few boys had them. Mine didn't. Eventually several crafts manned by the fathers were pushed into the water, and we mums looked on from the bank as our sons got into their canoes and hesitantly pedalled out into the river. Because now they were in no-man's land, a bit of fear took hold of them when the force of the water flow immediately engaged the small crafts in a haze of spray, and spun them out into the middle of the river. But all seemed to have gone off to a flying start after a few precarious wobbles, and screams of excitement, mixed with apprehension. We cheered them on as they were drawn midstream, and then they were out of sight.

We jumped into whatever vehicle was nearest and in trepidation took off downstream after the canoes with our sons in them. It was some distance before we caught sight of them again amongst the trees, as they were merrily being swept along some moderately flowing rapids. They kept on going. We kept on going, but the view was not always clear as bushes and clumps of trees obstructed our vision. Arriving at another clearing ahead we were suddenly struck by a cold, heart gripping fear as we realised that some of the canoes were no longer there.

Jumping out of the vans, we ran upstream along the bank overgrown with spinney bushes and it was rough going on foot. Soon the fathers in front also realised that some of the boys had not made it to the next bend in the river so they used the motorised boats to backtrack. The noise was deafening in this part of the river because of the number of big rocks obstructing its flow, as the water forced its way over and around them. The scenery was great but our fear was greater. Suddenly there was a lot of yelling and name-calling that gave us hope. The men had reached the missing canoes.

One had run aground and two had overturned after hitting rocks. The boys in these two canoes were scattered all over, some were hanging on to logs that were trapped between the rocks, and some were able to cling to their upturned craft that had veered off course when a large rock stopped its course downstream. Most importantly, all were accounted for. The boys were more or less battered, all were bruised, some were bleeding, and all were in a greater or lesser state of hypothermia. I collapsed in a heap, in a valley of tears when I saw my sons hanging on to the low branches of a tree near the riverbank, soaked to the skin. Thank God they were safe! They thought it was a great adventure! Even with their teeth chattering and bundled up in blankets, their excitement spilled over.

Residential Development

Ringwood was spreading as more and more people built their home further out of the city where cheaper land could still be found. The land across the road from us had belonged to a devoted Christian, elderly couple with many children. Bit by bit they had to subdivide and sell portions of their land so that they could survive through the increased costs of living, and their dwindling energies often required them to hire tradesmen to do the work they had previously done themselves. With age came failing health which became a greater burden on their finances as well.

Mr Clarke died the year after we moved into the area. Their children were scattered all over the state and some had moved interstate chasing work. Only the eldest son lived close by, but with eleven children of his own he didn't have much time for his elderly parents. He had ten boys and only one girl who was the eldest and between going to college and doing the shopping, she helped her mother with the younger children. Sometimes his young boys would come to cut the grass around the old house that had several additional lean-tos constructed as more children arrived, but more often the grandchildren came for gran's cookies. Old Mrs Clarke loved to bake in her ancient wood fired stove and would always have a boiling kettle on the stove, for anyone who popped in for 'a cuppa'. She often came around to us with some of her freshly baked cookies and for a chat, to see how our boys and then Regina were going, and to impart news of what was happening around the place. She was a fountain of knowledge about the area, both past and present. I could never figure out how she always managed to get the latest news about what was going on locally.

Initially our street had been just a graded road but with more people moving in, the town council had a bitumen road built. The costs associated with the new road were passed on to the landowners, as is always the case, by way of increased rates. These increases, however, were crippling our elderly neighbours and they had to relinquish a large irregular piece of land bordering on to the creek to pay for these rates. I believe that the Council took the land in lieu of payment and then on-sold to developers that subdivided the property into residential allotments. When the developers sent graders to the site to clear and grade the land for building, there was a loud uproar in the area. Like most environmentalists before us and to still to come, we vocally objected to the clearing of the natural afforestation. In my opinion, some of that rage transmitted itself to the children, both in their home and at school.

Here I am not trying to make excuses for the subsequent actions of a group of boys that included my two sons. What I am trying to say is that no one can accurately foresee what effect our words of anger may have on the young receptive minds of children, or how our passions for a cause may be interpreted by the young and inexperienced. How the words of adults may be misunderstood and absorbed by them. We don't fully understand how children assimilate discussions they hear at home that are not actually directed toward them, or when their underlying causes are not fully explained to them.

Work progressed at a rapid rate on the land by the creek, and then all of a sudden, everything stopped. For several days nothing seemed to happen, and then one day we had a visit from the local constabulary. We, and several other parents, were asked to attend the Magistrate's Court where a case was to be presented by the developer of the site showing a number of boys sabotaging some large earthmoving machines by introducing sand into the fuel tanks. Of course everyone was horrified. Parents rallied around.

But the damage was done. How can we handle this situation now? What the children had done was unpardonable.

My situation was simple. According to my husband, I was to blame. I did not supervise my (not our) boys well enough. I let them run wild! I did not teach them the difference between right and wrong. I didn't know what they were doing when they were playing with their friends. And, how was I going to pay for the lawyer that would now be needed to represent my sons? This argument went on for quite a while and it started to seriously undermine my respect for my husband. Weren't they our children?

Nevertheless, I decided I should get some regular paying work.

Making Ends Meet

Regina had started kindergarten now, and instead of continuing with my Avon cosmetics selling work, that in Allan's mind wasn't a job worthy of any consideration, or sewing for other people while he was at work in order to supplement his income, I realised that I should get a regular wage that we could rely on and be able to send the boys to a private school.

"What?" He shook his head in disbelief and asked, "Where did you get that idea from? Have you been talking to your crazy friends again?" he accused, and then stated, "You can keep sewing at home while the kids are at school."

I had just earned $700.00 after three months' work on eight formal dresses for a wedding group. He had no idea of how much work and how many hours had gone into the formal wedding gown of a budding young tennis player, her five bridesmaids, and her flower girl. Then, when all those dresses for the main wedding party were almost finished the mother of the bride, who had not been able to find something suitable, something that she liked ready made in the shops to wear to her daughter's wedding, asked me to make her an outfit as well. The style she chose for her formal long gown in a pale, multi-coloured chiffon (which is a very difficult material to work with) was thankfully not intricate but she also wanted a long silk shantung coat in a lovely cerise colour to pick out the darker swirls in the chiffon of her gown. The completed outfit, long dress and coat were very sophisticated, much in vogue at the time and well suited for the occasion.

On a whim, and so she would not feel left out of all this excitement, from the left over pieces of material, I made Regina a dress similar to the one that the official flower girl would be wearing. Needless to say, during one of the fitting sessions Regina also paraded in her little dress, and she was so tiny and cute that she got immediately snapped up by the mother-of-the-bride and educated in the acceptable etiquette of an attendant to the older flower girl.

The complete group made a stunning display on the day. The ceremony was attended by many well-known sporting enthusiasts, and widely photographed by the Glossies of the era. And me, always a 'softie', at the sight of my Mini Mouse unexpectedly walking in front, down the aisle toward the altar with the rest of the bridal party following her, sent me into an unexpected emotional state. Luckily I had a few tissues with me. I could have used a full box!

But there was so much work involved to complete this mammoth task that I worked long hours into the night when I had no unexpected interruptions from the family—when everyone had gone to bed. But of course my husband didn't know that, he was sleeping!

In the end I didn't get a full time job. We didn't send the boys to private school. We didn't get sued for the damage to the earth moving equipment. All the boys got away with a severe reprimand and no conviction recorded. They were all too young.

I phased out the sewing for clients, but I dedicated more time to my budding little business of representing the Avon Cosmetics Company, which had recently moved into the Australian market. By planning to call on working ladies in the evening, I not only accessed another group of people who were unavailable during daytime hours and had more disposable income, but it also got me out of the house after I had fed everyone. The dishes could wait till the morning.

The children would be ready for bed after they had finished their homework but often I would return late and find them still watching television with their father, instead of going to sleep at their regular time. Just watching TV, not talking, no meaningful interaction with them even when they were alone.

Thinking back, I wonder if it was my involvement with Avon that kept me sane. At least for those few hours away from home, spent in the company of others, I was able to communicate and indulge in a normal conversation on a variety of topics with adults who were engaged in different professions. From the beginning, when I was working with the young children in tow and when the skin care company had just commenced operations in Australia, to the end when I eventually decided on a career change, I was with Avon for a total of seven years. In that time, I became state manager and acquired a long list of useful household items that I probably would not have had otherwise, and other personal awards that included a genuine Omega platinum watch with twenty-seven diamonds (quite small, but brilliant) that I still have in some jewellery box somewhere to remind me of some of those good times.

One weekend we had a visit from Tonia and her young family. This was a rare occasion, as we lived many kilometres apart and as I was preparing lunch for us all, I unwrapped the lettuce to make a salad and an article caught my eye. In the newspaper wrapping I saw a last minute reminder for the Government sponsored course for adults who wanted to take advantage of a number of places now available for teacher training. Jokingly I announced to our guests that I would become a teacher after all. My husband gave me a lopsided, sarcastic grin, and made some remark that I missed. He wouldn't repeat it but Tonia's husband laughed, and she looked somewhat uneasy and embarrassed.

During the course of the afternoon they let us know that this was going to be their last visit, as the family was moving back to Germany. They were not selling their house so I took that to mean it may be a temporary move. But that was not the case. Tonia's parents had passed away, first her father died of cirrhosis of the liver caused by a lifetime of excessive imbibing, and then her mother who had suffered tremendous headaches the previous year caused by an undetected brain tumour. There was really nothing meaningful left to hold her back, and after such a rosy picture was portrayed to her of life back in Germany, she succumbed to her husband's wishes to return. But her parents' house was to remain in her name as a precaution and a financial safety net in case things didn't work out as her spouse predicted. In effect they didn't work out as well as she had hoped, and in the end she had to sell the old family house in St. Albans anyway.

A Career Change

My career change involved three years of going back to an institution to get a tertiary education. In spite of Allan's snide remark, which he made behind my back and that I didn't hear, I did apply for an entry application form. When I first saw the article in the national newspaper with the monetary incentive to be paid by the Whitlam Government to lure adults back to complete a primary teaching course, I perceived it as destiny. I sent the request for that application form on the very last day because we hardly ever got the daily newspaper. It was purely by accident that the article caught my eye at the last minute. I wasn't sure that it would get to its destination on time, but it did, and the formal entry application form duly arrived. I immediately completed it and sent it off.

It was several weeks before a reply came and by then I had given up hope that they had received it before the deadline had expired. Even if my application had arrived in time, had it been considered worthy? Much to my delight I was invited to sit for an entrance examination. It was to be held before the end of the school year in the Royal Exhibition Building, where many years earlier I had paraded down the catwalk together with professional models in the Haute Couture dress that my mother had made for my eighteenth birthday. Ironically, it was The Victorian Printing Works that printed the examination papers for all Higher School Certificates and Victorian University exams at that time, and I took that as a good omen—can't figure out why.

The bundles of booklets were sealed and delivered to the appropriate institutions under guard. The results didn't come out until the following February and this time I didn't bother to show any excitement, or pride as I made the announcement to my husband. I simply stated that I needed a car exclusively for my use, as my study times would be irregular and he would be required to take a more active role in his children's lives. As I expected, there were objections, and I told him we just had to adjust our lives around my new project.

His work environment had also undergone some changes and now that the company had grown, there were more employees and more flexible times, so all he needed to do was to arrange to start work one hour earlier so he would be home when the children arrived from school and he wouldn't need to travel by train to work so that also would save him time.

The school was within walking distance and I had often walked there with the children or back home together. Now I would get them ready and drop them off in the morning on my way to the university in Toorak, so they would only have to walk one way home in the afternoon.

Then I started looking for a car and soon found a beauty, but of course I was not allowed to have that one. It was a sports car with a foldaway roof. Way too sexy for his wife!

There was another hurdle that had to be overcome before the course actually got under way. Two references from people associated with the Education Department, who had known me for a certain minimum period, had to be submitted with my enrolment. One would easily come from the principal at Ringwood Primary School. But the first person to come to my mind was the person who would get the greatest satisfaction from my successful admittance. My old form teacher and Master of Ceremony at my wedding, but I had not kept in touch lately. We both have two more children than when we last met. No matter, he would understand and rather than ringing him I put my request in writing and then followed it with a phone call. As I expected, he was pleased that I had been accepted and proud that I had contacted him. I could not have asked for a more glowing reference.

Induction day arrived with all the fanfare and excitement of the imminent new phase in all our lives. But I soon found that I couldn't settle down to what was the norm for student life because I took my studies too seriously. I was on borrowed time and so I had to make it count. Now I understood how much more satisfying my time at university would have been if I didn't have the shackles of a family, if I had taken Mr C.'s advice and continued with my higher education studies straight after high school as my parents wanted me to do also. Being young and carefree, I would have revelled in that easy social environment on campus, where the majority of students would have been within my age group. Instead now, in my more mature years, my lectures were followed by intense work in the library then straight home for a different kind of work.

The first two years were pleasant enough and I coped easily, but by the third year the stress was building up and my health started to deteriorate. I was suffering from severe menstrual cramps, and when these overcame me, I could not tolerate being in the company of anyone, so intense was the pain that I had to lie down in a foetal position until the attack passed. The problem was that these attacks were becoming more frequent and more intense and I was diagnosed with severe endometriosis requiring an urgent operation.

"Can't it wait until the final exams?" I wailed in the gynaecologist's surgery.

"Not if you want a complete recovery," he countered.

Exams were scheduled for October, and now it was early September. I had to make some arrangements both at home and at the university before I was due to go into hospital. Luckily all practical work prior to exams was already done and the written tests were not due for some time except for the preliminaries. Armed with the surgeon's recommendations, I fronted up to the Dean of Faculties and asked for dispensation to not sit for these preliminary exams altogether and to have all other written exams delayed. My request was denied but an alternative was proposed. One of the lecturers would sit with me in hospital to oversee my effort with the preliminaries. I can't say that it was a brilliant outcome, but I scraped through. By the end of October I started to feel more optimistic as the date for the final and most taxing of the three examinations approached. I considered myself as well prepared as anyone, though I still tired easily and was still having drug therapy. What I neglected to take into account was the effect that these drugs were having on my short-term memory and I had to withdraw from the stream, in order to take alternative tests at a later stage. As graduation was not until later the following year, I was not unduly penalised.

But where schools advertised vacancies in advance, these places were taken up by those graduates whose results had come out first, and by the time I was ready to enter the workforce, the only schools on offer were those in the country which I was not in a position to accept because it would have meant relocating. And my husband was in his element.

Never one to look at anything from the bright side, he could not help himself. "What did I tell you? They want to send you out bush where no one else wants to go!" on and on he went, "Three years for nothing!" and he shook his head, "You will never get a decent job! And we all had to put up with all your late nights!" and he sighed in resignation.

"I beg your pardon?" I couldn't believe I was hearing this, "Who put up with my late nights?"

I had to listen to this kind of smug drivel for a few weeks until one day one of my numerous applications came good.

My First Teaching Appointment

It was not the kind of teaching that I had in mind but it was a good stop-gap, and by then I was fed up with listening to the derogatory remarks I got at home. Teaching adults English as a second language was a course that came easily to me, as I could empathise with the many and varied difficulties that immigrants faced when entering a new society, with language being only one aspect of the assimilation process. But one that my family had overcome relatively soon. (Actually my father struggled for a long time)

The venue in the heart of Melbourne still required quite a bit of travel time but the hours were flexible and with some work in the evening when other working students were able to attend the school, I thought it would be a great experience—and it was for that first term. Into the second term, however, I was introduced to a new intake of recently arrived adults. What I had not considered was the composition of the new classes. I nearly freaked out when I first saw my new class for the second term. Twenty long-frocked and long-sleeved Arab men, complete with headgear and sandals. And here I was in a mini skirt and knee-high boots, in the Western garb of that era. But where were the women? Their women! I knew that many Muslims had more than one wife why were they not there? I was not conversant with the Muslim faith. I didn't know at the time that Muslim women were not seen in public places and did not attend educational institutions. That it was entirely a male prerogative to be educated, while maintaining their women in a perpetual state of ignorance and subjugation. That I learnt later and it surprised me because an earlier school friend from a Muslin family had become a lawyer in Melbourne before the entire family moved back to Egypt.

However, the lecherous looks directed at me and at my totally acceptable attire under other normal circumstances, now made me feel unworthy—unworthy of what I challenged? I felt that I was exposing myself to a group of males who were mentally undressing me with their eyes. Did they feel that I should be stoned to death for indecent exposure? My confusion and embarrassment was almost palpable and the only way that I could end the day's session early was for me to pass on a series of homework sheets that had been planned for later in the course. It was too soon to distribute them, these people were not ready for that more advanced work but by passing it on now they knew what the class was expected to achieve.

I hurried off to the staff room for a strong cup of coffee in the absence of the infinitely more strongly desired glass of Scotch, to sustain me through the rest of the day. Alcohol and Islam are not compatible. That much I knew even back then!

Next day I came in earlier and dressed in the attire of an old schoolmarm—long skirt, with flat-heeled shoes. I marched right into the co-ordinator's office, with the same lack of respect that I had been subjected to myself the previous day by my new all-male class and demanded an explanation. Why had I been thrown in 'cold turkey' and without warning? If I were to continue teaching a non-conformist and disrespectful class such as that, which made me feel uncomfortable with their lecherous gazes and disrespected, then I wanted double the hourly pay.

I should have noted earlier that as a specialist teacher, my hourly rates were very generous to begin with, and probably twice those of my husband's, which shut him up and he stopped complaining for a while.

Now, I also knew that the Arab class that I was teaching was privately funded by their Emirates, and that they were paying handsomely for that privilege, so I was not really surprised that my demand for double pay was granted.

In the third and final term, however, the number of 'students' attending my class was considerably increased to almost double in fact, but by then I had learned to cope well and word of mouth had spread back to Saudi Arabia so we had a mutual state of 'almost respect'. I persevered with those classes until the end of the year and then a vacancy became available with the Victorian Education Department that I accepted, though it came with a substantial reduction in wages, but on the other hand, it allowed me more time at home and with my children.

Our Changing Neighbourhood

The entire side of our street now had houses and we welcomed the new neighbours into our small community. It was an interesting, eclectic mix of people and we became friends with all.

There was a young family with two female and two male children that was quite unique. The young wife was the daughter of a devoted, musical, Hungarian family that had emigrated from Eastern Europe several years earlier. The older parents had two daughters and four sons. The sons all had brilliant minds and became notable personalities both in Victoria and interstate, but they all inherited a gene that caused their growth to become stunted. They were somewhat deformed as children and never grew to normal height. The parents made sure that all their children had a tertiary education regardless of the boys' physique and the eldest son studied medicine in an effort to understand better the DNA code. He became a gynaecologist but died in his early forties. The second son became a barrister of some renown, but he died in his late forties. The youngest son lived longest, to the age of fifty-two. Within ten years the parents lost all their four sons. The daughters were perfectly normal but each one passed on this rogue gene to their own male children. In spite of all their problems and heartaches, they were a happy and close-knit family who coped well with their unusual handicaps. When a friend of the young wife inexplicably suicided, her baby boy was promptly taken into her care and subsequently adopted. Now there were seven in the family. When the grandparents visited their daughter and grandchildren, the very distinguished looking older gentleman would promenade up and down our still unmade road in the late afternoon, with his wife's arm through his, while he gently swung an ebony and silver walking stick and solicitously listened to every word that his lady had to say. They were such a devoted couple, obviously their lives and the problems that they had encountered throughout had only brought them closer together. It was a delight to watch them promenade and when the man died I kept in touch with his wife until she moved with the family to Brisbane

With another young family, we enjoyed fishing for eels at night. Apparently, the best time to catch these slippery and ugly looking pseudo-fish is at full moon, in the lagoons by the side of rivers, on a warm, calm evening. Eels are a delicacy on the Continent if they are prepared properly, and both our husbands had eaten the smoked eels that their parents had prepared many years earlier. But both sets of parents were deceased now, so there was no one handy to ask advice, not with the catching of eels, nor with the preparation or cooking of these slimy creatures.

It was our first attempt to find and catch them on calves' liver because that's what they like (so we were told by some self-proclaimed experts who had never caught any themselves). The meat is attached to the hook of a short fishing rod, but we were never told, and so we didn't know, that once they are hooked, they curled themselves around the line and make their way upwards. When I caught my first eel I squealed with glee, until the damn thing started to come toward me along my fishing rod! Then I squealed in disgust. It was much the same with everyone else too. The children thought it was a great joke to see their parents carry on like Banshees!

But we persevered and on the third night we went out to the backwaters of the Warrandyte River and there the pickings were plentiful. This time we vowed that we would not go home empty-handed no matter how long we had to watch the full moon. It was cold, but it was a beautiful moonlit night, even the kids couldn't sleep and were jumping all around us when one of us landed an eel on the hook. Between us we caught seven. We knocked them on the head with a hefty stick, stunning them and then dropping them in the Esky with ice. We said we would take them to my parents and clean them there, and perhaps they may be able to tell us what to do with them.

It was almost daylight when we got home for a few hours' sleep before heading all the way to Caulfield for instructions. The glorious moonlit night was followed by an equally sparkling day and when we arrived, Robert, Danny, and Regina raced up to their grandparents, "Guess what we caught, Nonna?"

Naturally, I had rung Nonna, to let her know that we were coming, they had a phone by now, but of course she acted suitably surprised and humoured the kids getting them to explain how it all transpired! With great fanfare and anticipation, the Esky was uncovered and the tangled up messy ropes of smelly, squirmy fish meat was tipped over onto the grass lawn at the foot of the Hills clothes line, and then to clean some of the slime, I cleverly (I thought) turned the hose on them. Immediately they got their second wind and another lesson was learned—not only do eels travel overland but they also crawl up Hills clothes' lines and had to be hit on the head yet again so that the men could gut them and clean them.

Apparently the best and tastiest way to eat eels is to smoke them first. So how do you do that? Well, we had built a large brick barbeque in our quite spacious back yard and to let the smoke flow out without getting into the eyes we also built a wide chimney. Perfect for smoking sausages and now eels!

But not so easy now, to be able to hang them down the chimney they had to have their heads still attached to their long bodies and their heads had to be speared through with a steel rod—not as easy as sausages either because they were different lengths. After much deliberation, Father and Allan hit on a plan, aided of course with a few stubbies to give them the courage that was needed in the face of these tenacious and slippery adversaries. We stayed on for Mum's pasta and salad, and dad's claret that we drank under sufferance, then left with enough time to get the fire started and the eels ready for smoking before it got dark that evening.

As usual we called our next door neighbours over, as well as our partners for the fishing expedition, to come and join us for a celebratory drink and barbeque while we sat and watched the ebbing flames smoulder and smoke with the aid of copious amounts of saw dust, while they did their work inside the chimney. The cooked, smoked eels were indeed a delicacy and with much finger licking, wiping the dripping oil off our chins and washing the flesh down with generous amounts of lager, some new ideas emerged as the evening became night. We decided to create an 'Eel Hatchery'.

In the bright light of day, we looked at the possible site for our new enterprise. In our ignorance, we believed that we could control these creatures. It's hard to believe that we actually went to all the trouble of lining a section of our front garden between the unfinished garage wall and the front steps with beautiful white quartz rocks that the whole neighbourhood went out to gather over the next few weeks from various places, some as far afield as Bendigo. We ended up with quite a lovely, fairly large pond and a trickling waterfall cascading from the corner of the steps. Now we had to go fishing again. The kids loved this part and still managed to get excited when one of us hooked these slimy creatures, but by the time we caught half a dozen between us the novelty was starting to wear off, so with them safely enclosed in the Esky we decided to call it a night.

With great fanfare, the next evening we all gathered for the introduction of the slimy critters to their new home. Three of the bigger eels didn't look too chirpy so we decided that they would be cooked, but the other three scuttled amongst the rocks and straight away made themselves at home. They looked quite comfortable there checking out every nook and cranny that we had thoughtfully created for them—and we congratulated ourselves, and each other on this new venture. We would check on them tomorrow.

Excitedly, we got up early next morning but the eels must be sleeping in their hollows. Fish do sleep you know! Later we all gathered around our pond to follow the progress of our hatchery, but where are the eels? Perhaps we should have done some research beforehand! The kids looked around perplexed, then at us and eventually accepted the fact that we were all idiots. Eels are able to easily move around land on the dewy grass of the early morning and ours obviously decided to migrate elsewhere.

So we ate the three I had cooked, and though they were much appreciated by all, in the future we chose to go to Victoria Market to buy them already cleaned and learned of other methods of preparing them from the amused stallholders. Eels in Aspic are also quite nice but I still prefer them smoked. And our lovely white quartz-stone pond grew beautiful purple water lilies.

Some Recreation

Allan's favourite form of recreation was card playing, starting early on a Saturday afternoon and continuing well past midnight. Because most of his friends lived in the vicinity of the parents' old home, we would tend to congregate at his older sister's house nearby. It was quite big and I could put the children down to sleep while the men played and drank, and the women sewed or knitted. The needs of the children were never a priority with my husband. This particular morning I had gone shopping alone and bought a lovely whole fish that I wanted to make into a chowder, so using the big aluminium boiler and quite a lot of water to cover the entire fish, I added carrots and potatoes and set this stock pot on the large hot plate to simmer while I proceeded to put the rest of the shopping away. But my husband was anxious to get going and it seemed that I was taking too long. He was getting impatient, so I left the large bunch of celery on the bench next to the hotplates thinking that it wouldn't take long to cook on the morrow, so it could be added later when the fish and other vegetables were ready. The children were dressed and ready to go. Quickly I gathered my work for that evening, and turning off the hotplate, I flew out of the door and into the waiting car where my family was becoming fidgety.

It was another Saturday night just like countless others. The men played cards, the women worked preparing dinner for everyone, then we all chipped in with the cleaning up and finally settling down to talk and knit woollen items for the children or sew. It was a routine that had become established over time. At least the families were socially gathered together.

The final card game ended after midnight and we gathered the sleeping children and bundled them into the back of the station wagon. The night was cold so that didn't take long, and soon we were ready to leave. It was a long drive home and even with the heater going, it was cold at that time of the year. The children were restless and Allan was driving erratically. We were not very far from home, travelling on the highway, when I noticed that we were being followed and cautioned my husband, who typically put his foot on the accelerator and let out a string of expletives. Flashing lights and the police siren forced him to stop. The older policeman looked into the back and saw three young children, wide-eyed and wrapped in blankets.

"You were driving too fast and all over the road. Why?"

"Sorry. I wanted to take the children home and to bed quickly," said Allan.

"I can smell alcohol on your breath."

"Yes, I had a couple of drinks, it was a special occasion."

"It's nearly two in the morning, and my shift is ending. I don't want to have to bring you in to the police station and do all that paperwork."

This fatherly figure turned to me, "Do you drive?"

"Yes," I meekly answered.

"Take over." He waited until we changed seats then he drove off with another warning. We breathed a sigh of relief and I cautiously drove off towards home, totally unaware that another nightmare awaited us there.

I parked the car in the dark garage and together we brought the children up the stairs to the front door. What confronted us when we unlocked the door had us reeling back in horror. The house was full of smoke and the stench of desiccated, burnt fish was nauseating. The night was cold but the house was hot, and the air dense and choking. A glow was coming from the kitchen and I knew instantly what had happened. The electric meter box was near the front door, so I turned off the power immediately. Luckily we always had a good strong torch with us when we went out, and we used it this time to take stock of the situation inside.

The large hotplate where I had placed the boiling pot with the fish in it was still glowing red-hot, as were the sides of the aluminium pot. There was smoke coming from above where the cupboard that housed the exhaust fan was black and scorched but had not yet burst into flames. The bunch of celery that I had left on the bench next to the stove was reduced to a pile of yellow, dried out reeds, and the part of the laminated bench top that had not been covered by the bunch of celery was black and blistered. The tiles behind the hotplates were covered in black soot, but what was truly amazing was the perfect, white, ashen backbone of the fish that was resting on the hotplate as if it had been placed there by a meticulous hand so carefully as to not to disturb a single bone of its skeleton. The base of the pot had completely burnt away as had the lid, which must have caved into the pot with the intense heat. What was left now was just the handle and the two screws which were obviously made of a different and probably tougher metal. These were delicately resting in the middle of the white backbone of the fish. It was such an artistic arrangement! I wish I could have photographed it, but at the time such frivolous action was far from my mind.

What had happened of course was very easy to explain. At four o'clock on the Saturday afternoon, in my haste to join the rest of the family waiting for me in the car, I had turned the knob of the hotplate to what I thought was 'OFF', but instead I had turned the knob too far and it had gone past the off and on to the 'FULL', so ten hours later, all the water had boiled dry, the metal saucepan had melted and turned everything black, the heat generated was threatening to set the kitchen cupboards alight. And probably what saved the laminated bench next to the stove from igniting was the bunch of celery that I had not put away.

Our first thought was to open all the windows to let some fresh air in and get the children into their beds. The main bedroom door was always kept closed to discourage inquisitive fingers delving amongst the Avon products that had been ordered for my customers but not yet delivered, so our room was relatively unaffected by the smelly smoke and my 'tired' husband was able to open the windows and blissfully slide between the cool sheets. Actually, there wasn't much that I could do until the morning light either, except worry about what could have been.

In the few years that we had been living in our home that we had so lovingly designed, and worked so hard to bring to fruition, we had come so close to losing it to fire on two separate occasions—and this time I would have been the one directly responsible!

Political and Economic Changes

Times were changing, and with a Labor Government now in power, it was obvious to me that not all the changes were for the better. The price of most commodities skyrocketed and inflation was high, and so was interest on home repayments. The banks were issuing bonds at a very attractive rate of interest, and that was great for those who had the money to invest, but what about the regular battler? The cost of houses was going up and up too. We were thankful that we already had our home. The next big project was to save up for a car and to finish building the garage because as the children grew the need for a bigger car became more urgent.

I could already see that our dollar was buying less and less, and it was going to take a long time to save the required funds. People were agitating for higher wages, but couldn't they see that with higher wages the cost of manufacturing or producing goods also had to go up? Everyone wanted 'more'. The country would be forever trying to catch up. By the time we would have saved the money that we now thought we would need, the costs of our purchases would be greater than they were right now. I tried to explain to Allan that was why people took out loans, to lock in their purchases at today's prices and repay the loan over a set time frame, but it was like talking to a brick wall. He would say time and time again, "But the banks charge interest for the privilege."

"But one gets to use the goods in the meantime!" I would wail in desperation.

Perhaps he was right, and the house was a big enough commitment for the moment. But that didn't stop me from thinking ahead. After my successful design of the garage with the swimming pool on the roof, I became inspired to design another addition to our humble house. The boys needed space to bring their friends home where they could play and study together.

The land at the back of the house sloped gently upward to the nicely landscaped, semicircular barbeque, and the vegie garden, with several fruit trees interspersed here and there, but there was quite a big area that was reasonably flat just outside the dining room. We had double glass doors opening outward in the original house design and it would not take much money, or effort to build another room that could house a billiard table there.

I took measurements and marked out on the ground the proposed dimensions of this new room. It had to be big enough to accommodate a three quarter size billiard table at least, and still allow enough room all around for several chairs. Then I realised that the room would be light and bright if we had another set of glass doors bringing the barbeque area into closer proximity and making it more useable during bad weather. It would become an indoor/outdoor recreation area all year round.

The proportions of the room grew and grew until I was afraid that my husband would be intimidated by its sheer size, but when I mentioned that now the room could hold a full size billiard table where he could also have his friends come and play, he looked more favourably at this new idea.

Now it was going to be his recreation area and not the children's. Emboldened by the lack of criticism for once, I put pen to paper and drew the room to scale, with sides and rear elevations, material uses to complement the existing house, and the roof line extension. It took several trips to the Council Chambers before the inspectors were happy with the final design and now we could make a start. In effect, the addition would be made up of two very large windows on each side, the rear wall made up of predominantly glass double doors, with another side door on the opposite side jutting out and fronting the street to enable people to enter via this side door without having to come into the main house at all. Essentially, there were four substantial pillars to hold up the roof.

Simple, quite cheap, and very effective. It would substantially increase the size of the house and we all started to get quite excited about this pending project. Once we got started, we couldn't stop and in the space of a few weeks we were ready for the flooring. This was the hardest and most demanding part of the whole job because I wanted a proper terrazzo floor that I could hose down, but would have to look good too.

Even back in the seventies, that was not a cheap alternative, so we did that job ourselves as well. We hired a grinder and polisher for two weeks because we knew that to get this right it would be a long, tedious, difficult process. And it was. In the fresh concrete, I broke brown beer bottles, green and blue wine bottles, and interspersed the bits of brown, green, and blue glass here and there between the pebbles before the cement dried..

Then came the hours, the days, totalling two full weeks of grinding everything down to a smooth, polished surface. The result was stunning, especially when the sun shone on all that coloured glass through the large windows!

The finished product made us quickly forget the aching backsides we had for weeks, after we all had to take turns, including the boys, to sit on this electric vibrating grinder and polisher for hours and hours at a time.

Part of the deal was that I would have a solid cover on the billiard table that would serve the purpose of being a table top for parties, as well as being a flat even surface for me to use as a materials cutting table.

The room was brilliant. Big enough for me to have a corner of it for my sewing machine without feeling closed in or crowded, yet I could enclose everything out of sight and clean it in minutes.

Me, an Investor?

Regina was in primary school now, but the boys were enrolled at the local high school, which I didn't think would extend their abilities sufficiently and my reason for working was to enable the boys to have a better education so that they would have a better chance in life. On a number of occasions Allan and I argued about the benefit of sending the boys to a private college but each time I had to take a step back. Allan's argument was that he never went to a private school and he couldn't see any benefit in spending all that extra money because that was only for the rich and we couldn't afford it. State high schools were good enough for the majority of children, so that should be good enough for our boys too.

Some family friends had purchased a block of land in a seaside village and were getting ready to construct their holiday home. It was going to be a house that they would live in permanently, but at a later stage, when they retired. Their plans for the future set me thinking.

Irena and I talked a lot. She was quite a bit older and had gone through everything that I had in the past and probably very much more, being one of a group of White Russians who were persecuted. I trusted her judgement. She had married late in life and they were only able to have one daughter who was now studying to become a veterinary surgeon. Their home was on a farm in Healesville, where they raised an assortment of cattle for milk and the abattoir, pigs and other animals. All three were consistent hard workers who had built a substantial future based on stock and property from virtually nothing, through sheer determination and forward planning. They had looked ahead. Way, way ahead and had remained totally focused.

Back at home I carefully looked at our savings and what they could bring us. I thought of Allan's argument and I thought of my own arguments. We had available $10,000 dollars between cash and my borrowing ability with the Teachers' Credit Union. I figured that if I took a chance, the risk would be fifty/fifty but I would willingly take full responsibility for my actions. I had been looking in the papers daily to keep up to date with the trends and one day an article caught my eye. Citibank was starting operations in Australia and to encourage initial private investments, they were offering a ten per cent return for a once only six months minimum investment of $10,000. After a sleepless night, in the morning I went to the Victorian State Bank where we had both our savings and our home loan to seek advice. I must admit that was a bit cheeky of me, seeing I was planning to withdraw all our savings, bar the one mandatory dollar to keep the account open. But I knew the manager at our local branch fairly well and his advice would be unbiased. Not only did he confirm that the offer by Citibank was a genuine, first time clients' only offer, but he also advised me to keep an eye out for our bank's forthcoming offer of Bank Bonds at an unprecedented generous rate. Not that I could do anything about that right now, no matter how generous the rates.

I took out the money we had there and headed for the Teachers' Credit Union for the balance to be borrowed. From memory I think it was at less than four and a half per cent annually and it wasn't for a large amount in any case. I would gain in six months a one off return of $1,000, from Citibank. How long would it take us to save those extra thousand dollars?

I must admit that I didn't sleep too well on many nights until my investment matured. It was the first time that I had acted without consulting Allan. In the meantime I kept myself occupied with the design for the house extension. The plans could be submitted directly to the Council provided they had all the necessary details itemised correctly and I already knew the correct procedure to follow having only a few months earlier obtained the 'Permit to Build' the garage.

I knew what I wanted, so I researched the Council Library and hounded their staff until I obtained from either one or the other of the building inspectors all the information I needed.

The garage was built first and had been completed in record time, much sooner than we had expected, as there were plenty of tradesmen around the area with the appropriate equipment who were keen to work the odd hour or so in overtime. It was building boom time. The garage was to be built in front of the house but connected to it and now it would be closer to the road kerb. The slope of our drive was very steep so the floor of the garage had to be excavated into the ground one meter to reduce the gradient of the slope of the driveway. The foundation of the house had to be reinforced in the dug-out section and the roof of the garage was to be made of concrete strong enough to support a swimming pool. The planning and computations for the garage roof had to be prepared by an engineer and had been much more complex than what I was working on now. Further up the backyard there was too much of a slope, and to put a swimming pool there would have cost more than we were prepared to spend for the few months of summer heat that Melbourne enjoyed.

Now not only was I involved with the plans, but I was also chasing quotes for materials and tradespeople. While this kept me busy, it was something that I found profoundly rewarding. All the input I was getting at home was the occasional nod, 'anything to humour her', I could almost hear the unspoken words. What I found hardest to cope with in my marriage was the lack of commitment and support not only for myself, but I felt so terribly sorry for my boys, who were missing out on the encouragement and bonding that I could see their friends were enjoying with their fathers.

By the time I got the plans through Council, the six months were almost up. However, unless we did a lot of the work ourselves on the house extension, there was still not enough money to repay my loan and buy the bigger car we so desperately needed, so I chose to keep the loan going and do what was still needed with the garage and then the billiard room, which also only took a few months to complete.

We were very fortunate to find an almost new Chrysler Valiant station wagon. So now we had both the car and the garage, and in a short while we could finish the recreation room and then the landscaping, with just a bit more monthly outgoings for the next couple of years.

This little exercise confirmed my theory that one could only get ahead by using other peoples' money, i.e. borrowing. Now, with the addition of a sizeable garage and swimming pool, a large recreation room and tasteful landscaping, the house became considerably more valuable and much more attractive.

Holiday House or Investment Property?

In the meantime, our older family friends had started building their beach house so often on a weekend we would go and help. Sometimes I felt that I was more in the way than a help to anyone, so I would take the children for a walk around the neighbourhood or to the beach.

One day in my wandering I came across a big old house with a 'For Sale' sign. It was quite old, a pre-war house, and in need of paint; the garden was overgrown with trees almost covering the roof and it seemed to be sitting on a triangular piece of land. It certainly looked neglected but it was only one house removed from the beach and the reason it was sitting on a triangular block on an angle was because the area was planned in such a way for the two tennis courts in front to form a square that was built diagonally across, so that all the four sides had houses across the four roads, on land that was triangular. My penchant for the abnormal or unusual was piqued. I had to talk to the selling agent. The house wasn't worth much, that was for sure, but the position was absolutely brilliant.

The agent turned out to be the local councillor, the local J.P., the local postal officer, and he owned the local newsagency, the local pharmacy, the local general store, and petrol pump. He was a busy man. My enquiry about the house had me running after him as he served his many customers, but eventually he got the message that I really wanted to see the house, so I followed him to the post office section of his enterprises where he reached up to take a key from one of the multitude of hooks hanging on the wall and gave it to me, telling me, "take your time."

Okay, so that is how business is done in the country.

My inspection of the house frightened me and I almost took the key right back. That was until I walked out onto the recently constructed, full-length veranda on the back and overlooking a veritable green haven. And guess what? There was a 'dunny' there—a 'thunder box' in the back yard that came to a point. It had a beautiful wisteria vine growing over the roof and a profusion of lilac blossoms trailing down and around the door. I had to see that!

It brought back memories of bygone days when my family and I had to negotiate the outdoors in all-weather when nature called, and we didn't have the blessings of a vine with perfumed blossoms all around the door.

But there was also a modern toilet installed when the veranda was built.

The house was fully furnished and, including the old enclosed side verandas or 'sleep outs', it had five bedrooms.

I did take my time wandering around and looking at the furniture that included an old and neglected grand piano, and an extensive library with many original issue books that were printed in the United Kingdom, plus a heavy eight-seater table with matching chairs badly in need of reupholstering. I took in all these details, before going back to make further enquiries.

Should I ask Allan to come to look first? I weighed the pros and cons of doing that, and decided I needed to know the price first.

The agent told me that the house formed part of a deceased estate and the beneficiaries had put a price of $19,000 on the property. Encouraged, my next question was, "The property, as it stands, is not worth that amount, and does it include all the chattels?"

"It probably does." I thought that response was a bit vague, but I told him that I liked the position and I wanted my husband to see the house.

"Keep the key and bring it back when you have finished."

Needless to say, I immediately got my usual negative answer from 'my dear better half'.

"The house was a wreck," I agreed,

"It needs a lot of work to make it liveable." I agreed.

"Who is going to do the work, me?"

I agreed, "And me."

Instead of always helping others, as he was doing now to build a completely new house, we could be working together on our own holiday home.

I took the key back and told the agent that we thought that the property was far too expensive. I let it rest for a few days, then on our next trip up to Somers, with the excuse of doing some shopping, I managed to corner the agent to ask if he had spoken to the beneficiaries. Much to my surprise, he had and they were willing to negotiate. Obviously there were not many people around willing to undertake such a major project. My reply needed to be thought out carefully because I wanted that property but no doubt the objections from Allan were valid and without his co-operation I could do nothing.

Mother liked the beach, but going to the beach on your own is no fun, so on our next visit, Mother came along. She had a lot of time for my husband, and he for her. In fact he had helped her to purchase a very well looked after car from someone who was moving to some overseas country and couldn't take the car with him. The Datsun Stanza was only one year old but Mother had never owned a car and had not learned to drive. However, once she had the car in her possession, it took her only a couple of months to learn through a driving school and practising with Allan whenever possible.

She enjoyed telling us about some of the antics that her instructor got up to. Apparently he was a minister or a priest who liked to chat. One day as she was approaching a pedestrian crossing that had some people fooling around and taking their time to go across, he said to her, "Just drive right through them, that will speed them up a bit. And if they say anything, we can just tell them you are a learner." He continued.

Luckily she knew better than to take that bit of advice (he was probably testing her) and she obtained her drivers' license soon after, on her sixty-fourth birthday. It was like a new lease for life for her. She had the freedom to move around, with or without her husband, who had always said she took too long to get herself and the children ready to go somewhere when Ondina and I were young. Now if he wasn't ready she could leave him behind as he had so often done with her in the past! Mum didn't forget.

Mother walked through the old house and shuddered at the amount of work needed to make it comfortable and fit for use, but she too liked the position, and the back sunroom and toilet were newly built, so I made her a proposition. If we could get the furnished house for $16,000 would she be willing to be the third partner?

We would need to put $5,500 each to cover costs. She agreed, as I knew she would, and now it would be up to me to convince my husband. Eventually he agreed, but only after I told him that once the house was improved we would be able to rent it to holidaymakers to help pay for it. Returning to the agent with a proposition that I knew was going to be turned down gave me more time to consider all the possible risks. I had offered to buy the house for $15,000 provided the beneficiaries left all the furniture and other chattels in the house, with settlement to be effected in thirty days instead of the usual three months that was customary in Victoria.

I wanted to have the first summer season for us to enjoy there while we worked to clear and clean the property and while I was on school holidays. Everything seemed to be so laid-back in this little village so I was surprised to take a telephone call the following day from the agent who had a counter offer from the beneficiaries. I held my breath because by now I was starting to get cold feet, but the counter offer really was better than I expected and exactly the figure I had proposed to Mum. $16,000 and they would leave most of the furniture except for the table, the eight chairs, and the grand piano. It was natural that they would want to keep the best pieces, but we needed to discuss this turn of events. Mother would agree, I knew that, and surprisingly, Allan also agreed that it would be a good investment. I suspect he had been talking to the friends whose house he was helping to build. Allan was not a slouch when it came to working. He enjoyed his considerable achievements. It was just that he was so non-committal and uninspiring in his general attitude. He was not a forward-thinking person.

The sale went through without a hitch and from then on we spent every free moment restoring our own holiday home. We were given the key when we first signed the contract, so in that unexpected extra month before we could settle the sale, we got a lot more work done before the school holidays were over. Then it was ready to rent. It turned out to be very popular with yachters, who booked it for their holidays from one year to the next. The agent was helpful in spreading the word in the nearby Yacht Club, just a couple hundred meters along the Esplanade. But we could only use it ourselves occasionally on some of the weekends, when it was vacant.

The long awaited table and chairs to match the daybed had been put on hold for a couple of years, and now finally they did materialise because there was more time to work on them. It was a joint effort, with a considerable contribution from me, especially in the latter stages of the more time-consuming work, like the sanding and polishing.

Every piece was meticulously crafted with turned legs on the four side chairs and the two end carvers' chairs, with matching side arms. The table had solid slabs of routed timber instead of legs for greater stability. The striking purple and gold material on the seats and back rests of the chairs stood out against the blond pine timber that in time turned darker and even more attractive, and the overall effect was really classy.

To complement and finish off the setting, I made a table runner with the stripes running length-wise, which also made the table appear longer, and I was very satisfied with the way the complete suite complemented the long drapes at the window, especially at night when we had the lights on and they shone on the golden stripes. We were pleased and proud that the end result produced a unique setting virtually from scrap timber and it served us well for a long time, even migrating with us to Brisbane, when we moved north some years later. Incidentally, the remains of that roll of fabric that I so jealously guarded for many years came in really handy when the seats of the chairs became tatty-looking, after years of constant use and spillages. It was a simple operation to remove the backing, release the staples, replace the old material with new covers and replace the backing. Voila! A new set of four chairs and two end carvers.

The following year, I was teaching a delightful class of fourth graders in Cranbourne. The children brought up in the country seemed free of inhibitions, naturally curious, keen to participate and friendly. It was probably the best class I ever had the pleasure to teach. Without exception, I loved them all, but once again the travelling time and the effort of driving the distance became a bit of a drag for me by the end of the year. Much as I enjoyed the working atmosphere in this up and coming country centre, I really didn't have enough time for me and the family, so I felt inspired to request a transfer to the small school in Somers, thinking that our boys would benefit from a change of scenery. They would be attending High School in Hastings. If we moved, I would have more time at home and Allan would be able to retire sooner because he was tiring more easily now.

With the new placements announced for the following school year, my request for the transfer to Somers was granted and we started to plan our move to the holiday house. Allan seemed happy because his eldest sister and new husband had also bought a piece of land on the other side of the minute Somers' CBD. They planned to build an ambitious residence on the cliff overlooking the Western Port bay, with the popular Phillip Island at its mouth.

The new husband was considerably younger than my sister-in-law and he had helped several builders while working and learning the many aspects of house building in Europe before migrating to Australia via France. He was ambitious and capable and in a very short time with help from his friends he built a big, solid house with a cellar underground and two storeys above ground. It was probably the most solid and biggest house within the greater area at that time and it was well positioned to take advantage of the sun in winter and breezes in summer, as well commanding a spectacular view of the Bay. But they were not quite ready to retire there yet. Still they often visited and came with a bottle to share with us, and that made my husband happy.

Trouble Follows

Once again the boys were left to their own devices and even though their father had time on his hands now, he did nothing to engage the boys' energies, like going fishing with them in this fishermen's haven, or learning to sail or going bushwalking. There were hundreds of opportunities for father and sons to become involved but Allan maintained that his fair skin could not tolerate the sun. And instead, the boys now fifteen and sixteen years, met some unsavoury elements on the beach where they spent a lot of time, and especially at nights they would congregate to smoke and drink. Had we gone out together as a family more often, to the numerous functions held for the residents at the nearby Yacht Club, things might have been different, but as it was, a street wise nineteen year old befriended the boys, who were lacking parental direction, and recruited them into a car-stealing gang. Luckily they were apprehended very early in their initiation stage and we as parents were called to appear in court at Mornington. As one of the local teachers now, I felt that I was the one being reprimanded and chastised, and I felt thoroughly ashamed, not only for myself and my sons, but infinitely more so for my husband who was referred to as lazy by his second son during the court appearance. That statement was hotly denied by both of us.

His father was not lazy. When he was well, he worked well. It was just that he never connected, or bonded with his sons. He let them do whatever they wanted, even now that he was retired and had so much more time to rest when he felt he needed to, while they were away at school. And I was powerless to intrude. It was already too late.

Maybe here I am making excuses, but even now, thinking back, I fail to see what more I could have done. I bought them tennis racquets and tried to entice them to play with me on the courts just outside our front gate. When that didn't work, I tried to enrol them with a tennis coach and local club. Again there was no encouragement from their father. He never even bothered to step outside the door to watch the boys at play. It was to try to change the direction that we felt the boys were heading that made us look at making a complete change.

During the September holidays, we headed north to Queensland. We had been there the previous year and liked the laid-back lifestyle of the locals, so we thought we would try again and if we still liked the area around Brisbane, we would look at buying something. Land, unit, house, or whatever we deemed suitable. The weather was more stable than southern Victoria and being warmer it would be kinder on our arthritic joints. Allan's especially.

We took three days to drive north, stopping at tourists' hotspot, and planned to do the same on the drive back. For the whole week we remained in the Brisbane outskirts, and from there we looked at the various possibilities and saw a number of real estate agents. In the evening we would discuss the pros and cons of what we had seen and return the following day for another look at different surroundings to those shown to us, to form a more balanced outlook.

We both liked the beachside suburbs but the houses seemed basic and flimsy, built to meet the demands of floodwaters rising. We saw nothing that appealed to us and in the end Allan said that perhaps we should build a house to meet our needs. We had seen a block of land that had possibilities, in an area that locals called the 'salad bowl' of Brisbane, in the Redlands. The agent referred to it as 'God's own country'. A bit far-fetched, I thought! And it was also a bit far from the city of Brisbane.

I had noted in our travels and inspections a two bedroom flat with a vast, open car garage, in a block of only four flats, not very far from the city and not far from where the proposed South East freeway was to be built in the near future, which I thought had more potential in the long run. It was close to the high school, had a good selection of private colleges, a hospital precinct that was in the process of being constructed. Across the main thoroughfare in the nearby hill were the extensive grounds of Griffith University and Toohey Forest, very easily accessible on foot or by bike.

So we were back to our usual dilemma where my husband liked one property and I liked another. We only had a couple more days before needing to make our tracks back. It had been raining heavily west of the ranges and we feared that if it continued we would need to detour. So we had to make a decision soon, if anything at all was to be accomplished during these holidays.

Looking at our finances, we only had enough money for the land. If we bought the land, we would need to start building soon and where would we live in the meantime? We would need to sell our Ringwood home where we had put so much effort into making it into the kind of home we wanted, but the market was depressed, inflation had been swift, and now the economy was stagnating, goodness only knew how long it would take us to sell our house. On the other hand, it was depressed in Brisbane too, that is why I thought we could negotiate a good price for the flat.

I made a proposition and held my breath while it was being digested. I had a good rapport with the Victorian Teachers' Credit Union and I knew that they would not hesitate to advance me a loan for an interstate investment property. I just had to convince my husband that we could have both the land and the flat if we planned it right and when the house in Ringwood was sold we could move into the flat and build on the block of land. The wheels started spinning, but very slowly and I knew from past experience that there was no point in talking further.

In the morning I went to see the agent and started negotiations, and by the afternoon asked for a contract to be drawn up at my price, which I knew would be counter signed, but at least I had something to bring to Allan.

In all the time he had to himself while the children and I were away, he must have seen the logic of what I was proposing because I didn't have much resistance for once, so while we waited for one contract to be returned, we went to the land agent and had another contract drawn up. This time Allan didn't want to negotiate, he just wanted the land, and I felt that we overpaid. *Ces't la vie!* The loan was to be in my name, as he was no longer working, but the title to both properties were to be in both names.

He might have been slow to appreciate what I was attempting to do for the benefit of all, but he wasn't stupid, or slow to see the benefit to himself!

In one day we had purchased two properties, and I had placed a noose around my neck, because on my pay we would be making the repayments on one residential home, one holiday home, one investment property, and a non-returning block of land.

It continued to rain. I started to feel a bit apprehensive and glad that on both contracts, I had insisted that one be dependent upon the settlement of the other, and both subject to the loan being approved in total.

It was wet and windy when we set off the next morning, homeward bound and quiet. We took the Cunningham Highway skirting Ipswich, through Warwick and intending to take the Newell Highway out of Goondiwindi, but only got as far as Yelarbon. What had been a hazy and dusty dry mirage for countless miles, on our way up north only ten days earlier, now that same area was an inland sea as far as the eye could see. We could hardly believe our eyes, looking around at the changes to the land all around us in such a short time, how could it have changed so quickly?

Where did all this water come from in such a short time?

The Macintyre River was in flood and it was impossible to proceed that way. We had to backtrack to Warwick and take the New England Highway to Tenterfield and continue to Glen Innes, Tamworth and south to Dubbo the long way. We all became short tempered and frustrated at the longer distances we were forced to travel with nothing to see along the way. Instead of enjoying the last few days of the school holidays, visiting more places of interest as planned, we were carefully treading water. Now that we had serious financial commitments, I could not take the luxury of time off work.

The year ended and our house still had not sold. The seeds of worry were becoming felt and I started to ask myself, 'what if'. The Queensland flat was rented and was paying its own way because I had renegotiated that contract for it to be freestanding. We moved out of Somers for the holidays and rented the five bedroom house at a premium for the six weeks before school resumed and so financially we were coping adequately. When we did have a sales contract on the house, we had three months to finalise everything, pack up and leave. It worked out well because this brought us to the end of the first school term. To leave the house in Somers vacant would have meant that in no time it would have reverted back to its neglected stage but thanks goes to our multi-skilled and talented, busy agent, who suggested a longer term rental for the teacher that would be replacing me. Tremendous, a win, win situation!

Something that we failed to take into account was my parents' future. Mother and Father had retired by now and Ondina was working in Tasmania. What were they going to do on their own in Victoria? The decision was quickly made that they would join us in Queensland as soon as practicable.

We settled into our flat and immediately set about enclosing the garage with a full width sliding glass wall. Once it was carpeted, the room was spacious, private and well lit with natural daylight and the boys happily settled in. I bought some established Lilly Pilly plants in big terracotta pots from a local garage sale to place in front of the glassed-in garage/bedroom/study to provide more privacy for the boys in the evening. Regina was happy to have the large bedroom all to herself, and it was tastefully decorated with her choice of colours. The next step now was to get them all enrolled at school. They were all attending high school now and I managed to get them all in together. Initially Regina was out of her depth because of the different education systems. She had completed grade six in Victoria and this marks the end of primary school, whereas in Queensland it is grade seven before a child is deemed ready to commence high school, so she was younger than most and she struggled a bit that first year.

As I had to resign from the Victorian Education Dept., I now needed to re-apply to teach in Queensland, and the first posting was with the primary school annexed to the high school that my children attended, but it was in a relief role for the times when one of the regular teachers was absent. This suited me perfectly because it left me enough time to plan for the house we were to build in the Redlands, some half an hour's drive away.

At the end of the second term we drove to Victoria to help relocate my parents. It was sad to say goodbye to the house where we had spent so much of our lives. We had become accustomed to all its shortcomings and taken them for granted, thinking about it, we realised that in all of those years not much had been changed. Once I was married and left, the house was quite adequate for three people; when Ondina left to work in Tasmania some ten years later, Mum and Dad certainly didn't need anything bigger. It was centrally located, walking distance to the racecourse and transport.

They had made some friends and had been content there.

But with no family nearby, and the grandchildren growing 'too quickly' they were glad to leave Melbourne behind, along with its 'four seasons in one day' reputation. We started looking for a house somewhere reasonably close to where we would ultimately be living and found one still under construction that only had a few weeks to go to completion, so they put that time to good use by holidaying up in far north Queensland. When they got back, their house was ready to move into, while ours was not yet started, so I had the time to help to establish their garden with plants suitable to the sub-tropical climate. These were not always what Mum would have chosen but she had no idea of how harsh the summers in Queensland could be yet, so as always she was willing to listen and compromise. As she said, "I don't want to become a slave to my own garden."

The only one source of contention was the house in Caulfield. Both Ondina and I felt that it should be rented out, instead of sold outright, because the position was irreplaceable and would be worth a lot more once we left this depression that was gripping the country behind us. But Mum and Dad didn't want to have the worry of maintenance at their stage in life and though we offered to take the maintenance issues upon ourselves, my parents felt that they would rather enjoy the fruits of their labours by using the money that would otherwise be tied up in the house, and we had to concede that it was their decision to do what was best for them. Everything seemed to be progressing smoothly. With the proceeds from the sale of our Ringwood home, we had paid off the land and started to build a solid, two storey home.

Once again, it was not to be your normal run-of-the-mill home. It took a while to find a builder that we could empathise with and when we did, it was through a friend that the boys had met at school. He was a young White Russian who lived with his old father and his Chinese mother in the house he had built for them nearby to where we now lived. He agreed to build our house only to the lock-up stage, as we knew we didn't have nearly enough money to complete it. We could have sold the flat where we were living but it was heavily mortgaged. It would be more sensible if we could sell the holiday house in Somers because it was unlikely that we would want to return there.

The economy was doing strange things. More people were selling their homes down south and moving north for the warmer climate, and though property still seemed to be more expensive in the southern states, the prices were escalating now in Brisbane as well. I contacted our multi-talented agent to enquire about the chance of quick sale.

"Not a problem!" He didn't mince words. "I can get you a good price too."

And he did! In a few short years, we got back nearly twice the amount we had paid for the old beach house. We could now settle the loan, pay Mother her fair share, and use the balance to proceed a little further with our new home building. When this money was exhausted, we told the builder that we would now take over and we moved into a very unfinished house.

The boys decided that at the end of the year they would start working in the Motor Car Industry. Not the type of work I would have chosen for them, but this time they had their father's support—he had become friends with the owner of the business that had offered the boys work! We could not foresee the damage that this kind of work would have on the boys' health, especially Robert.

The flat rented easily and paid for itself, but there was little money to put into the new building. Just a lot of work, but there was no rush. We planned to live there for a long time.

Flexible Itinerary – 1984

It was 1983 and the whole idea of going to Europe started out as a joke. A friend of the family who was a recent arrival in Australia was homesick for her elderly parents and homeland. Her husband was working and couldn't spare the time for a lengthy holiday, so one day I jokingly said, "We should go together."

Since arriving in Melbourne in 1951, I had never been out of the country except for a fortnight's cruise to Fiji way back in 1974. Now we were living in Brisbane and I was earning some money to supplement my husband's income as he was now retired and on a disability pension, so the idea of a visit to our respective homeland appealed to both Mira and me, but neither of us had enough money to spare for travel. Tentatively, I said that perhaps we should focus on a date twelve months hence to enable us to work and save toward this specific target. And twelve months later we were on our way.

We had decided to spend three months in Europe. This momentous occasion would also be the event of my first ever aeroplane flight. Yes, at the age of not quite forty-four years, I was flying for the very first time—and what an experience that would turn out to be. A unique experience to say the least!

Our respective spouses farewelled us at the Brisbane airport and we were on our way to Singapore. Spending a few days there seemed to be a good idea as the overall trip was very long and there was a lengthy stopover in Singapore anyway. Our three days there were taken up mainly with shopping expeditions, because back then in that emerging economy, prices were very competitive, and we were intrigued with the continual haggling that seemed to be a way of life in Chinatown. Walking along the side streets at night posed no danger, in fact we felt very safe even walking around at midnight and looking into the open homes of old people smoking some suspect pipes on their porches. Goodness, how things have changed now. None of those places are still standing in the new Singapore of today.

That first leg of our journey was uneventful. Our next stop was Ceylon, now known as Sri Lanka, and looking down as we were approaching the airport I noticed on the ground there appeared to be some commotion, some frantic activity that aroused a vague suspicion in my mind that perhaps something was wrong. We were flying very low and there were numerous vehicles in continual motion on the tarmac. Suddenly it seemed we were lifting rapidly again and circling for another landing, but no, we flew past the runway, we were being turned away and redirected to an area away from the main airport. After what seemed like ages, we came to a standstill in a rough and rutted section on the outskirt of the runways and several buses were approaching the plane. We were quickly loaded on board and whisked away. No one seemed to know why we had taxied to a stop so far away from the terminal but as we neared the area where I had witnessed all that frantic activity from up in the sky earlier, I noticed that the buses were driving through what appeared to be some sort of sewage slush and a reddish goo on the uneven ground, and they were hastily swerving around a lot of debris. The stench was unbearable in the heat and humidity of this near equator island country.

Everything was happening very quickly and when we reached the rear of the terminal, we were hastily ushered through the back doors and made to sit on benches where troops in full combat regalia and armed with automatic weapons inspected each one of us as we entered. By now we all knew we were somehow involved in an incident of major proportions. We were all very thirsty. There was no air conditioning and the nauseating stench was overpowering.

We were forbidden to move from our seats and all were at a loss for an explanation. None of the officials would say anything. For over five hours we sweltered in there, without water, and with only hastily contrived and very basic toileting facilities. Some passengers fainted from the heat, and the few young children were inconsolable, whimpering and fearful. Suddenly another group of officials in uniforms entered the hall and there was some movement in the immigration booths. Finally they were opening the shutters. An announcement declared that we were to approach the counters row by row. Each row had a detail of commandos accompanying individuals, and each person was minutely searched to the ninth degree so that no detail was left to chance. Earlier, during our stopover in Singapore, I had bought a silk blouse that had tiny covered buttons down the front, and much to my consternation, each button was closely examined by one of the security guards holding a detector not unlike a Geiger counter type contraption but this was also able to detect plastic explosives and he passed it all over my chest. Mira, my companion started to complain loudly when it was her turn to undergo such undignified personal treatment.

"Shut up. Do you want to get us both killed?" I whispered. I don't think she fully appreciated the seriousness of the situation we found ourselves in. But the fact that I had cautioned her didn't go unnoticed either, so we received some extra, personalised attention before it was our turn to pass through immigration checks and on to another line of waiting buses that transported us back to another waiting plane for the continuation of our journey. It was only later that we learnt of the very recent carnage on the tarmac. The previous plane to land had been bombed, killing thirty-two passengers and crew on board. The airport services were damaged and there was no water, electricity or sewerage. All things considered, we were extremely lucky to get out of there as quickly as we did, and without further incident.

Apparently there was some political upheaval in the country involving the Tamil Tigers and their ongoing claim for the tea plantations in the Highlands and that was, I believe, at the root of their conflict. In the light of the current global upheavals, terrorist attacks and counter attacks, territorial skirmishes and bombardments, it is worth noting that even so many years back in 1984 all those combat troops were strictly regimented and prepared to kill on instinct. In that instance, all were immaculately groomed, exceptionally good-looking young men and women, aged probably between eighteen and twenty-five years, and not one of them would have had a moment's hesitation in firing their automatic assault rifles at the slightest provocation. One could see on their set features there was no hint of emotion or humanity. These young and extremely disciplined soldiers looked without exception, as though their features were sculpted in marble, with life having very little meaning for any of them, and that included their own lives.

For me, I can look back on my first aeroplane flight as an astonishing event with unexpected, bizarre, even surreal encounters with another life. No more excitement for the rest of the flight to Germany, only some more delays with our luggage, and the difficulty of getting around one of the biggest airports in the world without being able to speak the language.

At Frankfurt airport, Mira and I parted company for a while. She was to go with her friends and relations, and we would join up again at a later stage.

A Shocking Reunion

I was met by the now grown-up daughter of my long-lost primary school friend, Tonia. Ruth, like her mother, was very adept at wrapping boyfriends around her little finger, and had managed to persuade one of them to drive down from the northern part of Germany to come and pick up a stranger from a busy airport. They waited and waited for over two hours after the expected arrival of our plane and then as a last resort they asked the staff to page me. I have no idea how I managed to hear, or understand my name over the loudspeakers and I don't know how many times they tried.

We travelled for several hours to a little place south of Hanover, which consisted of maybe half a dozen houses, and a fairly large sandstone block building that turned out to be the flourmill owned by Tonia and her husband. To me, it seemed in a pretty dilapidated state like the ones you see travelling around remote areas of Europe even now. Instead, as it turned out, it was a bustling ongoing and noisy concern, with machines grinding grain into flour, some others separating different grains, several machines bagging flour, grain, stock feed, pellets and other legumes. Vans were coming in, loading up and going away continually.

In another semi-detached building there was a residence from where the noises of grunting pigs could be heard, especially when someone opened the wide doors to emerge from there. When a young dark boy, who seemed to speak some English, came out, I asked about the noise and found that there was an attic the full length of the building that was used for the winter storage of fodder, and now there was also a sow that had just given birth to sixteen piglets.

To put this period into some perspective, this was before the Berlin Wall was taken down, and there was a lot of illegal migration between East and West Germany, as well as a lot of smuggling of food and provisions over the eastern border. People will do whatever is necessary to survive the harshness of the system they were obliged to live under.

The boy was living in the residence beneath the piggery with his father and two older brothers; they were asylum seekers from Albania and were working in the mill. Helping out would probably be a better legal description as they were given a roof over their heads and minimal pay. They were escapees from a country under the rule of the USSR, where many citizens were still being persecuted. Of course they were staying there illegally, working for cash, and lodgings until they found a country that would accept them, or until they would be denounced and deported back to whatever fate awaited them. Many of these people were in continual flight, going from one small village to another, and surviving from day to day doing whatever work they could find. Generally the locals were helpful and understanding and these illegal itinerants provided them with a cheap source of labour.

I spent a week with Tonia in total disbelief. How could a beautiful girl, who loved the gay life, the parties and the dancing, who had boyfriends by the dozen, was used to having music blaring all day long, a girl that went to the movies almost daily, an only child and the apple of her parents' eye, end up in an isolated, run down, medieval place like this?

I learnt that in winter when it rained or when the snows melted, the water in the river rose, and if it rose too high, it would flood the mill that was adjacent. The walls of the mill, built to hold these waters at whatever level they rose to, were always damp and covered with moss. The dampness permeated not only through the mill itself, making it smell of mildew, but it also rose to the main family residence above, where mould stained the walls and that sweetish sour odour of decay seemed to be everywhere. When the river was running fast carrying along an assortment of debris, logs, trees, dead animals, etc., the floodgates had to be opened to allow the water through, but the debris had to be fished out somehow first or it would lodge somewhere downstream and result in a fine from the local council. There was an old bridge spanning the river not far from the new road bridge recently built. This original bridge was made of great timber beams that Tonia's husband and son were continually patching up and bracing because though old, this bridge was needed to house the mechanism for the floodgates. During that first week I was there, I had seen with my own eyes the life my friend had been living for the past dozen or so years. Had I not seen it, I would never have believed it.

While I was staying there, one night the wind was blowing and rain was forecast. Husband and son were making a delivery to East Germany and were not expected back that day. The daughter Ruth was staying away with the boyfriend and in my opinion would have been useless there anyway, as I couldn't see her lifting a hand to help. In the meantime the forecast bad weather was approaching. The dark clouds rolled and rumbled, and lightning lit the sky but the threatened rain didn't come until 2 a.m. Another surprise was the intensity of the rain when it did come and how quickly it turned cold up here even in the summer months. I shuddered to think of the bleak and desolate landscape during the longer winter months in this northern part of Germany. There was no point in undressing for bed that night as I realised that Tonia would have to go out on that old and slippery bridge to work the floodgates by the light of a powerful hand held torch. I could not believe how antiquated everything was. There didn't appear to be any shortage of cash, so why didn't they improve their asset? It was another sixteen years before I got my answer.

The end of the week was approaching and as I prepared to leave that astonishing place with mixed feelings of sorrow, regret, pity, and love for the friend I had cherished throughout my youth, I asked myself, *What could I do? How could I leave her like this?*

In response to her pleadings for me to stay on, in the end I agreed to return before the end of my three months in Europe. But then a thought came to me, wouldn't it be nice if she could come away with me for a while. She had never had a holiday since leaving Australia and the only break from the mill was when she was rushed to hospital with a burst blood vessel to her head. After she was operated on and left hospital, she had some therapy sessions at a spa resort for a couple of weeks before returning to the grindstone.

I knew that if I left now without getting an agreement from her husband she would never leave, no matter how much she may have wanted to come away with me, so the next day I asked if I could go with him on a delivery on the pretext that I wanted to see the countryside. We left early in the morning and covered several precincts, dropping off goods in a variety of markets, Lebanese restaurants, farms, and camps, and the last drop off was at what looked like an elite Country Club, surrounded with well-kept parklands and a two-story mansion. That day I was introduced to the human trade.

A very distinguished and perfectly groomed middle age 'gentleman' greeted us at the security gate of an estate that had several well-kept buildings, a horse stable, and a state of the art manor. The 'gentleman' was a learned Pastor who was well known in the area and who was held in high esteem by my friend Tonia. Now her husband was conversing with the staff and doing the business that brought him here while I wandered along to the stables hoping to see some horses. What I saw and heard will forever remain with me, though I could never bring myself to mention anything to Tonia. I simply could not bring myself to shatter her faith in humanity! A group of men were drinking, laughing, and making merry in the horse stables nearest to me with a group of young girls in various stages of undress. The ages of these young girls would probably be somewhere between nine or ten years, to the eldest, who could have been any age from thirteen to sixteen years.

It was the eldest looking one who was closest to me, so my impression of her was, and still is, quite clear. As she looked up I saw that her eyes were glazed, with dilated pupils and sunk into their dark sockets, she had a pathetic, lost look about her. Her wrists and ankles had purple raised bruises, and her lips were swollen and garishly painted. I immediately thought of bondage, though I wasn't quite sure exactly what the term meant back then. Her blonde hair was lifeless and the skin looked like blemished parchment. It was so obvious that this young teenage girl had been put through the wringer, and sexually abused over an extended period of time and she appeared to be, even then, heavily drugged to keep her submissive and dependent. To me she looked like a walking ghost with sunken cheeks. What would be the fate of her younger companions? How long had they been there, where had they come from, and how many would survive to reach adulthood? All these thoughts flashed through my mind with the sharpness of lightning in just the few minutes that I stood there gazing inside the stables.

Shocked, I turned to walk away but my path was blocked by the 'distinguished gentleman' who turned on the charm and, smiling, invited me to share a drink with him. I shook my head and said, "No, but thank you."

"Wouldn't you like to see the house?" he then asked.

Again, an emphatic, "No," came from me.

"I would like to give you a present, because you are a friend of the family." Obviously this present would have to be drugs!

It was all I could do to stop my shaking legs from folding under me as I shook my head. He then pulled out 200 Euros and took my hand, wanting to put the money in it. It was a lot of money in 1984. In disgust, I pulled my hand away and just as things were starting to get ugly and out of hand with his facial muscles tensing and flushing threateningly, thankfully my host approached and I could turn my back on the 'Pastor', and shakily walk away, hoping that my legs would carry me as far as the van, without giving way under me. I could feel his gaze boring through me as I retreated to the van. It was a very quiet trip back home. I left the next day but not before I extracted a promise from my host that he would allow Tonia to come away with me for a week in Italy. I have no doubt that if I had mentioned anything to her about what I had seen and heard she would not have been going anywhere with me.

So this was silent bribery, and the unspoken words were, *She can go if you shut up*. I am under no illusion that he is an innocent bystander and my guess is that the Pastor had already been on the telephone to him to make enquiries and, perhaps, threats.

I had to ask their son, who had grown into a lovely young man, to take me to the station and promised him that I would be coming back soon and take his mother away with me for a long overdue holiday. The look I got from him could have meant two things: either he didn't believe I would come back, or he didn't believe his father would let his mother go away with me. I can't explain why but it was a look that worried me and I vowed to come back as soon as I could.

On the train I tried to concentrate on the scenery but my mind kept going back to those young girls in captivity. I had read somewhere that bands of gypsies roamed around Eastern Europe and kidnapped little girls, and sometime boys, to sell them on the open market in another country for the sex trade. Was that what I had stumbled on? Was there anything I could do about it? 'No', screamed common sense! Anything I did would only cause more pain, perhaps death. These gangs had been operating for centuries and it was a well enough known phenomenon to be written up about, so the authorities were well aware of their existence. These gangs were too well organised and as is the case in all big criminal organisations, they had people of influence to cover for them. Ergo, the Pastor! Who knew who his clients were? Police? Politicians? Drug Bosses? Extortionists? Once again it was the young and innocent who were being preyed upon by those who have no respect for life. That was corruption at its lowest level.

Revisiting The Past

A few months prior to our departure, I had asked Mother to write to all those relations that we thought I should visit. Of course, given the opportunity, I would like to catch up with all of them (not that there were many left) but that may not be possible, so she wrote to her only remaining sibling, her sister, because she was a definite person on my list to visit.

So once in Italy my first stop was to visit my youngest, and at that point, only surviving aunt. As a special surprise, Aunt Anna and her husband Nino planned a trip to Istria where they would take me back in time to show me the places where their generation had lived, and where I was born in the Italian countryside of the pre-war era.

It was a lovely summer's morning when we arrived by bus from Trieste. The trip was pleasant enough but not memorable. However, the quaint medieval township of Rovigno was a veritable gem. We spent several days in this ancient province where both my mother and my aunt were born, and even now after so many generations, we could feel a certain positive energy engage our psyche and draw us closer together.

I discovered that a number of Italians were able to return to their old properties by special dispensation. I thought to myself, *did they have to become communists to get that dispensation*? But the day was perfect and I didn't want to spoil it by asking the question.

Wandering arm in arm through the narrow streets (if one could call them streets. More like lanes or alleys), I became familiar with Mother's school, the church of *Sant'Eufemia*, the three story house where they were both born, the town piazza with the imposing square clock tower, and then we walked along the waterfront where now, in the late afternoon sun, hundreds of small fishing boats were coming in to tie up along the half a dozen or more piers for the night.

Such a good natured hive of activity, with the fishermen's families and children skipping along, laughing and singing, all coming to the waterside promenade to help with the cleaning and unloading of the day's catch.

As the sun went down and all that activity slowed and quietened, the lamplights came on to illuminate the promenade that was now buzzing with flying insects and fireflies. Their iridescent flashes of vivid colour complemented the stars above as they whizzed past, hovering in the lamplight all around the heads of young and old couples, walking with their arms around each other whispering, or humming some catchy tune in the soft breezes of the evening. Their shadows lengthening, thinning, before they are again caught up by the next lamplight. This was the calm serenity of the evening after a hot busy day, in the still early evening before the last meal of the day and the last drink for the night.

And then for us the magic of the night was seriously tested by our increasing hunger. The hunger won outright!

All that fresh fish made us think of barbequed whole trout cooked with nothing more than green virgin olive oil, fresh young parsley, and chopped garlic accompanied with young boiled potatoes and a green rocket salad mixed with tomatoes. My aunt immediately said that she knew just the place where we would be served such a meal to remember. The sprightly sixty year old had just retired after working all her adult life in the tobacco factory at the end of the town precinct of this picturesque medieval township, just before and in front of the boundary of Polaris, their old family farm that was confiscated by the Communists in the late 40's. She still smoked like a chimney!

We left the waterfront and headed toward the lively piazza where in a corner a group of locals were already enjoying their *'pasto di sera'* (evening meal), amid much clinking of glasses and good-humoured laughter. Pity, all the outdoor tables were occupied, so we entered a room with an eastern ambience, soft music, and incense exuded an exotic air. The silk, velvet, and gold-threaded cushions on low benches looked lavish and very inviting to our tired feet. We were ready for a sumptuous dinner too, after our long day.

When it arrived, we were not disappointed.

The fairly large fish came with all the side dishes we had ordered, and the presentation was as good as the meal. Nino ordered some light white wine that we sipped with much pleasure—and in abundance. It was so easy on the palate! There comes a time when one surreptitiously looks around for the 'his' and 'hers' sign on the wall, when the bladder also asks for attention. Not seeing anything that could pass for an amenities block, a passage or cubicle, I was obliged to ask the waitress who happily waves me in the direction of a wall covered in a dark red velvet drape. Blankly, I look at her, then at my aunt who nods and smiles too.

Now really mystified, I have to ask exactly where the toilets are. "Just go through the red curtains." I walked hesitantly to the curtains, obviously one must go through them. My hand parted the curtains. And oh, no! What I was confronted with was a whole row of holes in the floor. In horror, I stood there looking at these holes when a male with a long white robe came in next to me, went to one of the holes and squatted down. Gagging, I turned back and fled, not to the table where the others were waiting for me, but straight out the door. How could such a beautiful evening end like this? It was all I could do to hold the fish down in my stomach. It really was too nice a meal to bring it up. As I mentioned earlier, this particular area of eastern Italy has been influenced by the Turkish invasions of previous centuries and because it is so close to the Balkans, many of the old buildings both in town and in the country still had the very primitive facilities that I now encountered. Relieving oneself just so, in the Arab countries, is a matter-of-fact daily act. This person was going about his normal business but I would not give an ignorant Arab the satisfaction of seeing me throw up in this backward neighbourhood, so looking around in the starlit night, I forced myself to listen to the buskers in the piazza and wait for the others to join me.

Nothing was said about my shocked reaction. We wondered around for a while but the evening was ruined for me, and eventually we started to walk towards the private house, with modern toilet where we would be staying that night.

Breakfast the next morning was the typical continental fare, milk coffee, homemade bread with fresh cream and jam—as much as we wanted in quantity, but not much variety. The weather was very predictable in the region at that time of the year, with glorious mornings and brilliant afternoons, and we didn't have to hurry to catch our bus south, it wouldn't take too long to get there.

I didn't show much enthusiasm when it was decided to visit my place of birth because I really didn't have any good memories, but I did feel grateful that Anna and Nino were trying hard to make my visit memorable after such a long time away, so we ambled along to the bus stop carrying supplies for the day and in no time my aunt was pointing out sights that obviously meant more to her than to me. We followed the coastline for a while as the sun rose higher in the azure sky. The sea sparkled and danced against the white rocks and so close to the water, lots of stunted trees could be seen growing in terrain so rocky and with so little soil that I thought they could never bear fruit. I could not tell what species they were—figs, olives, lemons, pomegranates, cumquats, and prickly pears which were a local delicacy I was told, and soon we got to our destination.

We wandered along the Marina for a while, admiring the new sights of the rebuilt city that was no longer Italian. The new modern buildings left no trace of the atrocities that were committed there. Nevertheless, an uneasy feeling was settling on my chest, a feeling that I was unable to put into words. We circled the repaired amphitheatre. The Coliseum had been reconstructed and stood proud, and was almost as impressive as the one in Rome now, though in size it was more like the Arena of Verona, but this one was in much, much better condition as it had been reconstructed.

Along the Italian countryside, the scars of war were still evident in places where whole towns had been abandoned. People still shake their head in perplexity. After the leisurely walk along the water's edge, and the smell of the salty sea breeze, we now were beginning to feel some hunger pangs and in a beautifully landscaped and well-maintained park, we spread a rug under an apple tree in full bloom. Such a peaceful setting!

Aunt Anna opened her picnic basket, full of freshly baked Panini and mouth-watering fillings, several types of cheeses and olives to complement the firm, ripe tomatoes. Funny about country grown tomatoes! They have a taste that is hard to describe, they are more like a succulent fruit! We feasted on the thinly sliced prosciutto and washed it down with the slightly sweet local Prosecco.

Sated, Anna and Nino, her husband of only a few years, stretched out on the cool grass for an afternoon nap. The war had stood in the way of their marriage when they were young, but he was the father of their two adult children.

Why don't I do the same, they asked. That was when I voiced my concern, my uneasy feelings about the hill in the park. It was like an evil presence that hovered above my head like a dark, menacing, rumbling cloud. I told them that during the early 40's, the hill was a honeycomb of rock tunnels where citizens sheltered during the frequent bombing raids. Immediately they sat up as if I had personally insulted them,

"Impossible. It's just a beautiful park!"

"How can you say something like that?"

"What would you know?"

"How can you know?"

I let it go, and they calmed down, convinced that they had pacified me enough. Contentedly they lay back for their nap.

It wasn't long before that nagging feeling resurfaced and, unable to settle down, I stood and proceeded to circumnavigate this mysterious hill. Almost halfway around and the terrain changed, to predominantly rocks—big ones!

Still a beautiful park, but now I could see in the distance massive, black iron gates set into the hill. As I approached, my uneasiness got the better of me and I hesitated. But why? By now I was only a few meters away from the scarred hill face and the gates were not far beyond. *May as well go the whole way*, I thought to myself. What have I got to lose? It will either confirm, or disprove my theory. Either way, knowing is better than forever wondering. Confronted with this mammoth iron structure, I looked in awe at the gigantic, heavy locks and hinges. What type of machinery would be required to swing these gates open? The closer I got to this huge black hole in the hill face, the more certain I became that here, inside, I had spent many long hours, together with many other unfortunates. And then it dawned on me that I was one of the more fortunate ones. I had survived. How many had perished? I wondered if there was a roll of all those residents and ambulants who had used the shelter; and would our name be forever engraved there?

As I slowly made my way back, so shaken by the deeply buried memories of the years that had flooded back, I almost bumped into my aunt and Nino. They had gathered all belongings and were worriedly making their way back to the bus station, and wondering where I had disappeared. Here I was at the age of forty-four being chastised by my aunt for wandering away from them, without saying where I was going. Fair comment.

The bus trip back to Trieste was very quiet, with me deep in thought, and the two sitting next to me, sulking. From Trieste, my plan was to catch up with all remaining relations, my cousins and their children, and then travel back across Germany to the north to keep my promise to take my long lost friend from primary school on a holiday. But she had to wait a little longer. She knew from past experience that I would keep my word.

From Croatia to Italy

Mira wanted to spend some time with her elderly parents, but also wanted to see parts of Europe that were totally unknown to her, so we decided that I would go to the country town of her birth, spend some time there with her, then together we would travel through Croatia to visit parts that were unknown to me—and that was most of the country.

We visited some coastal areas and took buses to ancient historic towns like Sibernik and Split on the coast and then, because the area was so pretty, we decided to go a little bit further down the coast to a fishing village where the residents live by renting out rooms to tourists in the holiday season and cooking their daily catch for them at dinner time. There is nothing as mouth-watering as a freshly caught fish or lobster sizzling on the grill, and a fresh salad. In such an idyllic setting we passed the time of day swimming and sunbaking, eating, gathering flowers, strolling through the local markets and admiring the delicate handmade shell ornaments and leather ware. Daintily painted ceramic plates, vases and jugs told stories from the past, of the lives and loves; of the regions and the seasons, to strollers who took the time to look, listen and talk to the elderly locals. They were the ones who passed on the history in pictures.

We proceeded as far as Dubrovnik. Life seemed so simple then, but only a few years later, yet another war broke out in that zone. A civil war that involved another land grab and two young nephews of Mira who lived with their parents near Split were sucked into the fighting force. We had travelled by bus back along the coast to areas recently excavated to expose buried cities from the times of the Ottoman Empire now long gone, and it was one of the many we would see during our trip of discovery. Over the centuries cities were abandoned for a number of reasons, devastations from wars, seismic or alluvial movements, larger trade and commerce centres elsewhere; so over time these cities were covered up by the winds, and rains bringing soil down from higher ground.

Soon we needed to move on to Italy. We arrived at the port and booked an overnight boat trip across the Adriatic Sea starting at Zadar and disembarking in Ancona. Once again the plan was to spend some time in Italy visiting some of my relations and taking in some popular tourist attractions along the way. Our itinerary had to remain flexible enough for us to take in places of interest along the route that we needed to follow. With our Eurail Pass, we boarded a train in the morning that was headed for Napoli at the other end in the west, where we disembarked at the busy platform below street level. No point in asking anyone for directions, the Napolitani speak a language all their own, at least the written signs must have directions of national standard and the overhead boards had all the information we needed to get us to Pompeii.

Not that Mira was particularly interested in mountains of rocks and half buried ruins from the Roman era, but I wanted to see *'Gli Scavi Archeologici'* that I had read so much about. We arrived pretty early before the multitudes got there, which was just as well because it got very hot quite quickly and by the time we made it to the end of the viewing paths, we were both sweating in the sun. On the return path on the other side of the unique main street, we learnt that the double furrows in the centre had two purposes. These grooves were the exact distance apart from each other to allow the wheels of the Chariots to run smoothly inside them, and also in times of heavy rains they served as drains. Near the well were the preserved and still vividly tiled public baths. We were both overwhelmed to see the casts that have been made of corpses of the victims of that epic Vesuvian eruption in the year 79 AD that were buried under six meters of ashes not only Pompeii and its residents, but other Vesuvian towns in Campania.

"Okay, let's go to Sorrento, that's near the water and will be a lot cooler," I said, finally realising that she really had enough of these archaeological treasures for one day. It was a mistake to stop for lunch in such a popular tourist area, but at the time we knew no better. Of course the restaurant was crowded, and when eventually a place became available for us the male waiters were truly obnoxious and insulting, in particular towards Mira, knowing full well that she couldn't understand what they were saying. Of course that made me angry and I threatened to walk out and report their rude behaviour to their employers, after all it was the tourists, people like us, who were paying their wages. When I blew my top, they realised that I had understood and they became most apologetic but the damage was done. We remained for the lunch and we did pay—but no tip from us! Somehow the day was spoilt.

The waterfront in Sorrento was pleasant and cool in the mid afternoon. The pyramid shape of the Isola di Capri in the distance made a lovely backdrop for the boats, ferries, and pleasure crafts dotting the marina in the sparkling, sunlit bay. It was truly postcard scenery, so much so in fact that Mira enthusiastically took out her camera and while we were contemplating taking the ferry over to the island, she started taking photographs.

"Take one of me with the island in the background and the ferry behind me," she said, giving me the camera and posing. Without thinking, I took the camera and started to focus, moving to get the light and angle just right.

"Perfect, it should come out well," I said, just as the signal for the ferry's departure blared in our ears! No way could we make it in time to catch the ferry now. A bit disgruntled, we made our way back to the city centre browsing in the shops on our way to the station for our return trip to Napoli and to the hotel where we had left our luggage. Hopefully, we would find it intact.

No one likes one-nighters, and in Napoli they don't like to change the sheets for them either. I was suspicious when we came to the hotel. We not only asked to see the room but checked the sheets too. True to form there were hairs between the sheets and we had to ask management to change them, and in spite of his arguments, we stood our ground until he did.

For anyone visiting Pompeii now, my suggestion would be to base yourself in Sorrento, take some time to explore that enchanting area, enjoy the cuisine, and spend much more time in the leisurely study of an old, rich, and colourful culture in what is now a much more extensive section of the exposed plains of Pompeii.

From one place so rich in history, to another—Rome. Again, one night in Rome only whets the appetite for more.

Another cousin, now deceased, lived in one of the major arterial roads only a tram stop from *'Il Quartiere Barocco di Roma'*. At the time the older parts of *'La Roma Antica'* were not as well restored as nowadays, and even the Coliseum was only partly open. Most of that gigantic open-air stadium was encased in scaffolding and under restoration. Just a quick car ride around this colossal structure and one feels dizzy at its awesome proportions.

Gazing in awe at the numerous statues of all the popular deities of that day, we marvelled at the minute details sculptured in the candid marble. We were surprised to see so many in their various state of preservation and in awe that they are still standing today. All the wonders that we glimpsed during those two days were the seeds that germinated into a huge hunger in me to want to discover more. To travel back there sometime in the not too distant future!

Right now we had the idea of making our way north and just stopping for a while wherever we felt good vibes in some town along the way, and eventually parting at Trieste from where Mira would return to her family's residence and I would return to that northern township near Hanover where I had promised to Tonia that we would take a week to travel around parts of Italy together.

Garda – German or Italian?

When the train arrived in that northern village in Germany, the memories of my recent visit there troubled me and I made it clear that I didn't want to stay longer than a couple of days. Immediately there were objections from the Lord of the Mill but I stood my ground and reminded him of his promise. In the meantime Tonia was doing her bit to make sure that we would be ready early in the morning to be picked up by car and driven as far as the lakeside town of Riva del Garda in northern Italy. A busy and picturesque place perched on the northern shores of Lake Garda, which is a favourite holiday destination for many Germans. I didn't realise that she was paying her daughter's boyfriend to drive us, but it certainly was the quickest way to get there and a cheap way for them to have a holiday as well, in an area they would not have otherwise visited. Once they dropped us off in the middle of the action, the young ones immediately took off to do their own thing, while we wandered around to get the 'feel' for this northern part of the country that I had left behind more than thirty years earlier.

This area, so close to the Dolomites, seemed like a different country altogether, with the mountain peaks still glistening with compacted snow. It was unfamiliar and strange to me until I realised that it borders on to the Tyrol, with Austria and Germany as close neighbours. Understandably, if there is such an attractive, sheltered place so nearby, the people from neighbouring countries would flock around to take advantage of all the amenities the area had to offer. We could see them now, whole families, numerous as ants in their summer dresses, short shorts and colourful, brief bikinis enjoying this relaxed summer lifestyle. We were quite surprised to find that both the Italian and the German languages were spoken by the majority of shopkeepers and their clients, with many switching from one language to the other ever so effortlessly. The beaches and the streets had that carefree atmosphere of a holiday paradise and we were there at the height of the season. There were buskers with the fancy costumes of their regions and among them we found pretty, melodious, young singers. Little children in multi-coloured angel tulle and fluffy white, or gold and silver fairy wings were dancing, performing and reciting catchy poems. Cheeky magicians would come and pull a rabbit out of your bag, or a pack of cards from a bemused spectator's broad breamed sun hat to the amazement and laughter of those nearby. Harmless fun, without any malice, that enticed the multitudes to reach deep into their pockets and toss a coin or a note to those who made them laugh and forget their daily cares.

As the afternoon siesta ended, more and more beach umbrellas went up on the grassed parklands and by the edge of the water and we had to be careful not to walk in the path of a ball thrown by small and not so small players, or be run over or knocked down by bike riders who seemed to have all the rights in the world, all over the world.

To be able to walk along the water's edge, we had to buy a pair of Crocs for about ten times the price of what I could buy them in Australia, but there was no other way to negotiate the rocks on the 'beach'. When I talk about a beach, blue water and golden sand as far as the eye can see comes to mind and I assume that everyone thinks the same way—not so! Everyone here wears shoes to the beach! We did not have swimmers, so we had to be content with walking and watching the multitudes, with their assortment of bright plastic water toys having all the fun in the world in their once a year holiday experience.

It made me realise just how lucky we Australians are to still be able to find stretches of deserted beaches with clean sand, relatively close to major cities.

Finding accommodation here at this time of the year was going to be a challenge. The Reisen Bureau right in the middle of town had long queues of young people looking for the same thing—a bed for the night. So we kept our eyes open for any private notices where we saw home—owners advertising any vacancies on their letterboxes or gates. Soon we were able to find a room to share in one of the side streets, which was close enough to the Central District yet far enough from all the merry-making to be able to sleep at night (hopefully!).

The landlords were able to communicate with Tonia and we were both happy to take their suggestion for dinner 'al fresco'. We ate well and we slept well. Much refreshed and eager to continue on our next page of discovery, we took the bus to nearby Verona, stopping at Lasize for lunch and another walk around a very big, well-maintained Medieval Castle surrounded by massive rock walls. The huge courtyard had crowds gathered in front of just about every boutique featuring handmade shoes and bags of the highest quality and style (and price) that could be squeezed in the renovated rooms and restored halls of this popular lakeside resort that was also home to Harley Davidson devotees. We discovered that there are Castles in abundance in this region, most of them abandoned for lack of funds for their maintenance, but Lasize obviously had found many patrons.

Tosca at the 'Arena Di Verona'

The next letter Mother had written was to the cousin I had spent so much time with, when we were both in the care of our grandmother. He was the son of Father's twin brother whose family was also scattered around during the war. I figured he would remember me as we managed to get into so much mischief when Grandma wasn't looking. I felt confident he would remember the moonlit nights when we would climb out of the upstairs window on to the roof where the overhanging branches of the huge loquat tree, laden with ripe juicy fruit would supplement our meagre wartime diet. And the time on the beach when I cracked his skull with a rock in my anger, when he wouldn't give me the pail to make sandcastles—perhaps that is something I shouldn't remind him of, but I always felt guilty about that episode and Grandmother made such a big issue of it at the time!

It must have come as a bit of a shock to him, when one day out of the blue my cousin picked up the phone and on the other end of the line heard a stranger, with a strong foreign accent, who said "*Ciao*, I have just arrived from Australia. I am your cousin and I would like to meet with you and your family."

I could almost feel him swallowing a couple of times with surprise, but then he recovered and asked the obvious question, "*Dove sei?*" (Where are you?)

Good question, I had no idea where I was in relation to where he was, so I rattled off an address which he must have been familiar with, because we made a time for him to pick me up from there. What I neglected to say on the phone was that I had a friend with me. I thought I would explain that when we met. What he neglected to say was that our younger cousin, of whom I knew very little as I had never met him, had just married that morning at the Registry, and he and his new (second) wife were visiting their home. This must be what is called a 'Comedy of Errors'.

The two brothers came in a little Fiat Cinquecento. They alighted, and left the car on the footpath as Italians do and then they found themselves confronted with two dark haired, still pretty good looking, and fit females that they have never met before, at least not in their living memory. They knew one was a cousin because I had just recently called to say so. But which is the one? In confusion, the one I spoke to approaches my friend, because she is the one with the darker hair and looks more Italian than I do. We all laughed. But from there, I stumble and mumble in an effort to explain that after an absence of more than thirty years from my native land, my mother tongue had almost deserted me. I had not spoken Italian for so many years that when I had to use it now, I was really struggling to understand and make myself understood. But somehow we managed.

The four of us spent a wonderful afternoon together walking along the Ponte Garibaldi that had been almost totally destroyed by the Allied bombs in the 1940's. I think it used to be called Ponte Vecchio back then, and the Historic Centre. The Piazza delle Erbe, where banquets are sometimes held for special events, the well preserved and much photographed Musuleum dei Scaligeri, that are the sarcophagi of the aristocratic Scala family of Verona, and marvelled at the partially reconstructed Arena di Verona, where in the summer the annual Opera Festival is held, and that night the annual performance of Tosca was being presented. Remembering a time long gone, as a child, when I was bewitched by the spectacle of 'Immortal Aida', seen with my mother alone so very many years ago, where the dramas and pathos of life and death unfolded so sensually on the stage, and on the steps that I had in front of me right now, from this very same Coliseum. These nostalgic memories of the music and the artists so immersed in their role, reawakened a strong feeling of belonging that I immediately said to my cousins "I must see Tosca tonight. I must recapture that sublime, ethereal atmosphere of the live Opera".

We looked up at the sky that had been so clear all day and wondered, should we take a chance that the few drops of rain that were now lightly peppering the pavement would not get any worse as the evening progressed? What the heck! We mightn't be able to get any tickets anyway, but let's try.

The Arena is huge and seats an incredible number of people (some 25,000) but the Summer Opera Season attracts bus load after bus load of dedicated theatre goers from all over Europe and beyond. Tickets are pre-booked by Tour Companies from one year to the next so we didn't feel too optimistic of our chances of finding a spot. However, there are always a small number of seats that are kept in reserve for the last minute local release and about half hour before the starting time, we were able to obtain two tickets in a reasonable spot, and for a fairly reasonable price too!

The heavens favoured us as well because looking up at the sky again there was a full complement of constellations shining down on us. We thanked my cousins for being so helpful and accommodating, and they left us under the arches at one the entrances to the Arena to return to their wives who probably, and understandably, would be fuming by now. Putting myself in the situation of a newly wedded bride, be it for the second time, I certainly would not be listening or taking any excuses lightly if my new husband wandered off all day in the company of two other women that I didn't know from a bar of soap!

On the morrow, being Monday and a working day for my cousins, we had the day to ourselves, but in the evening we would be treated to yet another spectacle—a birds' eye view of Verona from the hill on via Ippolito, where the beautiful gardens of the '*Catedrale di San Giorgio*' looks down on the enchanted city of lights, of history and culture unrivalled. I nudged Tonia in the ribs, what a treat it would be to munch on a Pizza Margherita while sitting at dusk on the stone walls of the gardens, overlooking a drop of more than a hundred meters. Verona, viewed across the Adige River, the Ponte Garibaldi, Ponte Pietra and the fountain in the Piazza delle Erbe. But tonight 'Tosca' was a treat for me, and a new experience for her. Tonia had never been to an Opera, or the live theatre as she had never been interested in classical culture, so this was going to be totally new for her, and to make it a bit more meaningful, I explained some simple aspects of the Ancient Roman civilization, and the kind of entertainment that was popular at the time and how the theatre evolved. The music of now famous composers who lived a hundred or more years earlier like Wagner, with whom she was familiar and Mozart, List, Bach, Beethoven—and her face softened into a smile as she remembered another era, that to her now must seem a lifetime ago or in a dream; a time when we danced to the waltzes and tangos, and to the music that she loved so well.

"Do you remember the music of Vivaldi and the Four Seasons?"

"Or Puccini's music in 'Madam Butterfly?'" I asked her this because I knew that the music certainly was well known to her in the past, but apparently the names of the composers meant nothing to her. Softly I hummed some melody that I knew she would recognise and she would be transported back to a past well imprinted in her mind forever. I knew she would never forget the happy, long gone days when we used to dance to the lively music of Bizet's wild gipsy girl, 'Carmen'.

Tonight she would be introduced to another of Puccini's masterpieces—Tosca, but not until the night is dark. On the way in we were given two small party candles, one white, one red, and a card of matches. We weren't sure what to do with them until the overture commenced and all around us people lit their candles. The mind boggles if one thinks of 50,000 lit candles in a confined, though large enough area like an open air stadium. The sight was breath taking, and we looked in awe at the flickering star-lights all around us on the tiered steps that served as seating. The closest that I can describe this scene, is to compare a sight that may come close in similarity. And that would be a very bright glow-worm cave, but even that doesn't do tonight justice. Such an unusual spectacle must be witnessed! We forgot how hard were the rock steps that we were sitting on, as the stage lit up, then, as the candles died, the music seamlessly transported everyone into the *'Castel Sant' Angelo'* in Rome, during the Napoleonic period and the eternal lovers' triangle for another unparalleled music and song experience to be long remembered. We sat on those hard steps cursing our lack of foresight. Why didn't we take the cushions that were offered to us on the way in? Now our bottoms were numb, sore, and cold.

It was 2:30 a.m. when the night ended, which is pretty normal in Italy in the summer, and now the challenge was to find a taxi, but like all others we were still euphoric and not in a rush so we walked along the piazza where bars and cafes were still open with people happily talking, laughing, sipping and socialising under the stars in the balmy night, listening to the wistful sounds of a violin player. A little further on, a church choir was practising in one corner of the Piazza dei Signori. Most of Italy closes for the afternoon siesta and then, re-energised, the cities come alive again at night.

It was such a pleasure to watch the happy crowd, the amicable ambience, and the laughter. I looked around at the hundreds of people from a dozen different countries. Sure, some spoke too loudly, some laughed too loudly, some were obviously intoxicated but all were behaving impeccably while still having a 'jolly good time'.

I could not help thinking how different this was to our home pub scene, where young people feel they have to imbibe huge quantities of alcohol in record time to feel that they 'belong'. I asked myself— where do they want to belong, in their insecurity? The gutter? Many end in there, or in the back of a police car. What is the purpose of dressing up and putting on make-up, and ridiculously high heels, if you lose your dignity and self-respect? I feel so sorry for our young people today, they seem so misguided, lacking focus and integrity. And it worries me that television images of our young revellers are seen world-wide where judgements are made.

So day two in Verona we spent at leisure, until it was time to meet with our escorts again. Because my cousin was an editor and publisher of the Mondadori Books, he knew the northern regions of Italy probably better than most, but my impression was that he had become rather insular. He lived his life through the books he read rather than by live experiences. Nevertheless, we were eternally grateful that he was able to spend so much time with us, and we did meet the family, which consisted of only the wife, a lovely but timid lady, and their teenage only son, on whom they both doted. He later caused them much worry and anxiety by becoming a motorbike speed racer in summer and a champion snow-sledge surfer in winter, traveling down the snow covered peaks of the alpine regions at breakneck speeds.

Venezia, La Serenissima

Having allocated only three days to Verona, it was now time to move on to Venice. Thankfully, we were instructed not to disembark in Mestre, which was the station my family had departed from Italy so many years before and the only one I knew about at that stage. Our impending arrival had been announced to cousin Oliviero, the Mayor of Venice and his wife Anna, and they were gracious enough to meet us at the Santa Lucia Station, which is right in the centre of Venice. Appropriately, I remembered and commented that Lucia was his mother's name, the aunt who had taken me to view that unfortunate Opera, 'Lucia di Lammermoor', in the Arena di Verona in the early post-war period. Both the parents were now deceased and their kindred spirits had departed within four days of each other.

At that stage, I was totally unaware of his status in the city so when we greeted each other in that very public of places I averted an undercurrent of reserve or aloofness that was somewhat disconcerting, but I couldn't figure out why at the time. Both he and his wife were very elegant, unlike us after the train travel, we were somewhat dishevelled and it was a hot, humid day. We were taken on foot to a palatial residence nearby for refreshments, and then he excused himself, as he had to leave for work commitments. Anna was a lovely and gracious lady of class and obvious distinction, and she certainly tried to put us at ease and make us feel comfortable, needless to say, we felt awkward and unprepared for these classic surroundings. As I had no forewarning of where they lived, nor had I any idea of where we would be going, it seemed appropriate now that we had met, to finish our coffee and petit fours, and take our leave to go exploring for the rest of the day.

Thinking about the events of the day later on that evening, I had to congratulate Tonia for her aplomb and grace in handling such an unexpected situation so well. She certainly hadn't forgotten all the airs and graces of her youth even if she hadn't been able to practise them in the interim years!

Venice in August is hot and humid, and not very clean because there are always thousands of tourists at any time of the day or night. While the tourist dollar is always welcome and is probably what keeps Venice afloat, the hordes bring with them unwanted rubbish which one way or another, whether dropped or windblown, ends up in the Canal Grande and the view from 'Ponte di Rialto' is not always pristine.

Best taken in the evening, a romantic Gondola ride along the numerous canals is an exciting experience. We didn't have the time to wait for the evening so decided that now would do as well. The black and while liveried gondoliers, often not so young, but still seeing themselves as the irresistible heart-throbs of an era long gone, will sing the lilting, touching melodies for which they are famous, and sometimes they will stop in front of buildings that may have been the home of an iconic family like the aristocratic Dondolo or '*La Pieta*', the church where Antonio Vivaldi lived and composed some of his most famous works. Most notable, apart from '*La Basilica di San Marco*' is '*Il Palazzo Ducale*' (the Doges Palace) and '*Il Ponte dei Sospiri*' (Bridge of Sighs) that connects the prison across the canal to the Inquisitors' Interrogation Rooms of yet another era. But all this was too much history for my now tired friend Tonia who was, just like me, also upset at the number of empty coke cans that were floating down '*Il Canal Grande*'. It was a truly unforgettable day that was over too soon. Since we had not booked accommodation anywhere in Venice, we felt we should move on to '*Lago di Garda*' but I vowed that before this holiday was over for me, I would be back for a much longer and more in-depth visit, hopefully to reconnect with my first cousin and become better acquainted with his lovely wife. I was hooked on Venice.

Back on the train, the stretch from Santa Lucia to Mestre Stations that spans the sea to the mainland now became more meaningful to us because the trip we had taken on the Vaporetto, and the historic buildings we had visited, put the area into perspective and we could now see and recognise some of these famous buildings and appreciate the landscape better with our expanded knowledge.

Anyone who has visited Venice in the summer will have experienced 'holiday prices'. These can be three times dearer than in the off-season. By now, we were hungry and thirsty but the fare at the station was the typical American fatty fast food and not at all what we had expected, on top it was expensive. We waited until the train got past the tourist route, to where I knew the service would be better and the meals prepared by locals would be more tasty and plentiful. We had already experienced what a tourist paid compared to a local client who knew all the tricks. To break our afternoon thirst earlier, we had stopped at a bar for a beer.

"*Vuoi una fresca?*" (do you want a cool one?) Up goes the price if you say yes. Is there any other way to have a beer? I can't imagine a warm beer in summer.

"*Dentro o fuori?*" (inside or outside?) Up goes the price if you say inside, where it's cooler.

"*Ti siedi o al bar?*" (are you sitting or standing at the bar?) Up goes the price if you choose to sit.

And there is your three times mark-up. Once bitten, twice shy. We had learnt quickly!

Lunch by the Pre-Dolomites

In a pretty village with a welcoming park near the station we got off the train. We checked when the next connection would come by to make sure it would allow us plenty of time for a leisurely local meal at a family-owned restaurant that I knew would have wholesome, reasonably priced food. We were not disappointed, and the jolly chef even packed what was left of our meal for us to take for the overnight train trip to Riva del Garda. Gazing out at the approaching mountains and the beautiful scenery from the windows of the slow moving train, I said to Tonia, "It's no wonder my aunt and her family moved to this lovely area after they sold their house in the industrial city of Trento. I wouldn't mind stopping here for a while, just to say hello to them."

"We can stop if you like, then we can catch the evening train and continue on to Lake Garda. If all trains go as slowly as this one, it will take all night to get there," she commented. I looked at her and got the impression that she was trying to delay her return home by another day. I couldn't blame her! If it had been me, I would never go back.

So we alighted at the next stop. As we went through the gates, I asked the guard if all trains go so slowly through this alpine section. "No. Not usually," he replied. "There was a rock slide overnight just after the last train went through and they are still working on the line to clear it and make it safe. They are also checking for any other fissures that may cause more rocks to break away. All trains in both direction are travelling at much reduced speeds though the entire hillside. We have several crews working non-stop all along this section."

So I asked about the departure time for last train of the day, thinking that we may save on the price of another night's accommodation. We had a reasonably good rest the previous night so why not repeat the exercise?

After I made the phone call to alert her of this unexpected visit, we walked the fairly long stretch to my aunt's flat. We needed to get our leg muscles working again after the longer than usual train trip, and as soon as I rang the bell, she was there at the door welcoming us both for lunch.

I wasn't sure how Tonia would be received because of her background. I remembered that there was much hate between Italians and Germans after the 1943 attempted breakaway by Italy and the incarceration of 'il Duce', Mussolini. There are many versions of how the war affected the country but generally the people felt betrayed and when the Nazis advanced, whole regions revolted resulting in widespread massacres. Knowing that our family was deeply involved without actually understanding the intricacies of the situation, I now was a bit apprehensive.

I need not have worried. We were warmly welcomed and the family albums were brought out after we had finished the generous servings of homemade pasta, with the same meat sauce recipe that Mother makes back at home. Tonia remembered eating the same meal when she visited us when we were just children and her favourable comments were appreciated, only this time the meal was prepared by Nino, with the smiling blue eyes, who apparently did most of the cooking here. It was a pleasant, easy-going afternoon that we spent with them, with me trying valiantly to translate what was said, when I barely understood it myself.

The sun was setting at the end of the long summer day when we took our leave and made our way back to the train station. In the morning, I felt sure Tonia would feel more at ease on the shores of *Lago del Garda*. We had stopped there already earlier in the week when we came south from the Mill. The daughter and her ever-obliging boyfriend had taken a full day to drive us down and it was such a pleasant place to stop for a while to relax and meditate, that we had decided to return.

This time we found that the place was practically over-run by loud German tourists, many more people were wandering around, in and out of shops and restaurants. Walking amongst them we saw that the greatest number of businesses had bilingual services so I assumed that she would be able to converse and not feel as isolated or cut off from dialogue as she had been in our travels during the past week. Lucky for us, we found that the people who had hosted us in the vacant room the previous time, had a cancellation that morning so we were able to stay with them again in the comfort of their home.

For our two remaining days together, we let ourselves really unwind and enjoyed the holiday spirit in this idyllic playground at the foot of '*Le Dolomiti*', swimming, sunning ourselves, walking, shopping, and eating, just like all the other carefree holiday-makers. The days were quickly passing. Too quickly for friends who had not seen each other for so long. This was the second time that we had spent a week together, but only now Tonia had actually relaxed, away from the shackles of the mill and her home life. In the few days that she had been away with me, she had regained some of her composure, she looked better, with more natural colour to her cheeks, laughed more, and was happier, but as the last day approached, we each wondered if we would ever see the other again. We both had tears in our eyes as she boarded the train that took her back to the sow with the sixteen piglets, and the horses they had on agistment, the geese she was fattening for the Christmas dinner with her family, the kitchen garden that provided all their vegetables, the preserving of fruit and berries for the winter months when the swollen river flooded the mill, and nothing grew on the farm with its frozen soil. I must admit that I worried about her and her future, she was coping better than one would expect, but that was no life she was returning to, it was merely an existence!

We waved and waved until the train became just a speck in the distance. I would need to examine my loose itinerary to see if I could use the Eurailpass to meet again before returning to Australia.

Mother's Beloved Younger Sister

From Garda it was only a short trip back to my aunt in Rovereto, the train track had been cleared in both directions and now the trains travelled at their normal speed. I felt an obligation to go back and thank her and Nino for their hospitality toward me and my friend, who was a total stranger to them—an alien from Germany to boot. With Tonia, I had arrived for the day and stayed on for their appetising Tuscan pasta dinner, but now I intended to stay the night and I wasn't going to be put off with their excuses that they only had one bedroom, because by European standards, their home was quite a gem, a new apartment of generous proportions. I figured that if I had spent one and a half days flying time to get there, to meet up with them, then they could throw a blanket on their wide, beautifully sculptured blond leather lounge to accommodate me.

It's funny how one gets that knowing feeling about people immediately upon meeting them! And my feelings about my aunt was that she was used to getting her own way in whatever she wanted. She was the youngest and had a loud voice that she used to cajole, persuade, plead, or threaten, whichever the situation called for. Nino, as my mother had always said, was a treasure who did the cooking, had always looked after their children right up until now, even by helping their daughter, my cousin, who had recently married some flighty and, according to my aunt, unreliable, university lecturer and now they were building a house nearby. As she is currently working in government, it is not appropriate to name my cousin, but in my opinion she has taken after her mum in many of her ways. This time I got my way, and they did make up a bed for me on their lounge where I slept like the proverbial 'baby'. We laughed because they couldn't always understand the message I was trying to convey with my stilted Italian language and I could not help but feel very inadequate. As many emigrants before me, I was embarrassed to have forgotten the mother tongue and I consoled myself with the thought that they didn't speak English. But I made a vow there and then that I would become more proficient in my mother tongue in record time as soon as I got back home to Australia. Actually, I didn't wait even that long to start my own re-education.

We passed the two days in relative harmony until the end when I was going cross-eyed over the millionth photograph of children, grandchildren, and great-grandchildren of friends that I knew nothing about and relations long gone. In desperation, I blurted out, "Isn't it time to let the dead rest in peace?"

As soon as the words were out of my mouth, I bitterly regretted them. I could have bitten my tongue. One could be forgiven for thinking that I had stabbed her in the heart to hear all that wailing and lamenting.

"How could you be so insensitive? You are truly your mother's daughter to leave for a heathen land so far away and desert her own family in their time of need!"

Little did she know, or care about the hell we went through, but this time I didn't say anything!

"You have no feeling of love and respect for all of us that were left behind here." I bit my lip but kept my mouth shut.

That was my first inkling that my mother and her sister had not parted very amicably. And she raved on and on incoherently, until eventually Nino pacified her. What was the point of reminding her that when Mother wrote to her from Australia it was more often than not at least a year before an answer arrived? Or to remind her that Mother and Father had travelled back to visit, with the expected generous gifts for everyone, in 1967. It was the time of the war in the Suez Canal and the ship they were travelling on had to be diverted around Africa and the Cape of Good Hope. What was the point of asking why she had not written to find out if her sister had arrived back home safely? Did she even consider the possibility that her sister may be putting herself in danger by coming to visit her? Passing by a country that was at war?

It was time for me to leave for the third and last time. But I was glad that I had come back, we did have some good times together. There was laughter too and a reconnection. There was quite a lot to report back to Mother, who had never seen her sister's new home, or the new and modern suburbs that had sprung up around the old cities. The latest changes to the old country town where they had grown up and some of the people I had met in Rovigno who knew and remembered Mother fondly from way back. Yes, I was glad of the time we spent together. I could now tell my parents that I did not imagine the horrors we had lived through. They were real enough. But maybe that is something they really don't want to know!

The next time I saw my aunt and Nino was seventeen years later when I introduced my new Hungarian-born husband to them. That started them reminiscing about another era—one that was both before my time and his. An era when the Austro-Hungarian Empire had visions of annexing Italy or at least shrinking its borders!

It was with sadness that we heard of Nino's passing some time later, and much to the despair of his daughter who was very attached and still quite dependent on him. However, she never bothered to notify us, and we only found out via another cousin living in the United States some two years later that the person who was probably the best of that bunch, the one who was more grounded, who could converse and listen with genuine interest without creating too many dramas, the pacifist, the one with the 'smiling blue eyes', had gone to his final resting place.

My new husband and I did visit again quite recently but by then my aunt was in an advanced state of Alzheimer's, and seeing Steve with his attractive, shining white hair, she greeted him with a demonic screech that startled us both.

"Ah, you are my special angel, and you have come to take me away with you at last."

She died the following year.

A Medieval Wonderland

Now there was only one cousin left that I had not yet caught up with, and I wasn't sure how I was going to find my way to her hometown. Not that it was far from Rovereto, in the pre-Dolomites where I was now, but it was in an area called *'Le Vette Feltrine'*.

The town of Feltre in the valley of the Pedavena, lies between a peak in the Dolomites called *'Sass de Mura'*, which loosely translates to 'Wall of Rock', and is 2,550 meters high and the rich and fertile valley of the River Piave in the region of Veneto.

Edda was the eldest of all my cousins. I knew that she was a teacher with two sons (actually I didn't know about the sons at that stage) and she was married to a professor. He lectured at the University of Feltre, in History and The Fine Arts for many years, and that the name of the street where they lived was called *'via Mezzaterra'* (middle of the earth). She was from Father's side of the family and a daughter of *Zia* Lucia (Aunt Lucia, now deceased), in other words a direct descendant of the patrician *'de Costantini'* family. Other than this, at the time I knew no more.

She was already aware that I was in the area after I had visited Verona and Venezia, so when I finally mustered enough courage to make that phone call to her, she was more or less expecting it, and gave me detailed directions to the town of Feltre. That ended up confusing me more than I already was, but after a few false starts and many more kilometres than necessary, I did arrive in the ancient, walled city. If one can imagine stepping back in time several hundred years to a place that still engages in the sport of jousting, this is it! *'Il Paglio'* is held not only in Siena, Tuscany, but also on the more eastern region of Feltre. It is a festival that is held twice yearly, and all its' participants parade in the costumes of that bygone era. The whole town goes around in full medieval regalia for this re-enactment that can last up to a couple of weeks. That is what I walked into the day that I arrived in Feltre.

Feeling a bit overwhelmed, I dodged between the dancing and singing parades, sometime even getting unexpectedly caught up in the merriment of the moment as a cheeky young jester would hook his arm in mine and twirl me around the piazza.

The music emanating from more instruments than I was ever aware existed was pretty deafening. The singing and the cymbals were loud enough to crack the already cracked walls of the old town, but the euphoric atmosphere of the day engulfed young and old. Much impressed with the light-hearted fun that seemed to envelope all those around me, I eventually found a seat between two elderly couples who looked like they never ventured outside the massive walls and ramparts of this medieval town. These elderly people would surely know someone as distinguished as the '*de Costantini*'. Hey, just a minute, she had been married for some thirty or more years! What was her husband's name? Suddenly I wondered, did I have that information with me, or did I leave it at the bus station with my other gear? Much to the amusement of the old biddies sitting on either side of me, I proceeded to rummage through my bags, and yes here is the old envelope jammed between all the other detritus I was carrying with me, so I turned to one of them and showed them name and address, and their face lit up, here was a bit of interesting news to share—some foreigner with a poor knowledge of the language is looking for the professor and his wife. Of course they knew the address, it was just around the corner from where we were sitting, and what did I want with them? I told them that I was a cousin from Australia!

Well that was real news. It didn't come any better than that. They could fantasise about me and my past and connections, for at least the rest of the week! Another half an hour passed before I could get away.

I had taken only a small overnight bag with me, the rest I had left at the bus station in a locker, but in the bag was a change of clothing in case I was lucky enough to be invited to stay overnight. It was a safe and acceptable practice back before 9/11 to leave luggage unattended for a short break in the journey, and I would be travelling on to the eastern coast then north to Trieste from here.

Walking through the main archway and admiring the intricate carvings high above my head, I found myself in *via Mezzaterra*, all I had to do was climb the cobblestone hill and look for the number along the way. I saw the unique corniced fossil on the street wall before I saw the number on the door. There was no porch, no awning, just a heavy-set door in the two foot thick wall of the house, and a step. The only visible indication that we were now living in the twenty-first century was a modern looking button that I pressed to notify the residents that I had arrived. Eventually the front and only door opened and a beautifully dressed, mature lady appeared. My first thought was, *Oh, boy, she's going out*, but soon I discovered that that was the normal attire of the day for her, complete with pearls, stockings, and dress shoes. That lunch, the main meal of the day, was always taken downstairs four doors further up the hill and behind another heavy-set door with a number and bell, and an unobtrusive sign that said '*Ristorante Mezzaterra*'.

Okay, so it was past lunchtime and I had missed lunch, but I was probably a couple kilos heavier than my very svelte older cousin, I could undoubtedly skip the meal. I was led up two flights of beautifully polished stairs with an antique verdigris iron balustrade to where there was a kitchen-lounge-sitting room area with an amazing amount of natural light. My eyes were unconsciously drawn upwards to a glass roof that provided the light on this third floor and also on to another area up another flight of stairs that was the professor's study. This gentleman was now descending from his sky room and I could see that his dress code was as meticulous as his wife's, and his physique just as slim. With so many steps in the house, I bet they have never stepped inside a gym! Yes, they would have made a stunning couple in their heyday. They still do!

I was made to feel most welcome. It was obvious that Gianni, my cousin's husband, was very proud of his work that included the study of insects and butterflies as well as archaeological and fossil studies and cataloguing. Recently, in his spare time he had also started to paint a variety of insects, and the wall that ran alongside the staircase was lined with a multitude of very detailed and colourful paintings naturally enhanced by the full daylight that fell from such a strategically positioned glass roof. Their house was not unique in the area, but it was a museum in its own right. It had to be assessed by the Committee of Fine Arts, before they were able to renovate it many years earlier. They had to prove to the authorities that none of the networks of catacombs that crisscrossed the sub-terrain would in any way be disturbed or undermined by any of the restoration and renovation work, and that the outward appearance of the whole street and buildings would not be altered in any way. These were conditions that everyone undertaking any work on their own home had to respect.

The process of going through the building approvals took a staggering ten years, but when they finally moved into their 'new home' they had a very comfortable and modern house that would be the talking point of anyone visiting, for a long, long time.

There was only one bedroom (the main bedroom), nevertheless I was comfortably settled in a corner of the sitting room in a wide chaise lounge for the night, and in the morning I was introduced to their own private, subterranean catacombs and artefacts. Fossils and bones, both human and those of quadrupeds that had been buried for so long they had become discoloured and porous with their own network of termite tunnels. These passages meandered for hundreds of kilometres in that zone, but of course right through Italy and even farther afield, there are labyrinths of tunnels and caves where the persecuted Christians at the time of the Roman Empire had to find shelter. People in those days must have been of much smaller stature because I found that I had to crouch and bend down to fit inside these chambers.

What an unusually wonderful experience those few days have been for me to see how much history is hidden under the ground we walk on—we can only guess at the extent! Several other riddles have been solved for me too, regarding our family's background!

The conversation turned to my poor language skills, and I had to admit that there was no one I could converse in Italian with at home. I was Australian through and through, my children knew no other language and for my parents to communicate with their grandchildren they had to speak to them in the only language that they knew, and that was okay with everyone at home. But I felt I had let my native land down, and I promised them that I would try to remedy that shortfall once I returned, because now there were institutions that catered for people like me, who in later life wanted to re-establish contact with their roots. Did my teacher-cousin have any books (preferably novels) that she had finished with, and could spare to part with?

"*Si, certo!*" (Yes, of course!)

I did have a long bus trip when I left Feltre and that time could be well spent if I tried to familiarise myself better with the printed language. She came out of her own study, attached to the large main bedroom, carrying a bundle of hard cover books.

Wow! I can't carry that many! My baggage limit would skyrocket! So we picked one hardcover because she had used it in school for a number of years and now it was obsolete, but still very relevant for my restricted knowledge, and five other novels, so that when I left that evening I was already on my way to improving my Italian language skills, and the proficiency of my native tongue.

Though this was my first meeting with Professor Gianni, he presented me with an original painting of one of his most colourful and intriguing extinct insect studies as well as a reproduction of a fossil mounted on royal blue velvet. I have treasured both gifts ever since!

They walked me to the nearby bus stop and we warmly farewelled each other with promises to keep in touch. I pointed to the books under my arm indicating my intention to write them a long letter as soon as I managed to wade through these six books.

My first purchase once home was reached would be a comprehensive Italian Dictionary.

Nostalgia

I had to go back to Rovigno to see one last time that delightfully picturesque antique village of Mum's birth. I had been thinking of her life there and I wanted to have a final, private connection. I wanted to try to understand what it could have been like to live in such an enclosed environment, where everyone was a friend or a relation of the other, and what destruction of life and trust was wreaked by the havoc of war. I walked the streets, retracing her steps from her home where she said her last goodbye to her mother, the grandmother I never knew. Past the old restored stables that housed the Patriarch and Mother's youngest sister before they were demolished by the new Communist owners, so that they could build their new, modern town house. Along the waterfront, past the tobacco factory, '*I Bagni Nuovi*', the new Baths that formed one alignment of Polaris (the baths were demolished after the war) and beyond, to the newly constructed Jadran Youth Camp and its modern, spread out, resort-style buildings—where the young and carefree (and careless) pollute the pristine shoreline of a once much-loved and revered piece of fertile farmland that my ancestors had called Polaris. I sat for a long time in the sun on the huge rock that marked the nearest boundary to what should have been my inheritance. What should have been passed on, from generation to generation, and is now being degraded by these naked bodies in this nudist colony with their loud, blaring transistors and cassette players, their empty Coca Cola cans and bottles, their sweets wrappers and plastic bags that no one seems to notice, or care about.

But I was noted and talked about. I could feel the resentment in the demeanour of these usurpers. They resented my being there and watching the passing parade of naked bodies. My body was decently covered and theirs were not. They regarded me as a voyeur. If only they knew! Would they have cared? A resounding 'No'. Their arrogance was obvious in their demeanour.

Time flies when one is having fun and my fun, tinged with sorrow in this personal, morally engaging, picturesque part of the coastline was coming to an end!

A Soviet Experience

I was to use my train pass to meet Mira at her parents' home because she was feeling apprehensive about traveling alone. After that final trip of mine, alone in Europe, not ever having had a moment's concern up to that point, I could not understand it. My attitude, however, soon changed! After the trip that I was about to embark now, I could even sympathise with her. I boarded the train at Trieste that was to take me to Ljubljana then on to Zagreb.

At Zagreb I was to change train for a local one going north toward the Hungarian border, to a small country town in a farming community where Mira's parents had their home. But the property was quite a distance from the railway station with many twists and turns along the way so Mira was to meet the train in the morning when I was due to arrive. If one has travelled by train in Eastern Europe, he or she will have some idea of distances between major cities. They are much further apart than in the rest of Europe. The train left Ljubljana in the early afternoon and was expected to arrive in Zagreb some time during the night, so I kept myself occupied reading, writing letters, and conscientiously inspecting nature. Midnight came and went and the train was still speeding toward its destination. The night was bitterly cold in the full moonlight and though it was early September every other passenger was tightly rugged up with fur hats, and gloves, and rugs around their knees. The night seemed to last an eternity and though I was almost frozen, tiredness won out in the end and finally I succumbed and dozed off. I woke with a jolt to the shrill sound of the train whistle as it slowly pulled out of the station. Dazed, I looked around me and some of the faces were different. Oh, no! The station we were leaving must have been Zagreb!

The carriage door opened and in came the ticket inspector. He too was thoroughly rugged up with a fur hat and a full length, rough woollen coat in a khaki colour. Flustered, I handed over my ticket. It appears that my Eurail Pass was not valid in this section and he waved it threateningly at me with a flurry of unintelligible words. He doesn't speak English. I don't speak the Slavic language he is angrily addressing me in. He indicated that I was to follow him with my luggage. Luckily I was travelling lightly, with only one suitcase because the ride was getting rougher and rougher, and in the early morning light, I could see that the terrain we were now following was becoming wild, barren and inhospitable. Great, I thought to myself. I'm in the middle of nowhere, and I don't know where I'm going. After walking along the corridors for what seemed to be forever, we arrived at the front of the train, and my escort opened an amazing door that gave way into a sumptuous carriage lined with rich, glossy timbers and upholstered in luxurious soft red velvet. Highly polished brass fittings were everywhere and a large inlaid timber table depicting scenes of wild animals in the forest had a brilliant cut crystal chandelier hanging over it.

Wow! Who travels in here? I wondered. Then the worm of worry asserted itself in my stomach. *What am I doing here?* I asked myself. The inspector wandered away I imagine to complete his work and I was left alone sitting on these plush red cushions. Soon he is replaced by another two officious looking individuals, obviously Soviets of higher rank. Now I am truly worried. My Passport has been taken away. I don't know where I am. The train, I found out by consulting a map on one of the walls, is going to Belgrade. I don't know anything about Belgrade—I don't even know what language they speak there. But even more worrying, Mira will soon arrive at the station of her old village and will not find me on the expected train. She can't contact me, she has no idea as to whether or not I caught the train to Zagreb, and if I did, she has no idea of where I am heading now.

The two Soviets can't speak English either but one is holding my passport. Suddenly I realised I must get them to stop the train. But how? Easier said than done! Looks like they are not sure what to do with me either, so emboldened, I rummaged in my bag and took out a card I had received from Mira some time earlier giving the name of the station I was to alight from the country train that morning. The one I had missed by dozing off. I pointed to the name on the card, and then another brainwave hit me. Back into my handbag I rummaged to bring out a little folder with photographs of my three children when they were little, taken some time ago, but who were they to know?

So I pointed to the card, I pointed to the photos and I pointed to my watch. They left, and I am left in limbo while the train speeds on, and on! Now I am really worried and I don't know what to do as the hands on my watch tell me that the time too is speeding on. Am I imagining it, or is the train really slowing? I looked out the panoramic window of that surprisingly luxurious carriage, and yes it is. Outside the land was bare and desolate with no sign of life. Will they just throw me out and be done with me? After all I am travelling on an invalid ticket in this part of the country—what country am I in now? End of story, no one knows where I am. They don't have to say anything about ever having seen me—and they still have my Australian passport!

By now I should have panicked, but actually I am fairly calm, I need my wits about me to be able to think clearly. The door is flung open with a flourish and one of the guys, the one holding my passport, is now standing in the doorway and is beckoning imperiously for me to follow. In trepidation, I gathered my luggage and exited, then at the end of the hallway I saw that there was a door opening on to arid scrubland. As I approached the door, I held out my hand for the passport, and much to my surprise, he gave it to me with a smile. A surprisingly friendly smile that didn't crack his face, because right up until then all the three officials had been so serious and angry looking that I didn't think they knew how to smile, or that smiling maybe wasn't allowed in that region. I hadn't seen too many people smiling since I boarded this train. As I reached out to take my passport back, from behind us I could hear the sound of another approaching train, also applying the brakes to screech to a slow stop.

The two trains stopped side by side and there was an open door with a conductor on the other train beckoning me to step across. *Bless my soul! They really did it!* They stopped two trains going in opposite directions so that I could change over and go back to Zagreb and continue my journey.

I looked down at the great gaping gap between the two trains, and thought, *Here goes.* If I can't span that gap, I'm a goner anyway, no one is going to jump down and hoist me up again. So clutching my bag, I took a running leap and the other guy grabbed my arm as I precariously landed on the step, and he pulled me in. With shaking knees, I watched as my luggage also got propelled on to the second train, and we were off again. I waved madly and threw the Soviets a kiss as both trains continued on their interrupted journeys.

This was definitely a country train. It was still quite early in the morning and all the passengers were peasants on their way to the fields and markets with their baskets of goods for sale or barter. We looked at each other with the curiosity of young children observing an oddity. We could only smile at each other, as there was no other way to communicate. I didn't look like a very important person to them, so why did the trains stop for me? I knew that they would talk and wonder for the rest of the day, theorising and shaking their heads, the babushkas with their hair in buns and their headscarfs tied under the chin. The old-looking young men who have worked in the fields all their lives for a pittance, or just for survival; there were no children on this train. This was a slow, lumbering workers' train that stopped at every siding to drop off and pick up a person here, a person there.

Finally it stopped in Zagreb where I must look for the correct platform to board the other workers' train that will go in a northerly direction, but it is later in the morning and most of the peasants have already arrived at their destination so there will be fewer trains leaving Zagreb. The one I am looking to board will not arrive at its destination until thirty-five minutes past noon—five and a half hours late. It has been such a worrying morning! I know that Mira will have waited for two or three trains but surely not five and a half hours. I started pacing up and down the corridors, the anxiety not allowing me to sit still and I felt myself practically willing the train to go faster! But the minutes ticked by ever so slowly, and the countryside looked boringly the same mile after mile, it didn't seem to change at all, there was nothing to break the monotony until gradually the train slowed, then ground to a halt and I could see a small township in the distance. Of course I was the first to jump off, scanning the faces of the few people on the rutted stone platform as I headed toward the exit. And there, sitting at the edge of the platform looking alone and forlorn was Mira, deep in thought and resting with her back against a broken down timber fence. We silently looked at each other with such conflicting feelings written all over our faces, that the situation would have been comic, if it was not so poignantly, personal.

"I didn't think that you were coming"

"You won't believe what's happened to me," we said simultaneously, and burst out laughing, hugging each other in utter relief. Then with arms around each other, we slowly walked out of the station and on to the waiting bus.

We had not seen each other for several weeks, and we each had our stories to tell, but it didn't take me long to understand that Mira was not keen to stay any longer with her family, and she was in fact packed and ready to leave the following day. She felt that her mother whom she loved dearly but had not seen for several years was now weak and frail, and meekly resigned to her future fate of finding herself caught in the middle between a domineering daughter-in-law and an alcoholic husband. There was nothing Mira could do to make the situation more bearable for her ailing mother. Anger directed to her brother for not taking a stand to alleviate the household problems only caused more stress and anxiety for all, and it was best for those concerned if she went away soon, without any more fuss. I could understand her unenviable situation so didn't bother to unpack, and early the next morning we were ready to go. We were taken in the old horse and cart back to the station by the brother who could have done so much to ease the mother's suffering, could have been more kind, helpful and understanding in many domestic matters, but didn't bother.

Heading North via South

Back in the workers' train, we were now heading south to Zagreb. We had a few hours there to frit away before our regular train would arrive to take us back to Trieste. In the short time that it took us to find somewhere to eat and enjoy a strong cup of Turkish coffee, we changed our itinerary.

I told Mira how upset I was to see my old school friend Tonia living so far from what I called civilization, for want of a better word; how sad I was to see her having to return there after our brief holiday in Italy. How I feared that I would not see her ever again, and she would never return to Australia on her own now that her confidence had been so eroded and undermined by those around her, she wouldn't leave not even for a visit. So in those few hours of strolling around Zagreb, and pausing once again to savour a hot chocolate in another restaurant we made the executive decision to use our Eurail Pass to change direction and travel back north to Germany for another short and perhaps last reunion.

Overjoyed at seeing me again, Tonia made us feel most welcome, and even the husband gave up his double bed so Mira and I could sleep there, in the dingy room right next to the turbines that generated the electricity to run the flour mill. I think we stayed there for three days before we hopped on the train again amid the tears and goodbyes, to continue on our journey of discovery, southbound.

This time we were headed for an interesting looking place that I had discovered by browsing through all the literature I had picked up along the way. The train sped through serene landscapes and picturesque villages nestling in the valleys between gently sloping mountains that would soon be covered in meters of snow, on its way south, to end its run on the shores of the Bodensee, better known as Lake Constance

We knew nothing about the town of Lindau, other than on the map it seemed to consist of two parts: one, the older part, looked like a world heritage listed, small area sitting right at the end of a narrow peninsula in the water, or an island connected by a bridge. The map wasn't very clear and that's why it was intriguing. Two, the newer part on the mainland where the train would terminate at the station, seemed like any other township that we had already passed through, neat, tidy and well planned, and typically German, in the Bavarian Federal State. We arrived in the late afternoon but already evening shadows were falling as we set about to find a place to stay for a couple of nights. The next day we explored a truly delightful area. The old town was sitting in the lake, or sea as the locals referred to the large navigable body of water, and it was another amazing gem. All around us were the green covered mountains that in a month or so would become a skiers' paradise. On the slopes there were already a few people travelling up in the cable cars reaching high up to the ski resorts, and there was another, larger town on the opposite side of the lake. This area was so different to others that we had travelled through in the past two months that we decided to extend our accommodation for another night and take the cable car at Bregenz to the top of those far away ski slopes. From the top, we had a spectacular view of breathtaking contrasts of blues and greens of many hues, but already in early Autumn it was bitterly cold up there, with the weak pale sun shimmering on the dew covered grasses. Sleek horses of various sizes, obviously for riders of different ages, had heavy, colourful blankets on their backs and were grazing happily from leather bags slung across fence posts, but one or two paused in their chomping to gaze at us curiously.

In spite of all these wonders, my head was spinning, all of me was shivering uncontrollably, my chest was painful and I was wheezing. I was in the grips of the flu and I didn't have the clothes for the occasion, as Mira reminded me, I was wearing only light, open summer shoes. I noticed that my toes were wet from the damp grass and they felt numb from the cold, but I wasn't going to spoil this last day up here in the clouds by whingeing.

The waters of the lake at the bottom in front of us reflected the mountains around it, but the other end of the lake was lost in the hazy distance. We could see what looked like large vessels sailing into infinity. I consulted my map and it was interesting to note that this lake, or inland sea, formed the border of three countries: Austria, Germany and Switzerland. The vessels we could see in the distance were commuter ships travelling between Lindau, Bregenz, and Konstanz, with a number of other stops along the way, including a stop to an unlikely tropical island in the middle of this Bodensee. Or inland sea

What a pity that we didn't have enough time now to explore this intriguing island with its palm trees, hot houses for orchids and butterflies, and rookeries for baby turtles. It was a wonderland in the middle of an approaching winter landscape and the home of the Royal family of some local region or district. We were told that the immortal Marilyn Monroe had often spent time on this idyllic island, but stopping here for us would have involved several other stops that were not available on our preferred direct route.

I made a mental note to add this charmed place to my bucket list of possible future visits. My bucket list was getting fuller by the day!

Ah, Gay Paris!

We were elated to find that our Eurail Pass would cover our sea passage to the Swiss border, and from there we would continue on to 'Gay Paris' on a north westerly course by train and explore another part of Europe yet again.

We timed our departures so that the next two nights were spent on either the ship or the train as by now our finances were dwindling, and we still had about two weeks before leaving from Heathrow Airport for our final return trip back to Australia.

Apart from my flu, which didn't really hold me back (I just felt miserable), we had a dream run to Paris. We travelled alongside picturesque rivers flanked by the green mountains with white goats and their cute little kids clambering up steep inclines. Plains with row upon row of terraced grape vines all laid out symmetrically to follow the contours of the land. Nevertheless, that romantic, cosmopolitan, historic and hip city did not impress me at all and I never had any inclination to return to Paris.

Not one for my bucket list, mainly because we found that the French people were not really friendly or helpful to strangers in that period. They have since become more favourably disposed towards tourists and have toured more themselves in these later years.

It started at the *'Gare du Nord'* at the ticketing box when we tried to ask the attendant directions to the nearest station to our hotel. At first we were ignored—she didn't (want to) understand

English, Italian, Yugoslav or German, and she tried to dismiss us, but by then I was getting angry, tired, worn out, and not feeling well, and out of nowhere, much to my surprise a string of French swear words left my mouth. Stunned, the woman looked at me— "Ah, vous parlez Francais!"

Equally stunned, I delved into the dark recesses of my brain for the words I had not used for twenty-four or more years, and surprisingly found some that fitted the occasion. Eventually, we got the information we wanted and the direction where we could find a taxi that would take both us, and our luggage. Not all the taxies loaded suitcases and those that did demanded extra payment.

Sure, we did the usual touristy things and visited the places that everyone raves about in the week that we were there, but what remained impressed in my mind was the dirt, and the rain, and how everything looked a dirty grey.

The sky was grey. The Seine was a dirty grey with debris floating downstream alongside pleasure boats. The Notre Dame was grey both inside and out where the rain had soaked into the cement block brick construction and it felt damp inside. Even the view from the wind swept Eiffel Tower was grey in whichever direction we looked! I had to buy a raincoat to keep the rain out—and guess what? It was grey!

To top it off, we had to watch every step we took or the multitude of dog droppings would stick to our shoes or send us on a skid. Cute dogs of all shapes and sizes were paraded with their pretty, jewel-studded collars by their besotted and elegant owners all along the promenades of the Seine, but not one of the 'ladies', holding a fancy, lacy parasol in one hand and a fancy, embroidered dog leash in the other, ever bothered to carry a doggy bag to pick up their pet poodles' poo.

I guess that was below their dignity. That was something that I never could understand, looking around Paris. The 'capital of the fashion world', where the rich and famous flaunt their attributes to the rest of the world, and right then as we were walking the streets, the 'Autumn Fashion Shows' were being held, while at the same time even 'Mercedes Motors' were holding their next season's auto preview. Exotic clothes and ultra-sleek automobiles! This was the city of lights and romance, of the arts and music, with world-class museums and architecture. Where, unless one booked a table for dinner well beforehand in a restaurant, no seats were available. Why didn't anyone tell the Mayor or Councillors or even the cleaners of their nineteen arondisements that their city was downright filthy?

Fair Weather in London?

Personally I was quite happy to leave at the end of our week and move on across the channel to London. The wet, cold autumn weather was following us; by the time we arrived in Calais the waves were frighteningly mountainous, and we had to proceed north to Ostend, Belgium. From there, late in the evening we boarded a boat that got us safely through the rough seas and finally on to Dover the next morning.

The weather cleared by late afternoon and for the next few days London had unseasonal sunshine, and a day of sunshine makes a great difference to one's mood. A little lightness crept in almost undetected, to lift the spirit, not only ours but the mood of the throngs around us as well.

People were chatting gaily, and children skipped happily around their minders. To me it looked like some of the minders were not much older than their charges and I wondered if that was another source of employment for the large number of the unemployed in Britain. Isn't that the place where the nanny originated? Even back in the seventies and eighties the greater part of the female population had to go to work to supplement the family's income and it looks like the live-in nanny system has been nicely refined to fit in with school, work, holidays, and family time, with the nanny often becoming part of the family ably spanning the age difference between the young and the parents, forming an interesting bond of continuity.

A good and sought-after nanny is generally well-educated, and very attached and dedicated to the children who also become very close to her (or him). Yes, in a few cases I have seen presentable young men with as much flair and panache as women, who take to the vocation that once upon a time we used to call 'babysitting'.

London was interesting, if a bit too hectic for us both and we thought that 'Piccadilly Circus' was aptly named, with all the to-ing and fro-ing. The Thames was just as grey as the Seine but the red double decker buses and the phone boxes were a fun splash of colour.

The very-stately Westminster Abbey was a vast improvement on the dirty looking, besser block walls of the 'Notre Dame Cathedral' and in the feeble sun shining out of a cold sky, the huge buildings looked much more friendly.

A little further out, the countryside had that peaceful presence of timelessness that is so conducive to the relaxation of the mind as well as the body. Where poets can gaze at nothing and allow their creativity to blossom. That is until we caught up with the crowds, the tourists came in droves by cars and buses and were headed for Windsor Castle. What else could we do but join them? At least these tourists had some direction to follow, whereas we didn't at that point.

We found the massive walls of the Queen's residence every bit as imposing as a fortress of a bygone era and as we had seen in many other parts of Europe, but obviously this one is much better preserved, as befits the ruling Monarch of the Commonwealth. The tour took us inside the castle to all except the private suites daily in use by the royal family. Remembering the security that was in place that day, it really surprised us to hear that a few years later a usurper breached security and scaled the walls to gain access to the Queen's chambers!

The only blight for that week was the loss (theft) of a two-strand, long, coral necklace that I had stupidly left out in the open on the bed in our hotel room with the clothes that I intended to wear that evening, and of course no one knew anything about its disappearance when I asked the manager to make enquiries. More than the actual cost of the necklace, it was the sentimental value loss that I remember with chagrin as it was my first purchase in Venezia on the Ponte Rialto. The double strands of bright coral looked so suitably elegant on the black angora jumper I had planned to wear to dinner that night. Generally, I don't wear black very well, especially if I am not feeling a hundred per cent, my complexion tends to be a bit sallow and I need a splash of colour to be able to get away with it.

Our three months' holiday in Europe came to an end at Heathrow airport where we waited for our flight to Singapore where we would take care of the last minute shopping for bulky items to take home. Predictably our thoughts turned to our previous flight when we flew into Europe three months earlier and we shuddered in silence thinking of the circumstances that surrounded it. We were thankful that our return journey would not take us along the same route through Ceylon. Our flight would be to Geneva and then onwards, but what is this that they are now saying on the loudspeakers? The weather has turned really mean, with heavy squalls and storms, some snow and lots of lightning. Great! I have heard people say that if one is prepared for the worst, a good day is a bonus! My mantra has always been the opposite, at least since my old next door neighbour told me a lifetime ago, "smile and the whole world smiles with you. Cry and you cry alone. Be prepared for a good day, every day," was what the old gentleman had always advised. Could the few hiccups we had encountered along the way since leaving our homes in Brisbane now follow us back home?

Thinking back now, it has been an eventful trip. We got through our first flight, Singapore to Ceylon and the results of their political dramas there, without any personal sufferings.

One day when we were wandering around the streets in Naples during the soccer season, there was a riot about the obscene amount of money Italy had paid to get Diego Maradonna to play for their team, and when the Gendarmi got to the stadium precinct, pandemonium broke loose with groups of bikies terrorising people in the streets by encircling them, waving chains over their heads, and hooning around. Others pulled out knives and retaliated, resulting in the stabbing of five innocent spectators, right in front of our eyes. It happened so quickly that many other bystanders became unwittingly involved simply because they happened to be there. On the day that we were exploring the area around number 10 Downing Street, someone threw a hand grenade at the black door in front of us. We never found out why. It seemed that our trip was jinxed by a number of incidents outside our control, and now we were at the mercy of the weather. Can anything else go wrong? Our flight was called and we were on our way, a bit hesitantly as we looked up at the sky through the ceiling-high dark tinted windows, but apart from some brightly zigzagging bolts of lightning in the sky, strong winds, and some driving rain that caused the plane to jolt up and down a bit to the accompaniment of cries of fear and exclamations of anxiety from some of the passengers, the trip was uneventful all the way to Singapore.

What a change to the dreary ambience that was Heathrow! We gazed in amazement at the display in front of us. Why didn't we notice all this on our earlier stopover? Or did we come into a different terminal?

At Changi airport we found ourselves enveloped in the brightest kaleidoscope of live orchids to rival many time over the bright lightning flashes over Geneva and the Alps. Humid hot air from the tropics was such a welcome change from the wet, cold winds of London that over the last few days, seemed to have penetrated right through to our bones. Light, colour, and warmth was an added bonus.

We finished our duty-free shopping and wondered how we would get everything home. We were definitely overweight with our luggage but in those days, Customs was not so fastidious when they checked through our luggage, nor did they need to be, their main concern was keeping Australia blight-free and pest-free so any fruit, or fresh food in the luggage had to be disposed. Those who did not comply with our quarantine regulations got a hefty fine.

The barrier that I went through had an elderly gentleman in charge and when he saw me come through, he did raise his eyebrows at the overloaded trolley that I was pushing.

"What do we have here?"

"Sorry, I probably have too much stuff, but it's my son's 21st birthday back home, and I have been away for three months. I just wanted to bring him something special."

He cursorily went through all the bulky pieces of the stereo system that I had bought for Robert, then smiled and said, "Your son should like all this. He is a lucky boy!" and he waved me on. None of us were to know that when I got home, his father would commandeer the music system for himself.

A Slight Aside

What a contradiction we have here in Australia now with the Government allowing the importation of bananas, pineapples, berries, etc. to the detriment of our own farmers and the country people who have struggled with the elements all their lives, such as the fires and the droughts. They are required to follow the much more costly and stringent health regulations laid down here by the self-serving 'law'.

Through our so called 'Free Trade Agreements' farmers in particular have no chance of recouping those costs, as what is imported is so much cheaper, having arrived into our country without the same constricting regulation imposed on them by their country of origin.

Is it any wonder that so much farming land is allowed to lie fallow when the Australian Government gives compensation payments to people that have been told to destroy their perfectly good food bearing crops and fruit trees because cheaper crops can be imported from Third World countries.

What a farce! And how irresponsible of those politician who were elected to look after the interests of all Australian citizens including those who have lost their livelihood through cheaper imports, to now allow these countries' syndicates to buy huge areas of farmland and cattle country. I could mention a dozen or more instances of lost land to foreign investments, but the most recent and obvious one is the sale of the ninety-nine year lease of the Port of Darwin.

The Homecoming

If I thought that life at home would be any better when I returned from my three month vacation away from the family I was sadly mistaken. I got a barely lukewarm welcome from my husband and from my sons too, so I deduced that during my absence Allan played the poor martyr, a role that he could play so well and without the slightest effort. It was almost as though he was born into the role. I really have to struggle to remember any time at all when he put the feelings of others before his own. He simply never thought of anyone else's feelings. I could visualise how he would sweet-talk the boys to become his sympathisers and give him the moral support that he had never given them throughout their lives.

To begin with, no one at home was interested to hear of anything that I had seen and experienced. Where I had visited held no interest to them. They couldn't have cared less about their second cousins, or their grandparents' old home town and backgrounds, how they had lived or where, or any photographs that I brought over to show them. They barely glanced at any of the literature. Every effort that I could possibly make to get them somehow involved in the big world out there fell on deaf ears. My sons were not like that three months earlier, so what happened while I was away to make them so bitter against their own mother?

My older son was not allowed to keep the stereo system that I had purchased for him in Singapore, on the pretext that he would take it out of the house and let his friends muck around with it. So his father installed it downstairs in the billiard room and played his own taste of music on it, so I can only assume that my son thought that it was I who broke my promise to him, that I had given his father what was meant to be for him.

Nothing seemed the same and I felt like a stranger in my own house. I wondered if Allan had told everyone that I had left him and now he was giving me a hard time to prove his point. We learned to ignore each other but when people came to visit us the tension was palpable so we had fewer and fewer visitors.

Not even my daughter seemed the same, she was not a baby or an immature child that I had left behind or neglected, she was almost eighteen years old. They all knew where I was going and with whom.

Mira, her husband, and her one daughter, who was only eleven months older than my daughter Regina, were family friends and they often came to visit before our trip, as well as after our return, yet there was no animosity amongst their family, only interest and curiosity. So why was there such a radical change in the attitude of my own family?

Regina and I had been very close until we moved to the Redlands but once there, it seemed that she came under the spell of her brothers' friends, she became more distant, not only because she was getting older and becoming more independent, but more likely she was emulating the 'couldn't give a damn' attitude of the others.

Now back home, I had no job to return to and that was probably a good thing because by now my back was really playing up, I could barely turn my head and my right arm was too painful to lift. Whatever I had done to it at the end of our sojourn overseas wasn't going to go away simply by resting, so the doctor made a number of other suggestions, none of which worked.

Of course Mother and Father were starved for news of the old country and couldn't wait to hear about the few relatives that were still alive. They wanted to hear of the changes that had taken place and we traced the routes of my travels that criss-crossed several times. I could see that they were thinking of the distances and places I had visited and were wondering how I could have achieved so much in such a short time.

I spent a lot of time with them for the rest of that year, and then Father started to complain about his health. Even before I went away he didn't look well and, on doctor's orders, had seriously cut down his drinking. Now he was having trouble digesting food and had lost weight, one could tell that he was worried.

It was just before Christmas that Mum and I made plans to go shopping. When I arrived at their home that morning, Father excitedly announced that my eldest cousin, the Mayor of Venice, had rung the previous evening and they had all chatted together for a while. It was the first time it had ever happened and he could not reconcile the fact that the voices travelled across the globe so clearly, with only the slightest time lapse, and a slight hollow sound, as though the voices travelled through a tunnel. This was before mobile phones became widely used. Though they were invented in 1973, they were big and cumbersome so were not used much initially. Telephone conversations were not only expensive but also unreliable and not available everywhere. I was so glad that it had happened; that the aloof Mayor had made the effort to contact his uncle while he was still well enough to appreciate the communication.

Father didn't elaborate on their discussions, though he and Mother had spent some time with his nephew and his wife Anna during their visit in 1967. They had travelled with them to visit other people and places, so I imagine they would have had a lot more to talk about than I ever could with my limited mastery of the language. It was a good feeling for them and for me because my trip reconnected that family bond.

A Generation Apart But Similar

There was a notable resemblance in the character and mannerism between uncle and nephew. Both had difficult personalities and both responded to pandering. When we first met in Venezia, I felt somewhat overwhelmed by his reticence, not that he lacked in cordiality, I just felt a distance, a reserve that was almost a cover up for some deep seated insecurity; I didn't know what to make of it.

At that first meeting, I was puzzled but how could I delve into the personality quirks of a person I had just met after more than thirty years? Later I wondered if my friends had felt the same way when they first met my father during my school days and even subsequently.

Back in Venezia after having parted with both Tonia and Mira, I did come to understand my cousin better through his wife.

Recalling our youth, we had not spent much time together as children. In fact I only remembered him from one photograph. So to begin with, we were virtual strangers. Except for the deeply felt blood ties that seem to surface when people know that they are related and the obvious family resemblance of our features, I actually had no recollection of him as a child. Only hearsay.

When he married Anna, they formed a close and supportive relationship. She doted on her husband and he depended on her. A devoted couple who had no children, only a small in-house dog to keep her company when the Mayor was abroad. He apparently travelled to the States a fair bit in his capacity as the Mayor of Venice, but ironically never needed to learn English. Anna's family had always lived in Venice and they were the descendants of a long line of influential aristocrats. She was familiar with every nook and cranny, knew places of historic and touristic interest, and was very keen to take me around to the less frequented areas such as the dark, misty lagoons by the Lido, the small old churches with exquisite works of art not for public exhibition that were jealously guarded and kept in dark naves.

Close by were the presbyteries of priests who have accumulated, over many, many decades past, great treasures beyond comprehension. The might of the naval fleets of Venezia, that over centuries pillaged the exotic East for their jewels and silk tapestries, their gold, silver and copper vessels to be given in homage to the church back home. The greed and corruption of the church, the clergy and patrons were the ultimate causes for the downfall of the mighty Venetian Empire in the following austere period.

Anna had also studied the 'Divine Comedy' and obviously spent a considerable amount of time 'conversing with Dante Alighieri'. She could quote the 'Poeta Veronese' even more fluently than I had heard from my father, and like my father, her favourite passage was Canto VII from *'Inferno'* (Italian for Hell):

> In their first life these all
> *In mind were so distorted,* that they made,
> According to due measure, of their wealth,
> No use. This clearly from their words collect,
> Which they howl forth, at each extremity
> Arriving of the circle, *where their crime*
> *Contrary' in kind disparts them. To the church*
> *Were separate those, that with no hairy cowls*
> *Are crown'd, both Popes and Cardinals, o'er whom*
> *Av'rice dominion absolute maintains.*
>
> *(Dante Alighieri)*

I imagine this refers to those crazy with avarice and corrupted by greed.

Then there was the foggy mystique of the islands with their now little-frequented cemeteries that hide the dark secrets of the aristocracy that fell out of favour and were banished to the underworld, to join the not so noble rascals who were already there. "Ones of noble parents' fall from favour".

The narrow back 'streets' that only the locals are privy to, where the glass blowers of Murano perfect their colourful glass art for the privileged connoisseurs. Close by lies the island of Burano, where the nuns run the Convent of the Laces and where the still-wealthy locals commission great works of needle art that will take months to complete—just to wear to bed! The young novices who dedicate their lives to the church and live in the convent will, at the request of their patrons, stitch and embroider linens of such delicate texture and detail that ought to be displayed in museums rather than slept in. And it is quite common, even in this day and age, for a young girl to be given one or more objects of great beauty for her tenth birthday, as the first items for her 'Glory Box', to be followed by other treasures for the future, in the years before her wedding. Usually gifted to her by her Godmother, for the purpose of initiating the girl into the habit of starting young to accumulate beautiful pieces for her trousseau and establishing a large collection of linens and crockery for her future home.

Personally, my feelings at the time were that Anna got the rough end of the stick. She married for love, as my mother had so many years earlier, to a very similar man, with very similar idiosyncrasies. I found it interesting that both women were older than their spouses, yet looked naturally younger without the aid of any make up other than lipstick. Mother, however, did paint her well-shaped, strong nails a vibrant red for as far back as I can remember. That was one request from Father that she did ignore. He did however take his frustrations out on me when I first painted my nails the same colour using Mum's varnish. Once I started working I ignored him too, even though my nails were nowhere near as strong, or as evenly shaped as Mother's nails.

I believe there were many cousins from Anna's parents' families and she delighted in spoiling them and all their children. She was an only child herself and had been idolised by her own parents who had also stayed put during the warring years, refusing to become immersed in the fighting. Regardless of their non-involvement in the world-wide fracas, they were robbed of all their easily accessible, worldly treasures. They were left, maybe not quite destitute, but in greatly reduced circumstances.

Anna was such a gentle person with a depth of understanding and a need to please, she was a natural mother who only had a dog and a husband to love and spoil. And she did indulge them both. They both lapped it all up and begged for more. I liked her immensely and wished I had more time to spend with her but I didn't want to push my luck either, as I could sense that my illustrious cousin wanted his lovely and elegant wife to himself. We didn't get around to any of the fabled '*festas*' that I had been told were always on someone's agenda, because the best of those are held outside the peak holiday season when the crowds are more manageable. These are the more intimate and showy parties when the '*clique locale*' gather to compete for the glamour of style and colours, of gold and glass, of the beautiful, intricately embroidered and delicately painted jewelled masks and laces for which Venezia is famous. Of course the nightly soirees and daily musicals still entertain the masses throughout the year, but even these were mostly outside my financial standing at the time anyway!

In the Veneto, '*La Serenissima*' is a jewel in a region of excesses where every corner hides a secret. Where the very odour of the earth holds a spicy mustiness that hints at an exotic secret past. We walked past dark places in the middle of the day where the very air is heavy and pregnant with mystique, and where treason and deception formed the basis of Dante's 'Inferno', the first part of his Divine Comedy. All forty Cantos! I never discovered where he got the inspiration for 'Il Purgatorio', much less, 'Il Paradiso'.

In this unique place that will never reveal its inner pulse to the casual visitor, nor allow its long and convoluted history to unlock the multitude of secrets behind every door—indeed any door—I am lost for words. Shakespeare found inspiration here for many of his works, but probably one of his better known, 'The Merchant of Venice', reflects the reliance on commerce and greed of the era. Heavy, ancient tomes with leather covers encrypted with gold and encased behind glass in the local libraries and churches hint at intrigue by their very style of script.

 I could easily and most pleasurably live my life in Venice, in a world of my own making, recreating the past, moving around slowly within the pages of a romantic and historical novel of a colourful and interesting lifestyle. How tantalising it would be to take a peek at some of the scandals and intrigues of the likes of the Borgias and Medicis that have been the subject of countless books. But to follow the beaten track of tourism is like opening a book and looking at the pictures, the pages can be turned time and time again, but that is all one gets from the picture book, there is no soul. Had things turned out differently almost half a century earlier, Father would be in his element here. This is where his ancestors were from. This is where his remaining relations and family members still reside.

Life Goes On

Father went downhill rapidly. Not receiving much sympathy from his family, he probably felt he didn't have much to live for. I am ashamed to say that I was as uncommunicative with him as I had accused him of being in the past. And it is no excuse to say that I had a problem with my own back that started shortly after my return from Europe. We should all have been more compassionate, but especially me as the most senior after mother.

We cremated him in a simple family ceremony in February, just four months after I returned from Europe. If Mother felt the loss, she did not show it. But then she was good at hiding her feelings. Always had been! I had never seen her cry. Once I asked how she managed to keep her eyes always dry, because I am the exact opposite. I cry at the drop of a hat! She replied that she had run out of tears. That her life had been so sad in the old country that she had already cried herself dry. Another mantra of hers was, "No point in crying over spilt milk," meaning that what is done, is done, just get on with life and do better next time.

People will abuse their bodies when they are young, thinking that they are indestructible, until the body makes itself felt and then it's often too late.

"God helps those who help themselves," she would say to Father when the bottle was empty and he would start complaining about his health. I was never sure how to take that statement, feeling that it was open to so many interpretations and not all of them appropriate. I think she meant that if Father had stopped drinking earlier, his health may not have deteriorated so quickly and he might have lived longer.

We set about reorganising the house, changing furniture around and discarding what was no longer wanted in order to free some space because Little Sister Ondina, who was married now (in fact she had married on mother's seventieth birthday), was coming with her husband Wayne for a longer visit to Queensland. Much as they liked their work and their renovated home in an inner suburb of Melbourne, now that Mum was alone they felt an obligation to come closer to live. There was plenty of space there for them while they searched for a suitable abode.

They arrived shortly before I was scheduled to go into hospital for two laminectomies between the cervical sections of my spine. It appeared that nothing else would help my back as I was becoming increasingly restricted in my upper body movements and it was almost impossible for me to sign my name, yet surprisingly I could still drive. I suspect that is why I never got any sympathy or help at home from my immediate family—how could I possibly be able to drive a car if I couldn't even comb my hair? I was loath to ask for help, always looking for another way of doing things and being too independent, or stubborn by nature to let anyone think I couldn't manage without their help anyway!

This back problem was a puzzle to me too. I expected my back to cause problems sooner or later, but in the same area, the lumbar region, where in my youth I had previously torn ligaments, but no! This was a totally new and unexpected malady, nor did it heal as quickly after the operation as we expected. The anticipated period for recuperation after the laminectomies was to be six months. After fifteen months the specialist announced that I might have to consider the possibility that I would be in a wheelchair by the time I turned fifty. At which comment I baulked, stood up and told him I would cure myself.

"Thank you, and good bye."

Back to yoga and meditation. It took a while and a lot of perseverance, and there were times when giving up was very much an option, when I thought, "What's the use?"

Eventually I got there with the help of my mother, who insisted I spend more time with her, and less with my uncompromising family. The children were old enough to take care of themselves and help more with the house. While she loved them all dearly, Mother thought I was getting a raw deal at home that did not facilitate my healing process.

My husband was virtually a new man, with a new lease on life since medical advances in the early eighties allowed him to have a series of procedures to extract the dead bone that had been lodged within the femur for so many years. He was no longer plagued with suppurating poliomyelitis nor suffered any more inflammations. The entire family was relieved because his condition had affected us all. He could become more pro-active now! He should have been a happy man but I guess that after so many years of complaining and grievances, his mourning had become a habit and he still craved attention.

People kept telling me that reading alleviates stress, so I did a lot of reading and noticed that in our regional library there was a small children's section that had books in foreign languages, mainly Asian languages, but there were a few in other languages as well, including Italian. These were the languages that children could elect to study at school as a discipline, choosing the one that they were most comfortable with after a trial period.

Personally I couldn't see the sense in chopping and changing between languages because by the end of the year, the students had learnt nothing; they end up with a smattering of this and that, with no relevance and it is promptly forgotten by the end of the holidays. But for me it was time to really get serious about improving my mastery of Italian, or lack of. Obviously I wasn't going to find anything useful there but the librarian was helpful in suggesting institutions that catered for my needs.

Some of the books were not easy to read and I had to use a tiny dictionary that Mother had found in some corner of her room and so I was able to plough my way through, and the more I read, the more competent I felt.

Still unable to exert myself, I figured that activity could be replaced by a bit of mental exercising and it may even keep me from feeling sorry for myself while giving me the opportunity to meet like-minded adults.

About this time our tenants in Macgregor were moving out. It couldn't be happening at a worst time but necessity, they say, is the mother of invention. I advertised for three students from the nearby Griffith University and ended up with slightly more income than outgoings. I could survive!

It made me visit the University on a regular basis and I spent more and more time there enjoying the ambience and the resources.

Harder Times Ahead

To prove the point that he didn't need me around either, Allan decided to go back to Melbourne for three months "or more" to visit his brother and sisters. Was it payback time? I had taken a whole year to plan my trip. He just said, "I will be leaving next week and take my time driving down."

"Fine!"

My credit card was in the red to the tune of $4,000 and this was a lot of money 1985 and in one week I would have no car to get around in. Both the boys had their own set of wheels and most of their pay found its way into the modification process of the two classic Chrysler Valiants that they took so much pride in, and justly so. The body-line of the early model cars was great to look at.

They worked in a Motor Bodyworks workshop that belonged to family friends and so they were easily able to source tools and equipment in their free time to enhance the appearance and performance of their personal cars. It was becoming fashionable to use classic cars for weddings and these two Valiants were so tastefully trimmed and so highly polished to be often in demand, but they would only be driven by their owners! The boys would hire the uniforms of chauffeurs for the formal occasions.

My three children had become strangers in a very short time and now I had one week to sort myself out. My dilemma was not going to go away. What was I going to do once Allan drove off? The boys were hardly ever at home now. They were working and staying with friends, days on end. They were adults and I could not begrudge them their independence, in fact I had always encouraged it. But not alienation!

Regina was the only one who had applied for entrance to Griffith's University but at the end of the first year she wanted to defer for a year, intending to recommence her studies later. She was pretty young when she sat for her entrance examination and I thought maybe she did need to have a break from school, but deep down I knew that she wouldn't go back to resume her studies if she took that break. And so it was! My baby doll had grown up.

One sunny day she was getting herself ready to go out with her friends. The friends arrived shortly after I had asked her to put her clothes away and tidy up her room. "Yes, Mum."

Her friends arrived and she started to skip down the stairs to meet them.

"Did you clean up your room?"

"Yes, Mum."

And she opened the front door. No way could she have put her clothes away in that time. She was becoming a bit careless lately, so I went to her room to check and sure enough everything was left lying around. She had not even made an attempt to put her things away. That was the last drop in the already full bucket and the bucket spilled over.

I opened the window, picked up her clothes from the bed and the floor where they lay and threw them out of the window on top of her and her friends as they were all preparing to wander off. Suddenly, I had enough of being taken for granted. Obviously we were no longer friends who held a mutual respect for each other. It was time to change tack.

Picking up the phone, I called the local rag and placed an ad in the daily paper under the 'accommodation to rent' section to advertise a vacancy: 'Looking for a family to rent a large, fully furnished house for three months'.

Three days later, I interviewed a family with two children who had just arrived from New Zealand and were looking to buy a home and settle in the Redlands.

I commenced packing all our personal items, made the announcement to the boys when I next saw them, and told Regina she might as well go and stay with her friends, seeing that she was spending so much time away from home anyway. Perhaps I had been overprotective and she needed to develop in her own time and space. Seeing the way some of her friends, who were a little bit older, tended to protect her in a crowd, I was not too concerned that she would be adversely influenced. She might even learn to be more tidy living with them!

The tenants I had interviewed for the house were over the moon to have found such a lovely, big place that was fully furnished and I was pleased to meet the entire family who assured me that they would look after the property with all its inclusions as well as if they were their own.

I couldn't ask for more and I was paid the rent one month in advance which gave me enough money to make a decent payment on my credit card, as well as giving me some breathing time before the next payment became due.

It was definitely time for a change—a change of major proportions. I was emboldened with my experiences overseas. I had successfully navigated my way around several countries where I didn't even understand the local language, making a lifestyle change in one's own country can't be that hard. But I needed to get right away from familiar terrain. I didn't want to be located and snared back into the same set of surroundings and circumstances. If my family no longer appreciates me for who I was, I wasn't going to be used as a floor mat.

I made my way to the Gold Coast where I had a friend with two small children, who was struggling to juggle her time between motherhood and a career. She was looking for suitable accommodation within walking distance to nearby schools so the children could walk on their own. In the meantime the children needed looking after while she was at work. By my being there for a while, she would have more freedom to have some evening recreation time as well, whereas all I wanted was some rest and thinking time in a different environment, away from distracting influences. This move proved to be the turning point in her life that neither one of us could possibly have anticipated, while it also changed the direction of mine.

Jupiters Casino had opened its doors not many years earlier and it was the only international venue on the Gold Coast to provide accommodation and entertainment under one roof. It was new, it was smart, there were exciting international shows, lots of restaurants, several bars, and gambling. It was the place to go to be seen and people dressed well, in good clothes for an evening out.

Vicki wasn't a beauty but she was tall and had presence and youth on her side, as well as a bubbly personality and flaming red hair, so she stood out in a crowd. She didn't have much money to spare on clothes by the time the rent was paid and her young children decked out for school, but she had taste and could make a plain, everyday outfit into something special with the addition of a belt or a scarf or some cheap flashy jewellery and some ribbons or flowers in her hair. Neither was she too shy to ask her friends for a new change of clothing for the evening, usually choosing an assortment of mismatched items that no one else would think of putting together. She knew how to make the most of her attributes. We would look askance at the frivolous outfits that she would pick and choose, and then commandeer for the night. The excitement she was able to generate prior to an evening outing would involve half of the immediate neighbourhood, and the other half would offer to escort her.

During the time I spent with her, we would discuss what we could do to improve our general wellbeing and social happiness. We had totally different personalities, were at different stages in life, had not known each other very long but somehow we gelled. We got along well and made plans that included ways to meet a different group of people or society to the ones we had previously been associated with.

Vicki had recently landed a job with a Property Development Company that put her in contact with many transient people, so she was in a good position to get ahead with her 'go for it', career minded attitude. She would do well if I could take some of the pressures and responsibilities that the children presented, off her shoulders for a while.

The America's Cup

It was early 1987 and a lot had been happening in Australia, especially in Western Australia since the epic win four years earlier. The successful America's Cup Challenge by the syndicate that the entrepreneur Alan Bond formed in his bid to wrest that coveted trophy from the New York Yacht Club, with his fabled, sleek twelve meter, winged keel yacht that he named 'Australia II'.

It wasn't an easy win and it did take seven races over several weeks before the deciding heat that in the end called the race. The winning margin was only about forty odd seconds, but nevertheless the '83 Challenger win over 'Liberty', after America had defended and retained that massive trophy for some hundred and thirty years, sent shock waves throughout Newport, Rhode Island, and the rest of America.

The Louis Vuitton sterling silver cup loss was not the issue here. It was the loss of face that shook the Yankees out of their smug complacency, and once again reminded the American public that we Ozzies are not just mozzies, sometimes we do more than just buzz around.

Since that momentous day when the New York Yacht Club reluctantly relinquished its prized treasure, we had four years to work like crazy to be ready to host the next challenge, or rather the defence, in our own waters. It was to be a Regatta unrivalled for Australia.

The site for a new marina had to be chosen in Bond's own state, and once Fremantle was chosen as the preferred location, the new Challenger Harbour had to be constructed along with transport routes, accommodation facilities, entertainment hubs, just to mention some of the frantic activity Perth and environs would need to address. If we were going to host the elite of the world's glitterati, the Government that so far had made its own archaic rules and regulations to suit the land down under, would now need to wake up to 'world time'.

Changes to Liquor Laws, entertainment, and services including trading hours and a whole range of regulations must be overhauled and these must happen in double quick time!

Burswood Casino built in 1985 was probably one of the major shake ups to happen to Perth and though by cosmopolitan standards it's just a pea in a pod, that's when the laid back populace opened their eyes and realised that much more had to be done to house the influx of tourists who would augment the already-overflowing mining state coffers. Forward thinking businesses and enterprises had a mammoth task ahead of them if they were to obtain the required permits and licenses in time from the over-governed, cumbersome, red-tape, and Unions' shackled Parliamentary system this country is handicapped with.

Private business groups and syndicates came from around the globe to assess the terrain and the facilities available, and soon realised that not nearly enough of anything would be ready for January and February '87.

Sensibly, a private group chartered the 'Achille Lauro', a pretty big Italian Cruise Ship for the duration of the series. The ship's main viewing platform had a capacity for over one thousand four hundred spectators. Needless to say, it was by no stretch of the imagination the only cruise ship in the harbour but they were needed to supplement the scarce land accommodation available. The flotilla of private boats outnumbered many times the official parties attached to the 'America's Cup Challenge', and they were considerable.

"Australia is so far away!" How many times have we all heard this comment?

People don't generally come across the oceans over such great distances simply to view a boat race. The trip is expensive, it is time-consuming, it is tiring, and besides, people have seen some magnificent photography of this great, ancient country of ours. So diverse! Such contrasts! They are curious and they are sceptical—photographs can be enhanced.

"I want to see for myself if this is real!"

And they expect to see it all in a couple of weeks. After all, it's only an island isn't it? Almost eight million square kilometres! Invariably, people, be they Europeans or Americans, have no concept of the land mass that is Australia and gaze with amazement and disbelief when informed that it almost equals in area all fifty American states combined.

The people of Western Australia benefited from all the development, infrastructure, and cultural activities that were planned for that period. Being so far removed from other major cities, the southwest corner of the state started at least one year earlier to hold a number of festivities. The 'Boxing Kangaroo' became the emblem for sporting Australia and was quickly recognised in television commercials worldwide as our very own mascot, associated with a variety of trade, entertainment venues, and functions. Young and old smiled and nodded with amusement and affection. Many tried valiantly to mimic Matilda's whistle using the gum leaf, while koalas looked askance at the undermining of their food source.

The Festival of Sport included the World Sprint Car Championships and these events certainly put Perth on the world map, building up momentum for the main event. However, in spite of the best efforts of the crew and management of the Royal Perth Yacht Club, the challenger 'Stars and Stripes' won all of the first four races in the final series against the defender, 'Kookaburra III', and that was the end of that!

We felt as stunned and deflated as the Americans must have felt four years earlier when they were stripped of their pride and yachting fraternity joy. Tourists and competitors were now at a loose end, free to wander around the rest of the country and see for themselves the vastness, the beauty and the harshness of this immense island. So people came to the southern and eastern states to see where some of their ancestors had settled so many years earlier to make this country what it is today, and the rest of the country also took a share of the tourist dollar.

What does all this have to do with Vicki and me? Not much so far.

For the best part of the month, she had been coming home from work in the grip of cup fever. Where she worked at the 'Real Estate Developments' company, the excitement had been building up for many weeks, but not entirely because of the cup challenge that was taking place in Western Australia. Some high profile international investors had been gravitating to the Gold Coast and property syndicates were being set up to buy up big tracts of land.

The Japanese were particularly interested in the northern region of the Gold Coast and an alliance was formed with the Bond Corporation, resulting in numerous grand scale property purchases and developments including the establishment of the Bond University that initially opened its doors to students in 1989.

The influx of business people had to be entertained into the evenings so it was just as well that I was around to look after the children because their enchantingly captivating, tall, redheaded, light skin, freckled mother was a hit with the not-so-tall dark Asians, and she was in constant demand as an entertaining dinner companion.

One evening, a few days after the Americans reclaimed their trophy, she was to meet a group of post–challenge yachting enthusiasts who had come eastwards to admire the blue skies, golden sands, and sparkling, azure waters of the Gold Coast by day, and the scant flashing neon lights by night, at the Conrad-Hilton Jupiters Casino for pre-dinner drinks.

With all the excitement of the past weeks, she apologised for forgetting to tell me that the children had some school function to attend that evening and then they would be driven home by their friends' parents, so why didn't I join her and her group of revellers at Jupiters Casino? Why not, I had nothing better to do, so we spent the next few minutes getting into our glad rags and putting on the war paint, and off we tottered in our very high heels to the one place in town where one could bump into almost anyone. And Vicki literally did just that!

A rowdy group of Yankees were walking past as the lift doors opened and we practically fell into each other's embrace. Laughter and apologies all around, then we proceeded on our separate ways to the bar and the designated meeting place where we were to meet the Challenge supporters.

Amazingly, it turned out that this was the group she was to meet for dinner and the Follies Berger Show in the theatre afterwards. So the ice was already broken and the winners and the vanquished got on amazingly well throughout the evening, with raucous laughter at the risqué jokes and the raising of many glasses.

Later, while the revellers wanted to party on after the show, I excused myself with the pretext that I wanted to be with the children, but in effect I could see that Vicki was quite a hit with a particular cuddly individual and the last thing I wanted to do was to cramp her style. When I next saw her, two days later, she was smitten.

She had taken the next day off work and had gone sailing with some of the guys including the cuddly one who turned out to be a doctor—an ear, nose, and throat specialist from Arizona.

"Isn't that a bit far from the Pacific shores?" I commented, a bit sarcastically.

"Ahh, but…"

During the course of the next forty-eight hours—that was all the time they had before their plane took the group back to their regular lives in The States—they were given a thorough tour of the Gold Coast and the Hinterland, and to her credit she did come home to check that all was well with me and the children and to introduce her girl and boy to the V.I.P.'s who were suitably impressed with their manners. Before they left for the airport in the limousines organised by Vicki, all went out of their way to thank her for the time, knowledge of the local area, and her skills as a hostess, which were superb. She impressed me too, that was a side of her that I hadn't seen before.

For the next week, she was hard to pin down. I guess she had to make up time at work; but then she received an express delivery letter that sent her up on cloud nine. The ENT specialist was proposing marriage! With the touchingly romantic letter he wrote her, he enclosed a return-paid, first class ticket for Vicki to visit the U.S.A. for one month in the fall. As a gentleman, he vowed there were no strings attached. If at the end of the month they found that they were not compatible or that she didn't like him or his mannerism or his home, friends, and family, there was no compulsion for her to stay on. That was the reason that he was enclosing a two-way plane ticket, and he knew that as a mother, she would not want to stay away from her children for any longer than that. The least he could do then was to introduce her to his beloved country as she had done for all of them on the Gold Coast. Such a touching letter, it almost had me in tears too!

"What should I do? I really like him, he's fun." She was really asking me for my opinion and advice. This wasn't just girlie talk.

"He is a bit older than you are, but yes, he was fun," I nodded.

"I have never been overseas, it's such a big step." This was serious stuff.

"Which is the big step? Going overseas, or meeting up with a guy that you like?" I quizzed her.

I got that appealing lopsided grin of hers with her head to her side and, "You know me pretty well, don't you?"

"So, what should I do?"

I had to give her some 'older sister advice', "Vicki, you are not a pushover, you would never do anything that you didn't want to do. No one could persuade you to do something that you are not comfortable with, or not happy to go along with. Just go with your gut feelings." I threw the ball back in her court.

"But leaving the kids for a whole month, and that would be over the school holidays. That is a big ask." I could see the internal struggle she was having.

"But I would be willing to come over for the month and stay with them." She raced over and gave me a bear hug that winded me. I knew what was on her mind but we still had the time to work through logistics.

"You are the best of friends."

"Right now this best friend of yours needs a break. I need to go back to Brisbane and spend some time with my mother."

The Beginning of the End

It was also time for me to reorganise my own house for the return of its lord and master. Everything was replaced to the way it had been before he left for Melbourne three months earlier and when my husband made his grand appearance, I knew immediately that he would be staying in the house without me. I was through pandering to him.

To gather my thoughts, I went into the garden where the tranquillity and solitude always helped me to unwind or to focus. Being close to nature, the earth, the trees, the harmony and peace, it was so therapeutic and mentally calming that I was able to reorganise my mind and thought processes.

Taking off my recently remodelled engagement ring and wedding ring, I placed them safely in a corner of the BBQ bench where they wouldn't get dirty in the soil and weeds I would be working with. By the time my back told me that it had enough of my gardening and soil therapy, my decision was made.

Mother and I had a good understanding and when she didn't need the car for her bingo sessions, I could use it. I had it with me now. Having made my decision, I went inside for my bag and car keys, and yelling out that I would be at Mum's, I took off—no explanation, nor was one asked!

Unfortunately I forgot about retrieving my rings. Bad mistake because I had spent a lot of money to remodel both rings only recently. From all the wear over the years, the bands were pretty thin and a couple of years back, I had decided to use some old jewellery, a pair of earrings, with two pretty decent sized diamonds in the centre to reset the engagement ring into a pleasant modern design. That was the ring that I bitterly regretted taking off because I never got it back. Whereas the wedding ring was symbolic, it had seen better days as our marriage had. Now I felt that I no longer had a marriage anyway.

Apparently some Asian lady who quickly stepped into my shoes was now boasting of the generosity of an older Caucasian man. She didn't last long. She must have been a hard-working woman who had a young son whom she was sending to a private college because she genuinely believed that there he would receive a superior education. As she was also working odd hours, Allan was expected to take her son to school and musical events, functions and sports meetings when she was busy. He never did that for his own children whom he insisted go to state run schools.

Throughout our children's formative years, we used to have continual arguments about giving our boys a better chance in life through private education. Involving them in the broader, positive life experiences that are generally more widely available in a private college. My argument had always been that they would have been better prepared with the knowledge and tools for later successes in life. They would have been essentially endowed with the confidence that a person acquires when he has a sense of cohesion, of belonging, of working towards the achievement of a common goal.

So now the father of my children was immersed in the Asian culture, where parents will do anything to improve their children's chances of success in life. Where education is considered paramount and mostly their children come first in the parents' lives. This dedication is generally reflected in the children's superior marks at school. Not with my husband! After that first year this lady moved on to find someone more obliging. Taking my ring with her! In a monetary sense, my ring was worth peanuts in comparison to the rest of the goods and chattels that I left behind by walking out of my home.

But all the shackles that had made an emotional prisoner of me for twenty-seven years seemed to slide off my shoulders and I felt lighter, younger, and better. No more emotional blackmail.

After so many years of trying to hold a family together in spite of all odds, the realisation that I was slowly losing my identity, my sanity, and that even my personality was being undermined, hit me like a flash of lightning. Now I had a family that no longer wanted any input from me. And that was fine. The children were old enough to want to embark on their own life-learning journey, and make their own mistakes, unfettered. I could only hope that they had picked up enough common sense, experience, and sound knowledge in the early days when I had more influence on them.

A Student Among Students

Time spent with Mother was always calming. We had a good relationship, but I needed some form of mental stimulation, some engagement. I had to involve myself in something that would not only keep my body occupied, but my mind as well, because the most debilitating complex is boredom of the mind. How many times have we heard children say, "I'm bored"? But boredom afflicts all ages.

For all intents and purposes I was now on my own, so I had to function clearly and effectively on my own. I believed I could.

One of the three girls who were renting a room in the unit at McGregor had moved out, so I moved some of my personal items in the vacant room. It was the big double room with the full wall of sliding glass doors that had been a garage initially, so it had direct access to the outdoors.

As I didn't have my own car and I couldn't always keep using Mum's car, it made sense to move to Macgregor where I would be within walking distance to the University where I was fully immersed in a year of classic Italian language studies.

Finally my promise to my cousins in Italy was happening and I realised that the early start that I was lucky enough to have had during the early years at my first school in Italy was now helping me to appreciate sentence formation and colloquialism, but there was a lot of work to be done with grammar.

In class we giggled lot at our own mistakes, it seemed that we were getting nowhere for such a long time, and then imperceptibly, one fine day, everything fell into place and most of us were able to carry on conversations that actually made sense, with intonation and rhythm! Most of us were dedicated scholars but as usual a few dropped out for number of personal reasons, so the lecturer had more time for the rest of us as individuals and we made the most of our tuition time.

We read a lot to each other, in and out of class, and even though many had work commitments, we would try to meet for coffee somewhere and discuss our understanding of the more obscure sentences and meanings of the prescribed texts. The Italian lecturers would not accept 'near enough is good enough' when exams would start after the September holidays. But there would be enough time later to clarify misunderstandings, mistakes or misconceptions that were revealed after the papers had been marked. No one would be left wondering—"well, if I am wrong, just what is correct?" and we would be directed to a heap of other books.

Initially, when I started with these classes my health was still quite fragile, but the daily walk through the cemetery, that was still unfenced in those days, had me briskly exercising twice a day. The most frightening part for me was having to cross the four-lane highway, because sometimes my legs felt too weak to hold me upright and then any lamp-post or tree along the way would have to support me temporarily. Enjoying the leisurely walk one afternoon, on the way home from university, my legs did give way under me and I slowly sank onto the grass. It wasn't an isolated event, nor did it surprise me very much but in a flash the thought came to me, "Better here than on the road, at least the cemetery is more appropriate!" Gradually I got stronger and I could handle stressful situations better. I was enjoying life and living again. That year was so liberating!

In the fall, during our September holidays, Vicki's children and I went fishing in the canals in Surfers Paradise and the Nerang River while their mother experienced a totally new lifestyle in Arizona for a month. She wrote and rang often, and it was blatantly obvious from the tone of her voice and her written words that it was a lifestyle she would embrace fully, just as soon as practicable.

"Everything will be so different," she would say explaining something new and exciting, an event, or experience. "You will love it so much here." It was touching to read her notes to the children describing the warmth and affection she had received from the friends and relations, whom she hoped would become theirs as well, soon.

She promised that the children would never again need to walk to school in the rain on their own, and then come home to an empty, cold, dark old house like the one that they were renting now. She told them that they would truly love their new schools that she had already checked out. She went on to describe the different building styles for schools and houses, and the children that she had met were friendly, welcoming, and would make nice, new friends. She had been promised a big Cheyenne SUV, big enough to go away camping in the National Parks on weekends. That they would have their own clean and well-lit bedroom and if they wished they could choose their own pet to care for; play any sport they fancied.

It wasn't easy to get a green card to live in the U.S. of A. It wasn't easy to persuade the children's natural father to give permission for his son and daughter to leave Australia either. He had to be convinced that the move would be in the children's best interests and that they would benefit from the changes that were proposed for them. He wanted to make sure that his children would not suffer unduly from the separation from all those relations and friends that they held dear and had known all their lives, and that part of the agreement would enable them to return to Australia during their yearly school holidays.

All of these formalities took a full year to complete, and I believe the good Doctor had to call in a few favours from his many friends in government in order to expedite the arrival of his new family.

The following year, when I had occasion to travel to the States, I had the pleasure to be a guest at the new mansion that was in the process of having the finishing touches applied to the Olympic-size swimming pool. As a visitor and friend, I was treated as a V.I.P, not only by the people I already knew but also by the Doctor's family. The elderly parents, also doctors, had the time to spend with me and indeed both absorbed as much knowledge and information as I could impart in their sincere efforts to better understand the 'strange, likeable, young creature' from 'Down Under', we enjoyed each other's company immensely.

But all of that happened in the future!

And a couple years after that, on my next visit to the States, I understood the dedication to Yachting that now gripped Vicki and the family, as well as the Doctor, his family before him and those all around them.

For being instrumental in bringing about this union, I was rewarded with several trips around the countryside in the company of my hosts, and at other times accompanied by the parents, to witness many of the wonders that make America great. Everyone understood that if I had not made myself available that month in the fall of '87, none of these changes would have occurred.

Vicki grasped the opportunities that came her way and was quick to determine where her efforts should be concentrated. She worked hard to make incredible changes within her new community that, as she put it, was 'stagnating'.

Of course she trod on some toes, but generally she was well-accepted and welcomed as an entrepreneur who makes things happen on a grand scale. And in a country whose credo is, 'biggest is best,' she was going to go a long way!

Epilogue

Advice I Would Give Myself At 18

At eighteen, I could have had the world in the palm of my hand if I had been a bit smarter and a lot more patient. Not that I have any regrets about leaving school when I did. Sometimes I felt that life was unbearable at home, and looking for paid employment would not only make me more independent but also provide me with a different focus in life, broader horizons. That it did to some extent, but it did not entitle me to more freedom.

Once I landed my second job, which was truly rewarding, it should have opened a new chapter in my life that didn't have to include marriage at just nineteen.

Had I been a little more understanding of Father's alcohol problem and listened to the reasons behind his frustrations, we may have been able to reach a pact. If we had both been a little less stubborn and uncompromising; if we could have talked and listened, listened and talked, we might have come across a solution to benefit us both.

As the saying goes, I 'jumped from the frying pan into the fire' by marrying a physically-damaged, older man who had ever-so subtly conned me into believing that he really only had a short time to live. Naively, I wanted to make his short time on this earth as happy and pleasant as possible. Perhaps I was also unconsciously looking for a father substitute. I wanted someone that I could talk to, discuss problems, and find solutions in the way I was unable to do at home. And for a little while I could.

I should have stepped back and looked at the big picture in the cold light of day, thought of what it would mean to spend the rest of my life with that person, to have to share his family while relinquishing mine. To constantly feel obliged to give him moral support, but not receiving any in return in my time of need.

By the time we had our first child I realised that we were living a lie. He wasn't going to die anytime soon and in fact, he continued to destroy his family life by transferring the emotional blackmail he had used with me to his eldest child who became his carer later in life.

Certainly it would have been helpful if I had taken more notice of the marriages in his family and I should have taken the time to get to know his siblings better. Not one of their marriages had any meaning other than to produce their off-springs. Two couples remained together under sufferance, until one of the spouses died— both were still quite young males. In one case the husband had taken an overdose of drugs and the other died as the result of his erratic lifestyle.

The younger sister who partnered my husband in the folkloric dancing competitions; divorced soon after having one daughter, who in later years in turn married at sixteen like her mother, and divorced soon after.

Then there was the youngest brother who had many advantages over his other siblings and whom everyone had spoiled rotten since birth, so much so that I considered him a spineless walking wonder, whom only a fool would ever consider coupling with. Ironically, it was I who introduced him to the woman who eventually married him.

The parents openly hated each other, so now why would they feel any compulsion to be any different towards me? The obese, sick, old mother idolised her son and didn't want to share him with anyone, and particularly not with someone who was not of their clan. The bitter old man was only interested in who would cook his favourite meals when his wife died, which he hoped would happen sooner rather than later.

My parents no longer had an idyllic marriage either but they stayed together by respecting each other's space. I was brought up to believe that marriage is forever. One man, one woman before God. Faith can be shaken!

One of my Avon clients, in an ever-changing group of people, was a woman who bred Pomeranian dogs. I never found out if her husband had died in Europe or elsewhere, or even if she ever had husband as she gave different accounts to suit the situation. I guess I may have assumed that she did have one at some stage, because she was receiving a widows' pension that must have been quite generous, seeing she was a consistently big spender. In her own words she, "needed any help she could get."

I assumed that she was referring to her looks. What she probably meant was that she needed, or rather wanted, any help in any and every area but I wasn't to know that—yet! She was another one who had perfected the art of emotional blackmail and she managed to get herself invited to one of my regular evening gatherings for clients and neighbours in the old family home. It was just before we moved into our new house in Ringwood that had just been completed. This middle-aged German Frau who was many years older, and the mother of two teenage children, knew exactly what she wanted from the merging of bodies in that large, older residence that now belonged entirely to Allan's young brother. This 'lady' was barely inside the door when immediately she set about checking the number of bedrooms, size of the house, and the prized half-acre lot of land that the house was sitting on. Plenty of space to accommodate her paying hobby of breeding miniature Pomeranians. Then she turned on the charm, wooing the gullible young imbecile who owned the property now. Sympathising with him, mothering him, molly-coddling him, and even using my Avon Bubble Bath and Oils—without permission, I may add—to bathe him! The next day when I challenged her as she was coming out of the master bedroom, she said that she wanted, "To make him relax and give him a nice massage, poor boy." Her confidence was explosive!

"Relax from what?" Out of my mouth, unbidden, came the question, "He's never done a day's work in his life!"

There was no point in saying anything more. It was obvious what direction this farce was taking. Anyhow, that's what he always had in the past—people making excuses for him. Now he was getting what he always wanted—and more! A mother and lover all wrapped up in one, plus the stimulating company of her teenage children.

But she had her own agenda. On the pretext that she had hurt her back, once she stepped inside the front door, she never left the house, and together with her own two children, who also knew exactly what the mother wanted to achieve, they all wormed their way in and shamelessly quizzed and prized out every bit of information about his inheritance and also any possible resistance that might be encountered from the two surviving sisters. Both ladies were showered with expensive gifts but nothing would have changed if they had resisted, she would simply have changed her style of wooing and made herself out to be the victim!

They lived together, and bred and sold prized Pomeranians dogs for several years until the Department of Social Security finally woke up and cut her widows' pension—then they married.

How gullible people are, including me.

What a fool I was to think that our marriage would survive. And when I realised that my world was falling apart barely a couple of years after we had married, surely I should have had the sense not to believe that a child would patch up what was already fractured. Happy children are most often the result of a happy marriage, and I guess that was the problem, back then I didn't know many happy marriages.

Even now, in adulthood, my children are still plagued with feelings of insecurity and the effects of my toxic marriage.

As the years passed I have been alone for many long periods. This time enabled me to fully examine my actions and motivations of an era long gone, and I can honestly say that I have always acted in humanity's best interests, often putting myself in second place.

Many Years Later …

To Steve, My Soul Mate

As I sit on my balcony contemplating the tranquil ocean, I relate it to my life—the calm after the storm; and I reach for my husband's hand in a silent 'thank you'.

The compilation of my memoirs would never have taken place without the encouragement, help, and understanding of my best friend and lover, who on so many occasions bore the brunt of my frustrations. Since the turn of the century, he has listened to me, my family, and friends saying repeatedly, "Write your autobiography. Record your era and life. There is no one else alive who can do it."

Finally, one evening while we were out dining, Steve looked at me from across the table and as we raised our glasses, he asked me, "When will you start writing?" It was a serious question.

The underlying message was: 'each year seems to be passing faster than the previous year and too soon my time on this wonderful earth will expire'.

What you have experienced has been an unpretentious record of my life, neither exaggerated nor restrained. The events and views portrayed herewith are to the best of my knowledge and belief, true and correct. People and places are reflected as presented to me and if I have misjudged an occurrence or fact of any importance, I trust any resulting outcome to be trivial.